D0082440

THE HUMANISTIC TRADITION

4 The Age
of the Baroque
and the European
Enlightenment

THE
HUMANISTIC
TRADITION

4 The Age
of the Baroque
and the European
Enlightenment

Gloria K. Fiero

University of Southwestern Louisiana

WCB Brown &
Benchmark

Book Team

Developmental Editor *Deborah Daniel Reinbold*
Production Editor *Daniel Rapp*
Designer *Elise A. Burckhardt*
Art Editor *Miriam J. Hoffman*
Permissions Editor *Mavis M. Oeth*
Art Processor *Andréa Lopez-Meyer*
Visuals/Design Developmental Consultant *Marilyn A. Phelps*

 **Brown &
Benchmark**
A Division of Wm. C. Brown Communications, Inc.

Vice President and General Manager *Thomas E. Doran*
Executive Managing Editor *Ed Bartell*
Executive Editor *Edgar J. Laube*
Director of Marketing *Kathy Law Laube*
National Sales Manager *Eric Ziegler*
Marketing Manager *Kathleen Nietzke*
Advertising Manager *Jodi Rymer*
Managing Editor, Production *Colleen A. Yonda*
Manager of Visuals and Design *Faye M. Schilling*

Design Manager *Jac Tilton*
Art Manager *Janice Roerig*
Production Editorial Manager *Ann Fuerste*
Publishing Services Manager *Karen J. Slaght*
Permissions/Records Manager *Connie Allendorf*

Wm. C. Brown Communications, Inc.

Chairman Emeritus *Wm. C. Brown*
Chairman and Chief Executive Officer *Mark C. Falb*
President and Chief Operating Officer *G. Franklin Lewis*
Corporate Vice President, Operations *Beverly Kolz*
Corporate Vice President, President of WCB Manufacturing *Roger Meyer*

Main Cover Photograph:
Voltaire in Old Age, Jean Antoine Houdon, Chateau de Versailles.
The Bettmann Archive.

Cover Insets (top to bottom):
Ludwig van Beethoven. Courtesy of the Free Library of
Philadelphia.
Mint Marilyn Monroe, Andy Warhol, ca. 1962. Oil and silk
screen enamel on canvas. From the collection of Jasper Johns.
© 1992, The Estate and Foundation of Andy Warhol/A. R. S., New
York.
The White Cloud, Head Chief of the Iowas, George Catlin,
ca. 1845. Oil on canvas, 27¾ × 22¾ in. National Gallery of Art,
Washington, D.C. Paul Mellon Collection.

Copyeditor *Laura Beaudoin*

Photo Research by Kathy Husemann

The credits section for this book begins on page 167 and is
considered an extension of the copyright page.

Copyright © 1992 by Wm. C. Brown Communications, Inc. All
rights reserved

Library of Congress Catalog Card Number: 91–77640

ISBN 0–697–03789–4

No part of this publication may be reproduced, stored in a retrieval
system, or transmitted, in any form or by any means, electronic,
mechanical, photocopying, recording, or otherwise, without the
prior written permission of the publisher.

Printed in the United States of America by Wm. C. Brown Communications, Inc.,
2460 Kerper Boulevard, Dubuque, IA 52001

10 9 8 7 6 5 4 3 2 1

BRIEF CONTENTS

EXPANDED CONTENTS
(BOOK 4)

I
THE AGE OF THE BAROQUE   3

II
THE EUROPEAN
ENLIGHTENMENT 95

CHAPTER 24   THE PROMISE OF
REASON   97

CHAPTER 25   THE LIMITS OF
REASON   113

CHAPTER 26   EIGHTEENTH-CENTURY
ART, MUSIC, AND
SOCIETY   135

PREFACE

It's the most curious thing I ever saw in all my life!" exclaimed Lewis Carroll's Alice in Wonderland, as she watched the Cheshire Cat slowly disappear, leaving only the outline of a broad smile. "I've often seen a cat without a grin, but a grin without a cat!" A student encountering an ancient Greek epic, an African mask, or a Mozart opera—lacking any context for understanding these works—might be equally baffled. It may be helpful, therefore, to begin by explaining how the individual products (the "grin") of the humanistic tradition relate to the larger and more elusive phenomenon (the "cat") of human culture.

In its broadest sense, the term *humanistic tradition* refers to humankind's cultural legacy—the sum total of the significant ideas and achievements handed down from generation to generation. This tradition is the product of responses to conditions that have confronted all people throughout history. From earliest times, human beings have tried to ensure their own survival by controlling nature. They have attempted to come to terms with the inevitable realities of disease and death. They have devised methods of living collectively and communally. And they have persisted in the desire to understand themselves and their place in the universe. In response to these ever-present and universal challenges—*survival, communality,* and *self-knowledge*—human beings have created the tools of science and technology, social and cultural institutions, religious and philosophical systems, and various forms of personal expression—all of which we call *culture.*

Obviously, even the most ambitious survey cannot assess all of the manifestations of human culture. This text, therefore, focuses on the creative legacy referred to collectively as *the humanities:* literature, philosophy, history (in its literary dimension), architecture, the visual arts (including photography and film), music, and dance. Selected examples from each of these disciplines—though often abridged—constitute our *primary sources.* As works original to their age, the primary sources provide firsthand evidence of human inventiveness and ingenuity. The primary sources in this text have been chosen on the basis of their authority, their beauty, and their enduring value. They are, simply stated, the masterpieces of their time, and in some cases, of all time. They are, as well, the landmark examples of a specific people and place. As such, they offer insight into the ideas and values of the society in which they were produced. In order to delineate the entire "cat," the text also provides some discussion of the relevant political, economic, and social circumstances out of which the primary sources emerged.

The Humanistic Tradition explores ideas and values that belong to all of humankind; hence the text offers a global rather than exclusively Western perspective. Our multicultural approach maintains that the humanistic tradition is not the exclusive achievement of any one geographic region, race, or class of human beings. Yet, in the main, the primary sources examined in these pages were created by individuals with special sensitivities and unique talents for interpreting the conditions and ideals of their age. The drawings of Leonardo da Vinci, for example, reveal a passionate determination to understand the operations and functions of nature. And while Leonardo was far above average in his abilities, his efforts may be taken as a reflection of a robust curiosity that characterized his time and place—the Age of the Renaissance in Italy.

The Humanistic Tradition is a survey, not an exhaustive analysis of our creative legacy. The critical reader will discover many gaps, the most unfortunate of which is the relative lack of attention afforded the arts and ideas of Asia and Africa by comparison with those of the West. On the other hand, some aspects of Western culture that traditionally receive extended examination in humanities surveys have been pared down to make room for the often neglected contributions of Islam, Africa, China, and India. This book is necessarily selective—it omits many major figures and treats others only briefly. Primary sources are arranged, for the most part, chronologically, but they are treated in thematic or topical contexts. The intent is to examine the informing ideas of the humanistic tradition rather than to compile a series of minihistories of the individual arts.

The Legacy of the Humanistic Tradition

To study the creative record is to engage in a dialogue with the past, one that brings us face to face with the values of our ancestors and, ultimately, with our own values. Indeed, exploring the humanistic tradition is (or should be) a source of personal revelation; like Alice in Wonderland, our experiences will be enriched according to the degree of curiosity and patience we bring to them. Just as a lasting friendship with a special person benefits from extended familiarity, so our appreciation of a painting, a play, or a symphony benefits from repeated contact and close attention. There are no shortcuts to the appreciation of the humanistic tradition, but there are some techniques that may be helpful. We may, for instance, approach each primary source from the triple perspective of its *text,* its *context,* and its *subtext.*

The Text: The *text* of any primary source refers to its *medium* (what it is made of), its *form* (the shape it assumes), and its *content* (the subject it describes). All literature, for example, whether intended to be spoken or read, depends on the medium of words—the American poet Robert Frost once defined literature as "performance in words." Literary form varies according to the manner in which the words are arranged: for instance, dramatic dialogue, prose, or poetry. The main purpose of prose is to convey information, to narrate and describe, while poetry, which is founded on freedom from conventional patterns of grammar, is usually concerned with expressing emotions. Philosophy (the search for truth through reasoned analysis) and history (the record of the past) make use of prose to analyze and communicate ideas and information. In literature, as in most kinds of expression, content and form are usually interrelated. The subject matter or the form of a literary work usually determines its *genre.* For instance, a long narrative poem recounting the adventures of a hero is an *epic,* while a formal, dignified speech in praise of a person or thing constitutes a *eulogy.*

The visual arts—painting, sculpture, architecture, and photography—make use of such media as wood, clay, colored pigments, marble, granite, steel, and (more recently) plastic, neon, and computers. The style of the work of art depends on how the artist uses the formal elements of color, line, texture, and space—elements that lack denotative meaning. The formal elements of art may work to describe and interpret the visible world, as in such genres as portraiture and landscape painting. They may generate fantastic and purely imaginative kinds of imagery, or, they may be nonrepresentational—that is, completely without recognizable content. In general, however, the visual arts are all spatial—they operate and are apprehended in space.

The medium of music is sound. Like literature, music is a durational form of expression; that is, it is apprehended over the period of time in which it occurs, rather than "grasped" all at once. The formal elements of music include melody, rhythm, and harmony—elements that, like those of the visual arts, lack symbolic content. But while paintings and sculptures may imitate or describe nature, musical compositions are generally nonrepresentational. For that reason, music is the most difficult of the arts to describe in words. Dance is also a temporal art form. Its medium is the human body in its expressive dimension. Like music, dance is performance-oriented, but like painting and sculpture, dance unfolds in space as well as unfolds time.

In analyzing the text of a work of literature, art, or music, we might ask how its formal elements contribute to its meaning and affective power. We might also try to identify the style of the art work and ask whether and how that style reflects the personal vision of the artist. We may discover, moreover, that the creative artifacts of a specific period share certain defining features or characteristics. Similarities (both general and specific) between, for instance, Greek temples and Greek tragedies, between Chinese poems and paintings, or between postmodern fiction and pop sculpture may lead us to examine the relationship between such works of art and the cultures in which they were produced.

The Context: We use the word *context* to describe a historical and cultural milieu. In what time and place did the artifact originate? How did it function within the society in which it was created? Was the purpose of the piece decorative, didactic, magical, propagandistic? Did it serve the religious or political needs of the community? Sometimes our answers to these questions are mere guesses. Nevertheless, understanding the function of an artifact often serves to clarify the nature of its form (and vice versa). For instance, because much of the literature produced prior to the fifteenth century was spoken or chanted rather than read, that literature tends to feature repetition and rhyme, devices that facilitated memorization. We may assume that literary works embellished with frequent repetitions, such as the *Epic of Gilgamesh*, were products of an oral tradition. Then too, establishing the function of an artwork permits us to determine whether the created object satisfied an individual impulse or a communal need: the paintings on the walls of Paleolithic caves, which are among the most compelling animal illustrations in the history of world art, probably belonged to a sacred hunting ritual, the performance of which was essential to the survival of the community. Understanding the relationship between text and context is one of the principal concerns of any inquiry into the humanistic tradition.

The Subtext: The *subtext* of the literary or artistic object refers to its secondary and implied meanings. The subtext reveals the emotional or intellectual messages embedded in a work of art. The epic poems of the ancient Greeks, for instance, celebrate the virtues of male prowess and physical courage. State portraits of the seventeenth-century King Louis XIV of France carry a message of absolute and unassailable power. And, more recently, Andy Warhol's serial adaptations of Campbell's soup cans and Coca-Cola bottles mock the supermarket mentality of American culture. Analyzing the subtext of a work of art often involves an understanding of the implicit and explicit symbolism common to a particular age.

Beyond *The Humanistic Tradition*

This text is able to offer only small, enticing samples from an enormous cultural buffet. Students are encouraged to go beyond the tidbits provided here—to dine more fully from the table. And to feast most sumptuously, nothing can substitute for firsthand experience. Students, therefore, should make every effort to visit art museums and galleries, concert halls, and libraries. *The Humanistic Tradition* is written for typical students, who may or may not be able to read music but who surely are able to cultivate an appreciation of music in performance. The clefs that appear in the text refer to music listening selections listed at the end of each chapter and found on the accompanying cassettes, available from Wm. C. Brown Communications, Inc. The terms that appear in bold print in the text are defined in glossaries following each chapter. A list of suggestions for further reading also appears at the end of each chapter, while a selected general bibliography appears at the end of each book.

Acknowledgments

Writing *The Humanistic Tradition* has been an exercise in humility. Without the assistance of learned friends and colleagues, assembling a book of this breadth would have been an impossible task. James H. Dormon read all parts of the manuscript and made extensive and substantive editorial suggestions; as his colleague, friend, and wife, I am most deeply indebted to him. I am grateful to the following faculty members of the University of Southwestern Louisiana for their thoughtful suggestions: for literature, Allen David Barry, Darrell Bourque, C. Harry Bruder, John W. Fiero, Emilio F. Garcia, Doris Meriwether, John Moore, and Patricia K. Rickels; for history, Vaughan B. Baker, Ora-Wes S. Cady, and Thomas D. Schoonover; for philosophy, Steven Giambrone and Robert T. Kirkpatrick; for architecture, Ethel Goodstein; for geography, Tim Reilly; for science, John R. Meriwether; and for music, James Burke and Robert F. Schmalz.

The following readers and reviewers generously shared their insights in matters of content and style: Michael K. Aakhus (University of Southern Indiana–Evansville); Vaughan B. Baker (University of Southwestern Louisiana); Katherine Charlton (Mt. San Antonio Community College); Bessie Chronaki (Central Piedmont Community College); Debora A. Drehen (Florida Community College–Jacksonville); Paula Drewek (Macomb Community College); William C. Gentry (Henderson State University); Kenneth Ganza (Colby College); Ellen Hofman (Highline Community College); Burton Raffel (University of Southwestern Louisiana); Frank La Rosa (San Diego City College); George Rogers (Stonehill College); Douglas P. Sjoquist (Lansing Community College); Howard V. Starks (Southeastern Oklahoma State University); Ann Wakefield (Academy of the Sacred Heart—Grand Coteau); Sylvia White (Florida Community College–Jacksonville); and Audrey Wilson (Florida State University).

The University of Southwestern Louisiana facilitated my lengthy commitment to this project with two Summer Faculty Research Grants, as well as with an enormous measure of moral support. I am indebted to the energetic staff of Dupré Library, to the University Honors Program, which made available to me the research assistance of Kara D. DeRamus, Beth Jones, and Judy Guillot, and to the secretarial staff of the Department of History and Philosophy, especially Harriet Laporte, for her untiring and cheerful assistance. In preparing the time lines for the text, I have depended upon Glenn Melancon and the USL History Graduate Program. Special thanks go to the efficient personnel and staff of Wm. C. Brown Communications, Inc., and, in particular, to Acquisitions Editor Meredith M. Morgan, whose good humor and judicious advice lightened my burdens; and to Production Editor Dan Rapp, for his perfectionism and his unflagging support. Finally, I am deeply grateful to my students; their sense of wonder and enthusiasm for learning are continuing reminders of why this book was written.

Supplements for the Instructor

In addition to the books, a number of useful supplements are available to instructors using *The Humanistic Tradition*. Please contact your WCB representative for more information about these resources.

Instructor's Resource Manual

The Instructor's Resource Manual, written by Candace Waltz of San Diego City College, is designed to assist instructors as they plan and prepare for their classes. Possible course organizations and sample syllabi for semester or quarter systems are suggested. Each chapter corresponds to a chapter in the books, and features a chapter summary, chapter outline, and study questions, all designed to allow instructors to remove and copy as handouts for their students. There are two types of study questions: *Factual Questions* that allow students to recapture the important points of each chapter, and *Challenge Questions* that force students to think more deeply and critically about the subject matter. Each chapter has a correlation list that directs instructors to the appropriate music examples, slides, transparencies, and software sections of the other supplements. A list of suggested videotapes, recordings, videodiscs and their suppliers is included. The final section of the Resource Manual contains a Test Item File, divided by chapter and featuring multiple choice, true/false, short answer, and essay questions.

WCB TestPak 3.0

WCB TestPak, a computerized testing service, provides instructors with either a mail-in/call-in testing program or the complete test item file on diskette for use with IBM PC, Apple, or Macintosh computers. WCB QuizPak, part of TestPak, provides students with true/false and multiple choice questions for each chapter. These questions will be the same questions found on the TestPak service, so students can prepare for examinations. WCB GradePak, also a part of TestPak, is a computerized grade management system for instructors. This program tracks student performance on examinations and assignments. It will compute each student's percentage and corresponding letter grade, as well as class average.

Audiocassettes

Two ninety-minute audiocassettes are available for *The Humanistic Tradition*. Cassette One corresponds to music listening selections discussed in Books 1–3 and Cassette Two for music in Books 4–6. Each selection on the cassettes is discussed in the text and includes a voice introduction for easier location. These cassettes can be packaged with any of the six texts, or sold separately.

WCB Slide Bank

Available through Sandak, Inc., this customized slide set allows each instructor to choose slides that directly correspond to the text, or additional slides to illustrate similar concepts. Prices for the sets depend upon the total number of slides ordered. Contact your WCB representative for order forms and details.

WCB Humanities Transparencies

A set of 71 acetate transparencies is available with *The Humanistic Tradition*. These show examples of art concepts, architectural styles, art media, maps, musical notation, musical styles, and musical elements.

Culture 1.0 ©

Developed by Cultural Resources, Inc., for courses in interdisciplinary humanities, Culture 1.0 © is a fascinating journey into humanity's cultural achievements on Hypercard © software. Available in either IBM PC or Macintosh formats, this seven-disk program allows students to explore the achievements of humanity through essays, almanacs, visual, or musical examples. Each time period contains historical, political, religious, philosophical, artistic, and musical categories, creating an interactive, Socratic method of learning for the students. Culture 1.0 © also features note-taking capabilities, report capabilities, and a student workbook for more guided learning. Contact your WCB representative for preview disks or ordering information.

	To 1550	1600	1625	1650	1675

WORLD EVENTS

Catholic Reformation — Thirty Years' War — London Fire
Loyola: Jesuits — The Age of Absolutism —
Council of Trent — Louis XIV of France —

├ Elizabeth I of England — James I — Charles I — Civil War — English Commonwealth —
Cromwell

Philip II of Spain — French Royal Academy of Language and Literature
invades Dutch lowlands — Royal Society of London for Improving Natural Knowledge

Copernicus: heliocentric theory — Scientific Revolution —
Vesalius: *Anatomy* — Kepler   Galileo — Mathematics

├ Suleiman/Ottoman Empire —
├ Ming dynasty/China — Ch'ing (Manchu dynasty) —
├ Mogul Empire – Akbar — Jahangir — Shah Jahan —
Safavid dynasty/Shah Abbas

LITERATURE AND PHILOSOPHY

Loyola: *Spiritual Exercises* — King James Bible — Donne: meditations and sonnets — Crashaw: *The Flaming Heart* — La Rochefoucauld: maxims

Council of Trent: *Index Expurgatorius* — Bacon: *Novum Organum* — Descartes: *Discourse on Method* — Hobbes: *Leviathan*
Milton: *Paradise Lost*

Teresa of Avila: autobiography — First weekly newspaper published in London — Racine: *Phaedra*
Pascal: *Pensées*

Ming drama and poetry — Grotius: *On the Law of War and Peace* — Spinoza: *Ethics*

Safavid poetry

VISUAL ARTS AND ARCHITECTURE

Mannerism — the Baroque style —
Michelangelo: *Last Judgment* — Bernini: *Ecstasy of St. Teresa* — Wren: St. Paul's
Caravaggio: *Supper at Emmaus*
Parmigianino: *Madonna* — Poussin: *Arcadian Shepherds*
Tintoretto: *Last Supper* — Borromini: San Carlo
Safavid carpets — Van Dyck: *Charles I* — Lorrain: landscapes
El Greco: *Agony in the Garden* — Rubens: *Rape of the Daughters of Leucippus* — Rembrandt: *Return of the Prodigal Son*
Bichitr: Mogul court portraits
Vignola and della Porta: *Il Gesù* — Shajahanbad — Velásquez: *Las Meninas*
Imperial Mosque at Isfahan — Taj Mahal — Hals and Leyster: Dutch portraits
Ottoman court painting and metalcraft — Ming porcelains and silks — Peking: Forbidden City

MUSIC AND DANCE

Palestrina: *Pope Marcellus Mass* — Chromatic scale — First opera house Venice, 1637 — Lully: French opera
Victoria: church music — Violin, viola, cello, organ, and harpsicord perfected — Monteverdi: *Orfeo* — Modern oboe invented
Gabrieli: polychoral style; *In Ecclesiis* — Minuet

1675   1700   1725   1750   1775   1800

Dutch Republic

Excavation of Herculaneum

Louis XV ——— Louis XVI —— French Revolution

Glorious Revolution
William and Mary
Bill of Rights

Catherine the Great of Russia
Maria Theresa of Austria

American Revolution
Jefferson:
Declaration of
Independence

Declaration of
the Rights of
Man and Citizen

Reign of Terror
Napoleon

Linen napkins,
forks

Lavoisier:
Treatise on Chemistry

and experimentation —————— Industrial Revolution ————
Newton: *Principia Mathematica*

Flying shuttle   Spinning jenny   Watts: steam engine   Power loom

————— Decline of Mogul Empire —————

————— Enlightenment —————

Locke: *Essay Concerning
Human Understanding;
Of Civil Government*

Montesquieu:
Spirit of the Laws

Diderot:
Encyclopedia

Smith: *Wealth
of Nations*

Kant:
*Critique of
Pure Reason*

Corneille

Leibniz:
"philosophical
optimism"

Defoe

Swift: *Gulliver's
Travels*

Voltaire: *Candide*
Goldsmith: *Citizen
of the World*

Beccaria:
*On Crimes and
Punishment*

Pope: *Essay on Man*

Addison and Steele:
Tatler and *Spectator*

Gay: *Beggar's Opera*

Rousseau:
*Discourse;
Social Contract;
Emile*

Condorcet: *Progress of
the Human Mind*

Molière:
Le Bourgeois Gentilhomme

European Novel:
Richardson
Fielding

Ts'ao Hsüeh-chín: *Dream
of the Red Chamber*

Li Ju-chen: *Flowers
in the Mirror*

Pozzo: *St. Ignatius*

————— the Rococo style —————

Watteau: *Departure
from Cythera*

Fisher: Church of Ottobeuren
Vigée-Lebrun: portraits
Fragonard: *The Swing*

Clodion: *Intoxication*

Jefferson: University
of Virginia

Rigaud: *Louis XIV*
Le Vau and Mansart: Versailles
Perrault: Louvre
Girardon: *Apollo*

Boucher: *Venus
Consoling Love*

————— the Neoclassical style —————

Winckelmann: *History
of Ancient Art*

Wedgewood   Canova

David: *The Oath of
the Horatii*

de Heem: *Still Life*
de Hooch: *Dutch Courtyard*
ter Borch: *Suitor's Visit*
Vermeer: *View of Delft;
Goldweigher*

Chinoiserie

Hogarth: *Marriage Contract*
Greuze: *Village Betrothal*
Chardin: *Kitchen Maid*
Houdon: *Voltaire*

Soufflot: Ste. Geneviève
Adam: Osterly Park House
Gibbs: London churches

Vignon: *La
Madeleine*
Chalgrin: Arch of
Triumph

Piano invented

Feuillet: choreographic
notatIon

Vivaldi: *Four Seasons;*
concerto grosso

Handel: oratorio; *Messiah*
J.S. Bach: cantata; *Passion According
to St. Matthew; Brandenburg
Concertos; Art of Fugue*

Stamitz: Mannheim;
orchestra; orchestral
scores

Haydn: "Father of the
Symphony"; string quartets

Couperin: suites; *Art
of Playing Clavecin*

Mozart: *Eine Kleine Nachtmusik;
Marriage of Figaro*

Chinese opera

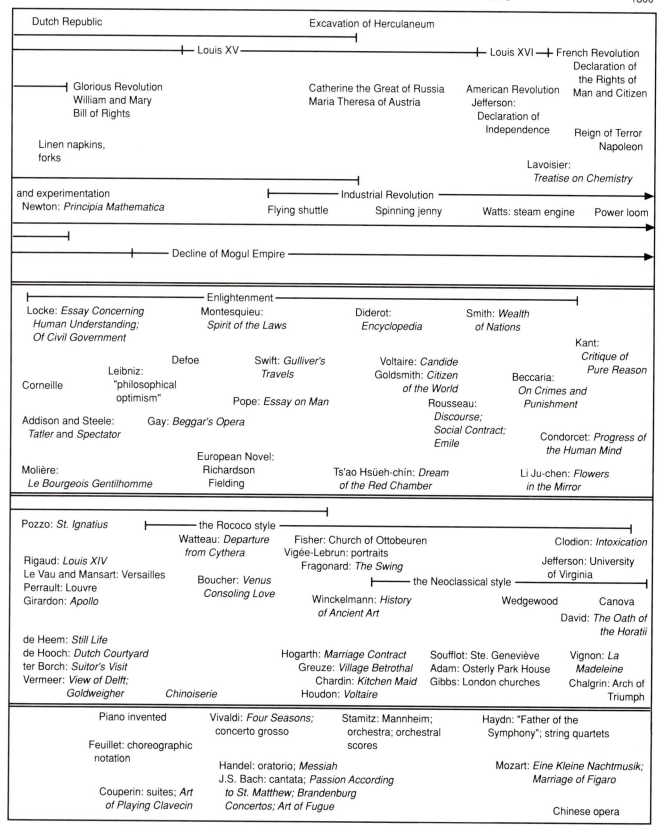

THE HUMANISTIC TRADITION

4 The Age
of the Baroque
and the European
Enlightenment

I

THE AGE OF THE BAROQUE

The period between approximately 1600 and 1800 was an age of contradictions. In Western Europe, deeply felt, even mystical religious sentiment vied with the rise of science and rational methods of scientific investigation. Nascent theories of constitutional government contended with firmly entrenched claims to divine right power among "absolute" rulers—monarchs who recognized no legal limitations to their authority. The rising wealth of a small segment of the population failed to offset widespread poverty and old aristocratic privilege. In Asia, as well, the seventeenth and eighteenth centuries brought major changes: Muslim rulers united the primarily Hindu peoples of India and proceeded to establish the glorious Mogul dynasty. The Ming emperors of China, who governed an empire larger than any other in the world, fell to Mongol (Manchu) tribes in the early seventeenth century. The Manchu rulers secured internal peace through rigid control of Chinese culture.

The early modern era witnessed the beginnings of the European state system and the establishment of the fundamental political, economic, and cultural norms of European and, by extension, American life. Rival religious claims following the Protestant Reformation complicated the scramble for land and power among European states. The first half of the seventeenth century witnessed the Thirty Years' War and other devastating conflicts between

Catholics and Protestants. In 1648, however, by the terms of the Treaty of Westphalia, which ended the Thirty Years' War, the principle of national sovereignty was firmly established: by that principle, each European state would exercise independent and supreme authority over its own territories and inhabitants.

In the economic arena, the prosperity of the sixteenth century was followed by marked decline in the seventeenth. Nevertheless, after 1660, commercial capitalism and the production of manufactured goods flourished in the West, where economic growth was tied to a pattern of global commerce. Asia, Africa, and the Americas—lucrative markets for European goods—were frontiers for European traders. And as global perceptions widened, Europeans realized that the "Old World" could no longer live in isolation.

In the West, the years between 1600 and 1750 were closely associated with a style known as "the baroque." Characterized by dramatic expression, theatrical spectacle, and spatial grandeur, the baroque became the hallmark of an age of exuberant expansion. The style also reflected the new, dynamic view of the universe as set forth by proponents of the Scientific Revolution. The baroque encompassed various phases: in Italy, it mirrored the intensely religious mood of the Catholic Reformation; in Northern Europe, it reflected the intimate spirit of Protestant devotionalism as well as the empirical character of the New Science; and among authoritarian regimes throughout Europe and Asia, it worked to glorify secular power and wealth.

The Age of the Baroque was fueled by the human ambition to master nature on a colossal scale. This ambition—inspired perhaps by a more detached and objective view of the self in relation to the world—is as evident in Galileo's efforts to understand and explain the operations of nature as it is in Louis XIV's attempts to exert unlimited power over vast territories and peoples. A similar kind of energy is apparent in the complexities of a Bach fugue, the cosmic scope of Milton's *Paradise Lost,* the spectacle of early Italian opera, the panoramic sweep of Dutch landscape paintings, the splendor of the royal palaces at Versailles, Delhi, and Peking, and the efforts of Ming and Manchu emperors to collect and copy all of China's literary classics.

Chapter 20, "The Catholic Reformation and the Baroque Style," examines the Counter-Reformation as an inspiration for the arts of seventeenth-century Italy and Spain. Major topics include the literary contributions of Ignatius Loyola and Saint Teresa, the sculpture of Bernini, the paintings of El Greco and Caravaggio, the music of Palestrina and Gabrieli, and the rise of opera. Chapter 21, "The Baroque in the Protestant North," explores selected examples of seventeenth- and early eighteenth-century Northern European literature, art, and music. The poetry of Donne and Milton, the art of Rembrandt, and the vocal music of Handel and Bach are examined as evidence of an essentially different religious sensibility from that of Catholic Europe, but one that shared the baroque taste for grandeur and dramatic expression.

Chapter 22, "The Scientific Revolution and the New Learning," investigates the ways in which advances in the sciences and the rise of early modern philosophy contributed to the formation of modern Western culture. The search for new modes of rational investigation in the writings of Bacon, Descartes, and Locke; the development of an empirically precise style of painting among the artists of the North Netherlands; and the birth of pure instrumental music are central, complementary themes in this chapter. Finally, chapter 23, "Absolute Power and the Aristocratic Style," focuses on the phenomenon of political absolutism in Western Europe and Asia and its influence on the arts. Under King Louis XIV of France, as among the Safavid Persians, the Moguls of India, and the Ming and Manchu emperors of China, there emerged an aristocratic style that aimed to glorify the majesty and power of the ruler. The chapter surveys the cult of majesty in France, the palace at Versailles, and the rise of academic neoclassicism. It also includes a delightful Molière play that captures the spirit of seventeenth-century French society. Beyond Europe, the aristocratic style is embodied in the Taj Mahal and other glorious Mogul monuments and in the Forbidden City of the Chinese nobility.

20

THE CATHOLIC REFORMATION
AND THE BAROQUE STYLE

The Protestant Reformation created a religious up-heaval unlike any other within the history of Christianity. Luther's criticism of the Roman Catholic church had encouraged religious devotion free of papal authority and had prepared the way for the rise of other Protestant sects (chapter 18). The rival religious beliefs that fragmented Western Europe became a major excuse for armed combat. The Thirty Years' War (1618–48), which resulted in the establishment of Protestantism in most of Northern Europe, caused the death of some five million Europeans. As Protestant sects lured increasing numbers of Christians away from Roman Catholicism, the Church undertook a program of internal reform and reorganization known as the Catholic or Counter-Reformation. While the Catholic Reformation introduced a more militant form of Catholicism to all parts of the world, it also encouraged, particularly in Spain, Italy, and Latin America, intensely personalized expressions of religious sentiment.

The Catholic Reformation

In the face of the Protestant challenge, the Roman Catholic church pursued a path that ensured its survival in the modern world. Between 1540 and 1565 churchmen undertook papal and monastic reforms that eliminated corruption and restored Catholicism to many parts of Europe. The impetus for renewal came largely from fervent Spanish Catholics, the most notable of whom was Ignatius Loyola (d. 1556). A soldier in the army of Philip II, the Hapsburg ruler of Spain, Loyola brought to Catholicism the same iron will he had exercised on the battlefield. After his right leg was fractured by a French cannonball at the siege of Pamplona, Loyola became a religious teacher and a hermit, traveling lame and barefoot to Jerusalem to convert Muslims to Christianity. In the 1530s he founded the Society of Jesus, the most important of many new monastic orders associated with the Catholic Reformation. The Society of Jesus, or Jesuits, followed Loyola in calling for a militant return to fundamental Catholic dogma and the strict enforcement of traditional Church teachings. In addition to the monastic vows of celibacy, poverty, and obedience, the Jesuits took an oath of allegiance to the pope, whom they served as soldiers of Christ.

Under Loyola's leadership, the Jesuit order became the most influential missionary society of early modern times. Rigorously trained, its members acted as preachers, confessors, and teachers—leaders in educational reform and moral discipline. Throughout Europe, members of the newly formed order worked as missionaries to win back those who had strayed from "mother church." With the aid of the Inquisition (chapter 12), the Jesuits were fairly successful in stamping out Protestantism in much of France, Southern Germany, and other parts of Europe. In the Americas, which became prime targets for Jesuit activity, missionaries learned Native American tribal languages and proceeded to convert thousands of native Americans to Roman Catholicism.

The Jesuit order was a fascinating amalgam of two elements—mysticism and militant religious zeal. The first emphasized the intuition of a god that transcended intellectual understanding, while the second involved an attitude of unquestioned submission to the Church as the absolute source of truth. These two aspects of Jesuit thinking—mysticism and militancy—are reflected in Loyola's influential handbook, the *Spiritual Exercises*. In his introductory observations, Loyola explains that the spiritual exercises should do for the soul what such physical exercises as running and walking do for the body. As aids to the development of perfect spiritual discipline, the exercises—each of which should occupy a full hour's time—engage the body in perfecting the soul. For example, in the Fifth Exercise, a meditation on Hell, each of the five senses is summoned to heighten the mystical experience:

> FIRST POINT: This will be to *see* in imagination the vast fires, and the souls enclosed, as it were, in bodies of fire.
> SECOND POINT: To *hear* the wailing, the howling, cries, and blasphemies against Christ our Lord and against His saints.
> THIRD POINT: With the sense of *smell* to perceive the smoke, the sulphur, the filth, and corruption.
> FOURTH POINT: To *taste* the bitterness of tears, sadness, and remorse of conscience.
> FIFTH POINT: With the sense of *touch* to feel the flames which envelop and burn the souls.

Loyola also insists on an unswerving commitment to traditional Church teachings. Among the "rules for thinking with the Church" is Loyola's advice that Christians put aside all judgments of their own and remain obedient to the "holy Mother, the hierarchical Church."

READING 71   From Loyola's *Spiritual Exercises*

THE FOLLOWING RULES SHOULD BE OBSERVED TO FOSTER THE TRUE ATTITUDE OF MIND WE OUGHT TO HAVE IN THE CHURCH MILITANT.

1. We must put aside all judgment of our own, and keep the mind ever ready and prompt to obey in all things the true Spouse of Christ our Lord, our holy Mother, the hierarchical Church.
2. We should praise sacramental confession, the yearly reception of the Most Blessed Sacrament, and praise more highly monthly reception, and still more weekly Communion, provided requisite and proper dispositions are present.
3. We ought to praise the frequent hearing of Mass, the singing of hymns, psalmody, and long prayers whether in the church or outside; likewise, the hours arranged at fixed times for the whole Divine Office, for every kind of prayer, and for the canonical hours.[1]
4. We must praise highly religious life, virginity, and continency; and matrimony ought not to be praised as much as any of these.
5. We should praise vows of religion, obedience, poverty, chastity, and vows to perform other works . . . conducive to perfection. . . .
6. We should show our esteem for the relics of the saints by venerating them and praying to the saints. We should praise visits to the Station Churches,[2] pilgrimages, indulgences, jubilees,[3] crusade indults,[4] and the lighting of candles in churches.
7. We must praise the regulations of the Church with regard to fast and abstinence. . . . We should praise works of penance, not only those that are interior but also those that are exterior.
8. We ought to praise not only the building and adornment of churches, but also images and veneration of them according to the subject they represent.
9. Finally, we must praise all the commandments of the Church, and be on the alert to find reasons to defend them, and by no means in order to criticize them. . . .
13. If we wish to proceed securely in all things, we must hold fast to the following principle: What seems to me white, I will believe black if the hierarchical Church so defines. For I must be convinced that in Christ our Lord, the bridegroom, and in His spouse the Church, only one Spirit holds sway, which governs and rules for the salvation of souls. For it is by the same Spirit and Lord who gave the Ten Commandments that our holy Mother Church is ruled and governed.

---

[1]The eight times of the day appointed for special devotions, see chapters 9 and 15.

[2]Churches with images representing the stages of Christ's Passion.

[3]A time of special solemnity, ordinarily every twenty-five years, proclaimed by the pope; also, special indulgences granted during that time.

[4]Church indulgences granted to Christian Crusaders.

Loyola's affirmation of Roman Catholic doctrine—especially the sacraments and the absolute spiritual leadership of the pope—were officially confirmed at a general church council that met three times between 1545 and 1563. The Council of Trent set clear guidelines for the elimination of abuses among members of the clergy and encouraged the regeneration of intellectual life within Catholic monasteries. Church leaders revived the activities of the Inquisition and established the *Index Expurgatorius,* a list of books judged heretical and therefore forbidden to Catholic readers. The Catholic Reformation supported a broadly based Catholicism that emphasized one's direct and intuitive—hence, mystical—experience of God. And although the Roman Catholic church would never again reassume the universal authority it had enjoyed during the Middle Ages, its internal reforms and its efforts to rekindle the faith restored its dignity in the minds and hearts of its followers.

The Literature of Religious Ecstasy

The passionate mysticism of Loyola's *Exercises* informed all aspects of the Catholic Reformation. Especially important in religious literature was the emphasis on heightening spiritual experience by way of the senses—a kind of mysticism that differed sharply from Hindu and Buddhist transcendence through the *denial* of the senses. The most famous of sixteenth-century mystics was the Spanish Carmelite nun Teresa of Avila (d. 1582), who was canonized in 1622. Teresa's activities in founding religious houses and in defending groups of Carmelites, who symbolized their humility by going without shoes, took her all over Spain and earned her the nickname "the roving nun." It was not until she was almost forty years old that her life as a visionary began. Teresa's visions, including the one described in the following autobiographical excerpt, marry sensory experience to spiritual contemplation. They address, moreover, the intriguing kinship between physical suffering and psychic bliss and between divine and erotic fulfillment. For Saint Teresa, love is the inspiration for oneness with God. And the language by which the saint describes that union—the reception of God's flaming arrow that leaves her "completely afire"—is charged with passion.

READING 72 From Saint Teresa's *Visions*

It pleased the Lord that I should sometimes see the following vision. I would see beside me, on my left hand, an angel in bodily form—a type of vision which I am not in the habit of seeing, except very rarely. Though I often see representations of angels, my visions of them are of the type which I first mentioned. It pleased the Lord that I should see this angel in the following way. He was not tall, but short, and very beautiful, his face so aflame that he appeared to be one of the highest types of angel who seem to be all afire. They must be those who are called cherubim: they do not tell me their names but I am well aware that there is a great difference between certain angels and others, and between these and others still, of a kind that I could not possibly explain. In his hands I saw a long golden spear and at the end of the iron tip I seemed to see a point of fire. With this he seemed to pierce my heart several times so that it penetrated to my entrails. When he drew it out, I thought he was drawing them out with it and he left me completely afire with a great love for God. The pain was so sharp that it made me utter several moans; and so excessive was the sweetness caused me by this intense pain that one can never wish to lose it, nor will one's soul be content with anything less than God. It is not bodily pain, but spiritual, though the body has a share in it—indeed, a great share. So sweet are the colloquies of love which pass between the soul and God that if anyone thinks I am lying I beseech God, in His goodness, to give him the same experience.

The sensuous imagery of Teresa's visions colored much of the religious verse of the seventeenth century, including that of her Spanish contemporaries, Saint John of the Cross (d. 1591), also a Carmelite, and Luis de Gongora y Argote (d. 1627). Similarly, in the poetry of such devout English Catholics as Richard Crashaw (d. 1649), the language of religious ecstasy mingled with brooding desire.

Born into a Protestant family, Crashaw converted to Catholicism early in life. His religious poems, written in Latin and English, reflect the dual influence of Loyola's meditations and Teresa's visions. At least two of his most lyrical pieces are dedicated to Saint Teresa: *A Hymn to the Name and Honor of the Admirable Saint Teresa* and *The Flaming Heart, upon the Book and Picture of the Seraphical Saint Teresa, as She Is Usually Expressed with a Seraphim beside Her.* The latter suggests that Crashaw was familiar with Bernini's sculpted version of Teresa's vision before it was publically unveiled in Rome (figure 20.1). Representative of the entire poem, the last sixteen lines of *The Flaming Heart,* reproduced in Reading 73, are rhapsodic in their intense expression of personal emotion. Erasing boundaries between erotic and spiritual love, Crashaw pleads that Teresa ravish his soul, even as she has been ravished by God.

FIGURE 20.1 *The Ecstasy of Saint Teresa,* Gianlorenzo Bernini, 1645–52. Cornaro Chapel, Church of Santa Maria della Vittoria, Rome. University Prints.

READING 73 From Crashaw's *The Flaming Heart*

. . . .

O thou undaunted daughter of desires!   1
By all thou dower of lights and fires;
By all the eagle in thee, all the dove;
By all thy lives and deaths of love;
By thy large draughts of intellectual day,   5
And by thy thirsts of love more large than they;
By all thy brim-filled bowls of fierce desire,
By thy last morning's draught of liquid fire;
By the full kingdom of that final kiss
That seized thy parting soul, and sealed thee His;   10
By all the heavens thou hast in Him,
Fair sister of the seraphim,
By all of Him we have in thee;
Leave nothing of myself in me!
Let me so read thy life that I   15
Unto all life of mine may die.

The Art of Religious Ecstasy

Mannerist and Baroque Painting

The religious zeal of the Catholic reformers inspired a tremendous surge of artistic activity, especially in Italy and Spain. In Italy, where the main centers of this activity were Venice and Rome, the art of the High Renaissance underwent radical transformation: the clearly defined, symmetrical compositions of High Renaissance painters and the decorum and dignity of the grand style (chapter 17) gave way to *mannerism,* a style marked by spatial complexity, artificiality, and affectation. Mannerist artists brought a new psychological intensity to visual expression. Their paintings mirrored the self-conscious spirituality and the profound insecurities of an age of religious wars and political rivalry.

FIGURE 20.2 *The Last Judgment,* Michelangelo Buonarroti, 1536–40. Altar wall of the Sistine Chapel, Vatican, Rome. Alinari/Art Resource, New York.

The mannerist style is already evident in *The Last Judgment* that the sixty-year-old Michelangelo painted on the east wall of the Sistine Chapel (figure 20.2). Between 1534 and 1541, only a few years after the armies of the Holy Roman Empire had sacked the city of Rome, Michelangelo returned to the chapel whose ceiling he had painted with the optimistic vision of salvation. Now, in a mood of brooding pessimism, the aging genius filled the space with agonized, writhing figures that press dramatically against one another. Surrounding the wrathful Christ are the Christian martyrs, who carry the instruments of their torture, and throngs of the resurrected—originally depicted nude but later, in the wake of Catholic reform, draped to hide their genitals. Michelangelo has replaced the classically proportioned figures, calm balance, and spatial clarity of High Renaissance painting with a more mystical and, at once, more troubled vision of salvation.

The mannerist style flourished in Italy with the compelling paintings of Parmigianino (d. 1540). Parmigianino's Madonna and child, commonly known as the *Madonna of the Long Neck,* introduces a new theatricality to the rendering of a traditional subject (figure 20.3; compare Raphael's *Alba Madonna,* figure 17.22). Perched precariously above a *piazza* adorned

FIGURE 20.3 *Madonna of the Long Neck,* Parmigianino, 1534–40. Oil on panel, 7 ft. 1 in. × 4 ft. 4 in. Uffizi Gallery, Florence. Alinari/Art Resource, New York.

FIGURE 20.4 *The Last Supper,* Jacopo Tintoretto, 1592–94. Oil on canvas, 12 ft. × 18 ft. 8 in. S. Giorgio Maggiore, Venice. Alinari/Art Resource, New York.

with a column that supports no superstructure, the unnaturally elongated Mother of God—her spidery fingers affectedly touching her breast—gazes at the oversized Christ child, who seems to slip lifelessly off her lap. Onlookers press into the ambiguous space from the left, while a small figure (perhaps a prophet) at the bottom right corner of the canvas draws our eye into distant space. Cool coloring and an overall smokey hue make the painting seem even more contrived and artificial, yet, by its very contrivance, unforgettable.

The degree to which the mannerists rejected the guiding principles of High Renaissance painting is nowhere better illustrated than by comparing *The Last Supper* (figure 20.4) by the Venetian artist Jacopo Tintoretto (d. 1594) with the fresco of the same subject by Leonardo da Vinci executed approximately a century earlier (figure 17.21). In his rendering of the sacred event, Tintoretto renounced the symmetry and geometric clarity of Leonardo's composition. The receding lines of the table and the floor in Tintoretto's painting place the viewer above the scene and draw the eye toward a vanishing point that lies in a distant and uncertain space beyond the bounds of the canvas. The even texture of Leonardo's fresco gives way in Tintoretto's canvas to vaporous contrasts of dark and

light, produced by a smoking oil lamp. Clouds of angels flutter spectrally at the ceiling, and phosphorescent halos seem to electrify the figures of the apostles. At the most concentrated burst of light, the Savior is pictured distributing bread and wine to the disciples. While Leonardo focused on the human element of the Last Supper—the moment when Jesus acknowledges his impending betrayal—Tintoretto illustrates the miracle of the Eucharist, the moment when Jesus initiates the sacrament by which the bread and wine become his flesh and blood. Yet Tintoretto sets the miracle amidst the ordinary activities of household servants, who occupy the entire right-hand portion of the picture.

The mannerist passion for pictorial intensity was most vividly realized in the paintings of Dominikos Theotokopoulos, generally known, because of his Greek origins, as El Greco (d. 1614). A master painter who worked in Italy and Spain in the service of the Church and the devout Phillip II, El Greco produced visionary canvases marked by bold distortions of form, dissonant colors, and a daring handling of space. His fervent, slender saints and martyrs, highlighted by ghostly whites and yellow-grays, seem to radiate supernatural halos—auras that symbolize the luminous power of divine revelation (figure 20.5). In *The Agony in the Garden* El Greco creates a moonlit landscape

FIGURE 20.5 *The Penitent Saint Peter*, El Greco, ca. 1598–1600. San Diego Museum of Art.

in which clouds, rocks and fabrics billow and swell with mysterious energy (figure 20.6). The sleeping apostles, tucked away in a cocoonlike envelope, violate rational space: they are too small in relation to the oversized image of Jesus and the angel that hovers above. El Greco's ambiguous spatial fields, which often include multiple vanishing points, his acrid greens and yellows, and his "painterly" techniques—his brushstrokes remain visible on the surface of the canvas—all contribute to the creation of a highly personal and, by our standards, "modern" style that captured the mystical fervor of the new Catholicism.

If mannerism, as reflected in the art of Tintoretto and El Greco, was the vehicle of Counter-Reformation mysticism, the *baroque style* conveyed the dynamic spirit of an entire age. Derived from the Portugese word *barocco,* which describes the irregularly shaped pearls commonly featured in ornamental European decoration, the term *baroque* is associated with such features as ornateness, spatial grandeur, and theatrical flamboyance. In painting, the baroque style is characterized by asymmetric compositions, strong contrasts of light and dark, and bold, illusionistic effects.

The baroque style originated in Italy and came to dominate European art in the years between 1600 and 1750. Italian baroque artists worked to increase the dramatic expressiveness of religious subject matter in

order to give viewers the sense that they were participating in the action of the scene. Such was the ambition of the north Italian artist Michelangelo Merici, known as Caravaggio (d. 1610). The leading Italian painter of the seventeenth century, Caravaggio flouted Renaissance conventions of dignity and decorum, even as he flouted the law—he was arrested for violent acts that ranged from throwing a plate of artichokes in the face of a tavern keeper to armed assault and murder. In his controversial paintings, Caravaggio used strong contrasts of light and dark to give his figures sculptural force. A golden light bathes Christ and his disciples in *The Supper at Emmaus* (figure 20.7): Caravaggio "spotlights" the moment when, as related in the Gospel of Saint Luke, Christ's followers recognize him as he lifts his hand to bless the bread. He further underscores the dramatic moment of recognition, or revelation, by means of vigorous gestures: the disciple on the right flings his arms outward along a diagonal axis, while the one on the left grips the arms of his chair as though to rise. Unlike the visionary El Greco, Caravaggio brings sacred subjects down to earth with an almost cameralike naturalism. Where El Greco's saints and martyrs are ethereal, Caravaggio's are solid, substantive, and even ordinary looking. Their strong physical presence and frank homeliness eliminate the psychological distance between viewer and subject.

Caravaggio organized traditional religious compositions with unprecedented theatrical power and daring. In *The Crucifixion of Saint Peter,* he arranged the figures in a tense, off-centered pinwheel that caught the eccentricity of Saint Peter's torment—he

FIGURE 20.6 *The Agony in the Garden*, El Greco, ca. 1585–86. Oil on canvas, 40 1/4 × 44 3/4 in. The Toledo Museum of Art. Gift of Edward Drummond Libbey.

FIGURE 20.7 *The Supper at Emmaus,* Caravaggio, ca. 1600. Oil on canvas, 69 in. × 55 1/2 in. National Gallery, London.

FIGURE 20.8 *The Crucifixion of Saint Peter,* Caravaggio, 1601. Oil on canvas, 90 in. × 69 in. Santa Maria del Popolo, Rome. Alinari/Art Resource, New York.

was crucified upside down (figure 20.8). The saint's powerful physique is belied by the expression of vulnerability in his face. By placing the strongly modeled figures so close to the viewer and illuminating them against a darkened background, Caravaggio "stages" the action so that it seems to take place within the viewer's space—a space whose cruel light reveals such banal details as the executioner's dirty feet. True to the ideals of the Catholic Reformation, Caravaggio's paintings appealed to the senses rather than to the intellect.

Italian Baroque Sculpture

Gianlorenzo Bernini (d. 1690), Caravaggio's contemporary, brought the theatrical spirit of baroque painting to Italian architecture and sculpture. A man of remarkable technical virtuosity, Bernini was the chief architect of seventeenth-century Rome, as well as one of its leading sculptors. Under Bernini's direction, Rome became the "city of fountains." Richly adorned with dolphins, mermaids, and tritons, the fountain—its waters dancing and sparkling in the shifting wind and light—was a favorite ornamental device of the baroque era.

Bernini's most important contribution to baroque religious sculpture was his multi-media masterpiece *The Ecstasy of Saint Teresa* (figure 20.1), executed between 1645 and 1652 for the Cornaro Chapel of Santa Maria della Vittoria in Rome (figure 20.9). The piece, which typifies the intense religiosity of the

FIGURE 20.9   Cornaro Chapel, anonymous, ca. 1644. Oil on canvas. Church of Santa Maria della Vittoria, Rome. Staatliche Museum, Schwerin, Germany.

Counter-Reformation, brings to life Saint Teresa's autobiographical description of divine seduction. Bernini depicts Saint Teresa with head sunk back and eyes half-closed. A smiling cherubim resembling a teenaged cupid gently lifts Teresa's bodice in order to insert the flaming arrow of divine love. "Completely afire with a great love for God" (as she herself reports), Teresa swoons in ecstatic surrender. The uncertain juxtaposition of the saint and the cloud on which she reclines suggests the experience of levitation described in her vision. Sweetness and eroticism are the central features of this extraordinary image, whose sensuous impact is increased by bold illusionism: marble draperies flutter and billow with tense energy, and marble clouds float in heavenly space.

But Bernini went beyond the sculpture itself to achieve theatrical effects. In an effort to bring to life

FIGURE 20.10 Saint Peter's Basilica and the Vatican, Rome. Apse and dome by Michelangelo, 1547–64; dome completed by Giacomo della Porta, 1588–92; nave and facade by Carlo Maderno, 1601–26; colonnades by Gianlorenzo Bernini, 1656–63. Height of facade 147 ft., width 374 ft., height of dome 452 ft. Alinari/Art Resource, New York.

Teresa's mystical vision, he combined the tools of architecture, sculpture, and painting: he situated Teresa beneath a colonnaded marble canopy from which emerged a set of gilded wooden rays (representing supernatural light). Since real light entered through the glazed yellow panes of a concealed window above the chapel, the saint would appear bathed in a visionary golden glow—an effect comparable to the spotlighting in a Caravaggio painting. At the ceiling of the chapel a host of angels appears to descend from the heavens—the ensemble illusionistically conceived in paint and stucco (a plaster substance). Agate and dark green marble walls provide a somber setting for the gleaming white and gold central image. And, on either side of the chapel, the members of the Cornaro family (conceived in marble) behold Teresa's ecstasy from behind prayer desks that resemble theater boxes. These life-size figures extend the supernatural space of the chapel and reinforce the viewer's role as witness to an actual event. It is no coincidence that Bernini's tour de force appeared contemporaneously with the birth of opera in Italy, for both share the baroque concern for dramatic expression on a monumental scale.

The Architecture of Religious Ecstasy: The Italian Baroque Church

Adorned with hundreds of fountains and churches, the city of Rome carries the stamp of Bernini's flamboyant style. Commissioned to complete the *piazza,* the broad public space in front of Saint Peter's, the central church of Western Christendom, Bernini designed a trapezoidal space that opens out to a larger oval—the two shapes comprise, perhaps symbolically, a keyhole. Bernini's courtyard is bounded by a spectacular colonnade that incorporates 284 Doric columns (each thirty-nine feet high), as well as ninety-six statues of saints (each fifteen feet tall). In a manner consistent with the ecumenical breadth of Jesuit evangelism, the gigantic pincerlike arms of the colonnade reach out to embrace an area that can accommodate over 250,000 people (figure 20.10)—a vast proscenium on which devotional activities of the Church of Rome are staged to this day. The proportions of Bernini's colonnade are symbolic of the baroque preference for the grandiose, a preference equally apparent in the artist's spectacular setting for the Throne of Saint Peter and in the immense bronze canopy (*baldacchino*) he raised over the high altar of the cathedral (figure 20.11).

FIGURE 20.11 *Baldacchino*, Gianlorenzo Bernini, ca. 1624–33. Bronze with gilding, height, 93 ft. 6 in. Saint Peter's, Rome. Alinari Archivi/Art Resource, New York.

FIGURE 20.12 Il Gesù, facade, Giacoma Vignola and Giacomo della Porta, Rome, ca. 1575–84. Height, 105 ft. width, 115 ft. Bildarchiv Foto Marburg/Art Resource, New York.

FIGURE 20.13 Il Gesù, interior. Alinari/Art Resource, New York.

Seventeenth-century Italian architects designed churches that reflected the mystical and evangelical ideals of the Catholic Reformation. Il Gesù (the Church of Jesus) in Rome was the mother church of the Jesuit order and the model for hundreds of Counter-Reformation churches built throughout Europe and Latin America (figure 20.12). Designed by Giacomo Vignola (d. 1573), Il Gesù bears the typical features of the baroque church interior: a broad Latin cross nave with domed crossing and deeply recessed chapels (figure 20.13). Lacking side aisles, the sixty-foot-wide nave allowed a large congregation to assemble close enough to the high altar and the pulpit to see the ceremony and hear the sermon. The wide nave also provided ample space for elaborate religious processions. Il Gesù's interior, with its magnificent altarpiece dedicated to Ignatius Loyola, exemplifies the baroque inclination to synthesize various media, such as painted stucco, bronze, and precious stones, in the interest of achieving sumptuous and ornate effects.

The exterior of Il Gesù, completed by Giacomo della Porta (d. 1604), is equally dramatic. Its design—especially the elegant buttressing scrolls—looks back to Alberti's two-storied facade of Santa Maria Novella (figure 17.8). But in contrast to the linear sobriety of his model, della Porta's facade, with its deeply carved

FIGURE 20.14 Facade, San Carlo alle Quattro Fontane, Rome, Francesco Borromini. Begun 1635, facade 1667. Length, 52 ft., width, 34 ft., width of facade 38 ft. Alinari Archivi/Art Resource, New York.

decorative elements, has a dynamic sculptural presence. For dramatic effect, the architect added structurally functionless pilasters and numerous decorative details. An ornate **cartouche** (oval tablet) and a double cornice accent the central doorway, inviting the worshiper to enter. While the Renaissance facade was conceived in two dimensions, according to an essentially geometric linear pattern, the baroque church-front is conceived in three. Like a Caravaggio painting, Il Gesù exploits dramatic contrasts of light and dark and of shallow and deep space.

The most daring of Italian baroque architects was Francesco Borromini (d. 1644). Borromini designed the small monastic church of San Carlo alle Quattro Fontane (Saint Charles at the Four Fountains, figure 20.14) to fit a narrow site at the intersection of two

FIGURE 20.15 Interior of dome, San Carlo alle Quattro Fontane, Rome, Francesco Borromini, ca. 1638. Alinari/Art Resource, New York.

Roman streets. Rejecting the rules of classical design, he combined convex and concave units to produce a sense of fluid and undulating movement. The facade consists of an assortment of deeply cut decorative elements: monumental Corinthian columns, a scrolled gable over the doorway, and life-sized angels that support a cartouche at the roofline. Borromini's aversion to the circle and the square—the "perfect" shapes of Renaissance architecture—extends to the interior of San Carlo, which is oval in plan. The dome, also oval, is lit by hidden windows that flood the interior with light. Carved with geometric motifs that diminish in size toward the apex, the shallow cupola

appears to recede deep into space (figure 20.15). Such inventive illusionism, accented by dynamic spatial contrasts, characterized the Roman baroque style of church architecture.

But the theatricality of the baroque style went further still: by painting religious scenes on the walls and ceilings of churches and chapels, baroque artists turned houses of God into theaters for sacred drama. Such is the case with the Church of Sant'Ignazio, the barrel-vaulted ceiling of which bears a *trompe l'oeil* vision of Saint Ignatius' apotheosis—his elevation to divine status (figure 20.16). A master of the technique of linear perspective, the Jesuit architect and sculptor

FIGURE 20.16 *Apotheosis of Saint Ignatius,* **Andrea Pozzo, 1691. Fresco. Saint Ignatius, Rome. Alinari Archivi/Art Resource, New York.**

Andrea Pozzo (d. 1709) made the walls above Sant'Ignazio's clerestory appear to open up, allowing us to gaze "through" the roof into the heavens that receive the levitating body of the saint. Pozzo's cosmic rendering—one of the first of many illusionistic ceilings found in seventeenth- and eighteenth-century European churches and palaces—may be taken to reflect a new perception of physical space inspired by European geographic exploration and discovery. Indeed, Pozzo underlines the global ambitions of Loyola's mission by adding at the four corners of the ceiling the allegorical figures of Asia, Africa, Europe, and America. The vast, illusionistic spatial fields of Italian baroque frescoes also may be taken as a response to the new astronomy of the Scientific Revolution, which presented a view of the universe as spatially infinite and dynamic rather than static (chapter 22). Whatever its inspiration, the spatial illusionism of baroque painting and architecture gave apocalyptic grandeur to Counter-Reformation ideals.

The Music of Religious Ecstasy: Italian Baroque Music

In an effort to rid sacred music of secular influence, the Council of Trent condemned complex polyphony and the borrowing of popular tunes, both of which had become popular in religious music since the late Middle Ages. Above all, the reformers stressed the comprehensibility of the sacred text. The Italian composer Giovanni di Palestrina (d. 1594) took these recommendations as strict guidelines: his over one hundred polyphonic masses and 450 motets feature clarity of text, skillful counterpoint, and regular rhythms. The *a capella* lines of Palestrina's *Pope Marcellus Mass* flow with the smooth grace of a mannerist painting. Called "the music of mystic serenity," Palestrina's compositions embody the conservative and contemplative side of the Catholic Reformation rather than its aggressive, dramatic aspect. In the religious compositions of Palestrina's Spanish contemporary Thomas Luis de Victoria (d. 1611), there is a brooding but fervent mystical intensity. Like El Greco, his colleague at the court of Phillip II, Victoria brought passion and drama to religious themes. And, recognizing that the Council of Trent had forbidden Palestrina to compose secular music, Victoria wrote not one note of secular song.

The Genius of Gabrieli

At the turn of the sixteenth century, the opulent city of Venice was the center of religious musical activity. Giovanni Gabrieli (d. 1612), principal organist at Saint Mark's Cathedral in Venice and one of the greatest composers of his time, ushered in a new and dramatic style of choral and instrumental music. Gabrieli composed expansive **polychoral** religious pieces featuring up to five choruses. Abandoning the *a capella* style favored in Rome, he included solo and ensemble groups of instruments—especially the trombones and cornets commonly used in Venice's ritual street processions. Because Gabrieli was the first composer to indicate a specific instrument for each voice part in the musical composition, he has been called "the father of orchestration." Like baroque painters and sculptors, who sought sharp contrasts of light and shadow and dramatic spatial effects, Gabrieli created coloristic contrasts in sound, writing into his scores the words *piano* (soft) and *forte* (loud) to govern the **dynamics** (the degree of loudness or softness) of the piece.

Gabrieli was also the first musician to make use of a divided or "split choir" employed in *concertato,* that is, in opposing or contrasting bodies of sound. At

Saint Mark's, an organ was located on each side of the chancel, and four choirs were stationed on balconies high above the nave. The antiphonal play of chorus, instruments, and solo voices produced exhilarating sonorities (evident in the excerpt from Gabrieli's motet, *In Ecclesiis*♭) that met and mingled in the magical space above the heads of the congregation. In some of Gabrieli's compositions, echo effects produced by alternating voices and the use of unseen (offstage) voices achieved a degree of musical illusionism comparable to the visual illusionism of mannerist and baroque compositions. Like the extremes of light and dark in the paintings of El Greco and Caravaggio, Gabrieli's alternating bodies of sound (chorus versus chorus, solo voice versus chorus, chorus versus instruments) and contrasting musical dynamics (loud and soft, high and low) created strong harmonic textures and rich, dramatic effects. The *concertato* technique was the essence of early seventeenth-century baroque music, and in Gabrieli's hands, it was nothing less than majestic.

Gabrieli's music incorporated a new concept in musical organization: that of **tonality**. Tonality refers to the arrangement of a musical composition around a "tonic" or "home tone." Baroque composers employed the **chromatic scale** (the twelve tones—seven white and five black keys—of the piano keyboard) to construct chords around a tonal center. In baroque music—as in most music written to this day—all of the tones in the composition relate to the home tone. Tonality provided baroque musicians with a way of achieving dramatic focus in a musical composition, somewhat similar to the manner in which baroque artists used light in their paintings. The even progress of Renaissance polyphony, like the even lighting of the Renaissance painting, gave way to a theatrical accentuation of individual voices and breathtaking choral and instrumental contrasts.

Monteverdi and the Birth of Opera

The master of baroque vocal expression and the greatest Italian composer of the seventeenth century was Claudio Monteverdi (d. 1643). Monteverdi served the court of Mantua until he became chapel master of Saint Mark's in Venice in 1621, a post he held for the rest of his life. During his long career, he wrote various kinds of religious music, as well as ballets, madrigals, and operas. Like Gabrieli, Monteverdi discarded the intimate dimensions of Renaissance chamber music and cultivated an expansive, dramatic style. His compositions reflect a typically baroque effort to imbue music with an expressiveness that reflected the

---

♭See Music Listening Selections at end of chapter.

FIGURE 20.17 The Teatro Regio, Turin. Painting by P. D. Olivier of opening night, December 26, 1740. Five tiers of boxes are fitted into the sides of the proscenium, one even perched over the semicircular pediment. Note the orchestra, without a conductor, the girls distributing refreshments, and the armed guard protecting against disorder. Courtesy of the Museo Civico, Turin.

emotional content of poetry. "The [written] text," declared Monteverdi, "should be the master of the music, not the servant." Monteverdi linked "affections" or specific emotional states with appropriate sounds: anger, for instance, with the high voice register, moderation with the middle voice register, and humility with the low voice register. With Monteverdi, the union of music and speech sought in the word painting techniques of Josquin (chapter 17) blossomed into full-blown opera: that form of theatrical expression that combined all aspects of baroque artistic expression—music, drama, dance, and the visual arts.

Opera emerged from Renaissance efforts to revive the music-drama of ancient Greek theater. While humanist-composers had no idea what Greek music sounded like, they sought to imitate the ancient unity of music and theater. The earliest performances of Western opera resembled the Renaissance masque, a form of musical entertainment that included dance and poetry, along with rich costumes and scenery. Baroque operas were more musically complex, however, and more dramatically cohesive than Renaissance masques. The first opera house was built in Venice in 1637, and before 1700 Italy was home to

seven hundred more such houses, a measure of the vast popularity of the new genre. By the end of the seventeenth century, Italian courts and public theaters boasted all of the essential features of the modern theater: the picture-frame stage, the horseshoe-shaped auditorium, and tiers of galleries or boxes (figure 20.17). Some of these houses, resplendent with sculptures and illusionistic frescoes, bear strong similarities to Catholic Reformation churches and chapels (see figures 20.9 and 20.13).

Monteverdi's *Orfeo,*[§] composed in 1607 for the duke of Mantua, was Monteverdi's first opera and one of the first full-length operas in music history. The *libretto* (literally, "little book") or text of the opera was written by Alessandro Striggio and based on a classical theme—the descent of Orpheus, the Greek poet-musician, to Hades. *Orfeo* required an orchestra of more than three dozen instruments, including ten viols, three trombones, and four trumpets. The instrumentalists performed the **overture**, an orchestral introduction to the opera. They also accompanied vocal music that consisted of **arias** (elaborate solo songs or duets) alternating with **recitatives** (passages spoken or recited to sparse choral accompaniment). The aria tended to develop the character's feelings or state of mind, while the recitative served to narrate the action of the story or to heighten its dramatic effect.

Monteverdi believed that opera should express the full range of human passions. To that end, he contrived inventive contrasts between singer and accompaniment, recitative and aria, soloist and chorus. He also employed abrupt changes of key to emphasize shifts in mood and action. And he introduced such novel and expressive instrumental effects as *pizzicato,* the technique of plucking rather than bowing a stringed instrument. A multi-media synthesis of music, drama, and visual display, Italian opera, whether secular or religious in theme, became the ideal expression of the baroque sensibility and the object of imitation throughout Western Europe.

Summary

In the wake of the Protestant Reformation, the Roman Catholic church launched a reform movement that took late sixteenth-century Europe by storm. Loyola's *Spiritual Meditations* and the autobiographical writings of Saint Teresa of Avila set the tone for a new, more mystical Catholicism. In the spirit of Saint Teresa's ecstatic visions, such Catholic poets as Richard Crashaw wrote rhapsodic lyrics that fused sensual and spiritual yearnings. The arts of the seventeenth century reflect the religious intensity of the Catholic Ref-

[§]See Music Listening Selections at end of chapter.

ormation, even as they mirror the insecurities of the religiously divided and politically turbulent West.

The baroque style, which came to dominate Western Europe between 1600 and 1750, was born in Italy. The mannerist paintings of Parmigianino, Tintoretto, and El Greco anticipated the baroque style by their figural distortions, irrational space, bizarre colors, and general disregard for the "rules" of Renaissance painting. Italian baroque art, as typified by Caravaggio's paintings and Bernini's sculpture, featured dynamic contrasts of light and dark, an expanded sense of space, and the operatic staging of subject matter. Counter-Reformation churches, embellished with visionary paintings and sculptures, were ornate theaters for the performance of Catholic ritual. Bernini's *Ecstasy of Saint Teresa* and Pozzo's ceiling for the Church of Saint Ignatius in Rome achieved new heights of illusionistic theatricality. Addressing the passions rather that the intellect, baroque art broadcast the visionary message of Catholic reform to a vast audience that extended from Europe to the Americas.

Rome and Venice were fountainheads for Italian baroque art and music. Palestrina's polyphonic masses and motets emphasized clarity of text and calm sublimity, while Gabrieli's lofty polychoral compositions, performed at Saint Mark's Cathedral in Venice, featured dynamic contrasts between and among voices and musical instruments. The daring contrasts, rich color, and sheer volume of Gabrieli's music find their parallel in the canvases of Caravaggio.

The most important development in seventeenth-century European music was the birth of opera. Borrowing themes from classical mythology and history, Claudio Monteverdi integrated text and music to create the new and noble art of music-drama. In its synthesis of all forms of performance—music, literature, and the visual arts—Italian opera became the supreme expression of the theatrical exuberance and spiritual vitality of the baroque style.

GLOSSARY

aria an elaborate solo song or duet, usually with instrumental accompaniment, performed as part of an opera or other dramatic musical composition

cartouche an oval tablet or medallion, usually containing an inscription or heraldic device

chromatic scale a series of twelve tones represented by the seven white and five black keys of the piano keyboard; see **scale** in chapter 6 glossary

concertato (Italian, *concerto* = "opposing" or "competing") an early baroque style in which voices or instruments of different rather than similar natures are used in an opposing or contrasting manner

dynamics the degree of loudness or softness in music

overture an instrumental introduction to a longer musical piece, such as an opera

piazza (Italian) a broad, open public space

pizzicato (Italian) the technique of plucking (with the fingers) rather than bowing a stringed instrument

polychoral music written for two or more choruses, performed both in turn and together

recitative a textual passage recited to sparse chordal accompaniment; a rhythmically free vocal style popular in seventeenth-century opera

tonality the use of a central note, called the *tonic,* around which all other tonal material of a composition is organized, and to which the music returns for a sense of rest and finality

SUGGESTIONS FOR READING

Bazin, Germain. *The Baroque: Principles, Styles, Modes, Themes.* New York: Norton, 1978.

Burke, Peter. *Popular Culture in Early Modern Europe.* New York: New York University Press, 1971.

Dickens, A. G. *The Counter-Reformation.* London: Thames and Hudson, 1968.

Lavin, Irving. *Bernini and the Unity of the Visual Arts.* New York: Oxford University Press, 1980.

Martin, John Rupert. *Baroque.* New York: Harper, 1977.

Norberg-Schulz, Christian. *Baroque Architecture.* New York: Rizzoli, 1986.

Petersson, Robert T. *The Art of Ecstasy: Teresa, Bernini and Crashaw.* New York: Atheneum, 1970.

Wallace, Robert. *The World of Bernini, 1598–1680.* Library of Art Series. New York: Time-Life Books, Inc., 1970.

Wittkower, Rudolf. *Art and Architecture in Italy: 1600–1750.* New York: Viking, 1959.

———, and Irma B. Jaffe, eds. *Baroque Art: The Jesuit Contribution.* New York: Fordham University Press, 1972.

MUSIC LISTENING SELECTIONS

Cassette II Selection 1. Gabrieli, Motet, "*In Ecclesiis,*" (1615) excerpt.

Cassette II Selection 2. Monteverdi, *Orfeo,* Aria: "*Vi recorda, o boschi ombrosi,*" 1607.

21

The Baroque in the Protestant North

Throughout Italy, Spain, and other areas in the West, the baroque style mirrored the spirit of the Catholic Reformation; but in Northern Europe, where Protestant loyalties remained strong, another phase of the style emerged. The differences between the two are easily observed in the arts: in Italy, church interiors were ornate and theatrical; but in England, the Netherlands, and Northern Germany, where Protestants as a matter of faith were committed to private devotion rather than sacred ritual, churches were stripped of ornamentation, and the mood was more somber and intimate. Protestant devotionalism shared with Catholic mysticism an anti-intellectual bias, but Protestantism shunned all forms of theatrical display. In Northern Europe, where a largely Protestant population valued personal piety and private devotion, the Bible exercised an especially significant influence on the arts. Pietism, a seventeenth-century religious movement that originated in Germany, encouraged Bible study as the principal means of cultivating the "inner light" of religious truth.

If the Bible was a shaping influence on the arts of the Protestant North, so too was the patronage of a rising middle class. Having benefited financially from worldwide commerce, middle-class merchants demanded an art that reflected their keen interests in secular life. And while princely patronage in the North did not slacken during the seventeenth century, the landmark examples of Northern European art pay tribute to the vitality of this wealthy commercial class.

Civil War and the Rise of the English Commonwealth

In England, Queen Elizabeth I (1558–1603) was succeeded by the first Stuart monarch James I (d. 1625), during whose reign Shakespeare wrote his last major plays. A Scot, and a committed proponent of absolute monarchy, James ruled England by personal decree. His son, Charles I (d. 1649, figure 23.18) followed his example, alienating large segments of the English population, including the growing number of Puritans (English Calvinists who demanded church reform and greater strictness in religious observance). Allying with antiroyalist factions, mostly of the middle class, the Puritans constituted a powerful political group. With the support of the Puritans, leaders in Parliament raised an army to oppose King Charles, ultimately defeating the royalist forces and executing the king on charges of treason. The government that followed this civil war, led by the Puritan general Oliver Cromwell (d. 1658), was known as the "Commonwealth." Bearing the hallmarks of a republic, the new government issued a written constitution that proposed the formation of a national legislature elected by universal manhood suffrage. The Commonwealth, however, was unable to survive without military support. When Cromwell died in 1658, Stuart monarchs were invited to return to the throne; but Parliament's place in English government was firmly established, along with its authority to limit the power of English monarchs.

In the 1680s, when King James II (d. 1688) attempted to fill a new Parliament with his Catholic supporters, the opposition rebelled again. They expelled the king and offered the crown of England to William of Orange, ruler of the Netherlands, and his wife, Mary, the Protestant daughter of James I. During the "Glorious Revolution" of 1688, Parliament enacted a Bill of Rights prohibiting the king from suspending parliamentary laws or interfering with the ordinary course of justice. The Bill of Rights also enforced religious toleration and other civil liberties. Most importantly, however, the " bloodless revolution" reestablished constitutional monarchy in England and struck a major victory for popular sovereignty.

The King James Version of the Holy Bible

These dramatic political events, so closely tied to religious issues, occurred in the years following one of the most influential cultural events of the seventeenth century: the new English translation of the Bible. If, indeed, tradition is formed by the perpetuation of systems of ideas, then, surely, English tradition and Western European culture in general owes a major debt to the 1611 publication of the King James Version of the Bible. Drawing on a number of earlier English translations of Scripture made during the sixteenth century, a committee of fifty-four scholars recruited by James I of England produced an "authorized" English language edition of the Old and New Testaments. This edition of Scripture emerged during the very decades in which Shakespeare was writing his last major dramas (chapter 18)—a time when the English language reached its peak in eloquence. Along with the writings of Shakespeare, the King James Bible had a shaping influence on the English language and on all of English literature.

The new translation of Scripture preserved the spiritual fervor of the Old Testament Hebrew and the narrative vigor of the New Testament Greek. Like Shakespeare's poetry, the language of the King James Bible is majestic and compelling. Some appreciation of these qualities may be gleaned from comparing the two following translations. The first, a sixteenth-century translation based on Saint Jerome's Latin Vulgate edition and published in the city of Douay in 1609, lacks the concise language, the poetic imagery, and the lyrical rhythms of the King James Version (the second example), which drew directly on the original Hebrew texts.

READING 74 *The Twenty-Third Psalm* (from the Douay Bible, 1609)

Our Lord ruleth me, and nothing shall be wanting to me; in place of pasture there he hath placed me.

Upon the water of refection he hath brought me up; he hath converted my soul.

He hath conducted me upon the paths of justice, for his name.

For although I shall walk in the midst of the shadow of death, I will not fear evils; because thou art with me.

Thy rod and thy staff, they have comforted me.

Thou hast prepared in my sight a table against them that trouble me.

Thou hast fatted my head with oil, and my chalice inebriating, how goodly is it!

And thy mercy shall follow me all the days of my life.

And that I may dwell in the house of our Lord in longitude of days.

The Twenty-Third Psalm (from the King James Bible, 1611)

The Lord is my shepherd; I shall not want.

He maketh me to lie down in green pastures: he leadeth me beside the still waters.

He restoreth my soul: he leadeth me in the paths of righteousness for his name's sake.

Yea, though I walk through the valley of the shadow of death, I will fear no evil: for thou art with me; thy rod and thy staff they comfort me.

Thou preparest a table before me in the presence of mine enemies: thou anointest my head with oil; my cup runneth over.

Surely goodness and mercy shall follow me all the days of my life: and I will dwell in the house of the Lord for ever.

English Literature of the Seventeenth Century

John Donne

One of the most eloquent voices of religious devotionalism in the Protestant North was that of the poet John Donne (d. 1631). Born and raised as a Roman Catholic, Donne studied at Oxford and Cambridge. He traveled widely before converting to Anglicanism and becoming a priest of the Church of England. A formidable preacher as well as a man of great intellectual prowess, Donne wrote eloquent sermons that challenged the parishoners at Saint Paul's Cathedral in London, where he acted as dean (figure 21.1). At

itself; every man is a piece of the continent, a part of the main. If a clod be washed away by the sea, Europe is the less, as well as if a promontory were, as well as if a manor of thy friend's or of thine own were. Any man's death diminishes me, because I am involved in mankind, and therefore never send to know for whom the bell tolls; it tolls for thee. 15

---◆---

Donne's poetry was as unconventional as his prose: both abound in "conceits," that is, complex and ingenious images, and in shocking and extravagant metaphors—devices that have prompted critics to describe his poetry (and that of many other seventeenth-century English writers) as "metaphysical." Metaphysical poetry reflects a baroque affection for the dramatic juxtapositions of opposites, for intellectual imagery, and for frequent shifts of viewpoint. These features are apparent in some of Donne's finest works, including the group of religious poems known as the *Holy Sonnets*. In the first of the following two sonnets, Donne challenges Death in conceiving itself as powerful and influential. Instead of regarding Death, according to convention, as a "mighty and dreadful" ruler, Donne demeans Death as a slave who keeps bad company ("poison, war, and sickness"); he concludes with the artful device of Death itself "dying." Donne's defiance of Death stands in contrast to the submissive tone of medieval preachers (chapter 12), but his view of physical death as "a short sleep" from which "we wake eternally" is confidently Christian.

In the second sonnet, Donne compares himself to a fortress that has been seized by the enemies of the Lord. Donne describes Reason as the ruler ("Your viceroy in me") who has failed to defend the fortress. He now pleads with God to "ravish" and "imprison" him. The poem abounds in intriguing paradoxes that link sinfulness with deliverance, conquest with liberation, and imprisonment with freedom. Donne's unexpected juxtapositions and paradoxical images are typical of English metaphysical poetry, but his rejection of conventional poetic language in favor of a conversational tone (much celebrated by modern poets) represents a revolutionary development in European poetry.

FIGURE 21.1 Saint Paul's Cathedral, Christopher Wren, London, 1675–1710, west facade. © A. F. Kersting.

Saint Paul's, Donne developed the sermon as a vehicle for philosophic meditation. In *Meditation 17* (an excerpt from which follows), Donne pictures humankind—in typically baroque terms—as part of a vast, cosmic plan. His image of human beings as "chapters" in the larger "book" of God's design is an example of Donne's affection for unusual, extended metaphors.

READING 75 From Donne's *Meditation 17*

All mankind is of one author, and is one volume; 1
when one man dies, one chapter is not torn out of the
book, but translated into a better language; and every
chapter must be so translated. God employs several
translators; some pieces are translated by age, some by 5
sickness, some by war, some by justice, but God's
hand is in every translation, and his hand shall bind up
all our scattered leaves again for that library where
every book shall lie open to one another. As therefore
the bell that rings to a sermon calls not upon the 10
preacher only but upon the congregation to come, so
this bell calls us all. . . . No man is an island entire of

READING 76 From Donne's *Holy Sonnets*

Death be not proud, though some have called thee 1
Mighty and dreadful, for thou art not so;
For those whom thou think'st thou dost overthrow
Die not, poor Death, nor yet canst thou kill me.
From rest and sleep, which but thy pictures be, 5

Much pleasure, then from thee much more must flow,
And soonest our best men with thee do go,
Rest of their bones and souls' delivery.
Thou art slave to fate, chance, kings, and desperate
    men,
And dost with poison, war, and sickness dwell,   10
And poppy, or charms can make us sleep as well,
And better than thy stroke; why swell'st thou then?
One short sleep past, we wake eternally,
And Death shall be no more; Death, thou shalt die.

* * *

Batter my heart, three-personed God; for You   15
As yet but knock, breathe, shine, and seek to mend;
That I may rise, and stand, o'erthrow me, and bend
Your force, to break, blow, burn, and make me new.
I, like an usurped town to another due,
Labour to admit You, but oh! to no end;   20
Reason, Your viceroy in me, me should defend,
But is captived and proves weak or untrue.
Yet dearly I love You, and would be lovèd fain,
But am betrothed unto Your enemy.
Divorce me, untie, or break that knot again,   25
Take me to You, imprison me, for I
Except You enthrall me, never shall be free;
Nor ever chaste, except You ravish me.

The Genius of John Milton

John Milton (d. 1674) was a devout Puritan and a defender of the Cromwellian Commonwealth that collapsed in 1658. His career as a humanist and poet began at Cambridge University and continued throughout his eleven-year tenure as secretary to the English Council of State. Though shy and retiring, Milton nevertheless became a political activist and a persistent defender of religious, political, and intellectual freedom. He challenged British society with expository prose essays on a number of controversial subjects. In one pamphlet, he defended divorce between couples who were spiritually and temperamentally incompatible—a subject possibly inspired by his first wife's unexpected decision to abandon him briefly just after their marriage. In other prose works, Milton opposed Parliament's effort to control free speech and freedom of the press. "Who kills a man kills a reasonable creature," wrote Milton, "but he who destroys a good book, kills reason itself."

Milton's verse compositions included lyric poems and elegies, but the greatest of his contributions were his two epic poems: *Paradise Lost* and *Paradise Regained*. Milton wrote both of these monumental poems during the last decades of his life, when he was totally blind—a condition he erroneously attributed to long nights of reading. Legend has it that he dictated the poems to his two young daughters. In *Paradise Lost* Milton created a cosmic (and earth-centered) vision of Heaven, Hell, and Paradise comparable to that drawn by Dante (chapter 12) but more philosophic in its concern with the issues of knowledge, sin, and free will. Considered the greatest of modern epics, *Paradise Lost* is impressive in its vast intellectual sweep, its wide-ranging allusions to history and literature, and its effort to address matters of time, space, and causality.

When Milton resolved to compose a modern epic of the majesty and significance of the epics of Homer and Virgil, he was already fifty years old. At the outset, he considered various themes, one of which was the story of King Arthur. But he settled instead on a Christian theme that allowed him to examine an issue particularly dear to his Protestant sensibilities: the meaning of evil in a universe created by a benevolent god. The twelve books of *Paradise Lost* retell the story of the fall of Adam and Eve, beginning with the disobedience of Satan and culminating in the expulsion of the First Parents from Paradise. The poem concludes with the angel Raphael's explanation to Adam of how fallen Man, through Christ, will recover immortality. This august theme, rooted in biblical history, permitted Milton to explore questions of human knowledge, freedom, and morality and, ultimately, to "justify the ways of God to Man." In *Paradise Lost,* the last major epic to be written in the English language, Milton rivaled the achievements of Shakespeare. Like Shakespeare, Milton used blank verse: unrhymed lines of ten syllables each with accents on every second syllable. This form allowed Milton to carry the thread of a single thought past the end of the line and thereby group ideas in rich, verse paragraphs. The language of *Paradise Lost* is intentionally lofty; it is designed to convey epic breadth and to narrate (as Milton promised) "things unattempted yet in prose or rhyme." The following excerpts from the beginning of Book I convey some sense of the power and majesty of Milton's verse.

READING 77   From Milton's *Paradise Lost*

Of man's first disobedience, and the fruit   1
Of that forbidden tree, whose mortal taste
Brought death into the world, and all our woe,
With loss of Eden, till one greater Man[1]
Restore us, and regain the blissful seat,   5
Sing Heav'nly Muse, that on the secret top
Of Oreb, or of Sinai,[2] didst inspire

---

[1]Christ.

[2]As was the case with epic poets of old, Milton here invokes a divine source of inspiration. Milton's muse, however, is an abstraction of Judeo-Christian wisdom, identified with the muse that inspired Moses at Mount Horeb (Deut. 4.10) or on Mount Sinai (Exod. 19.20).

That shepherd, who first taught the chosen seed,
In the beginning how the heav'ns and earth
Rose out of chaos: or if Sion hill   10
Delight thee more, and Siloa's brook³ that flowed
Fast by the oracle of God; I thence
Invoke thy aid to my advent'rous song,
That with no middle flight intends to soar
Above th' Aonian mount,⁴ while it pursues   15
Things unattempted yet in prose or rhyme.
And chiefly thou O Spirit, that dost prefer
Before all temples th' upright heart and pure,
Instruct me, for thou know'st; thou from the first
Wast present, and with mighty wings outspread   20
Dove-like sat'st brooding on the vast abyss
And mad'st it pregnant: what in me is dark
Illumine, what is low raise and support;
That to the highth of this great argument
I may assert Eternal Providence,   25
And justify the ways of God to men.

---

³A spring near Mount Zion in Jerusalem, where in the Hebrew Bible, God spoke to his people.

⁴In Greece, the Muses were thought to live on Mount Helicon, also known as the "Aonian mountain."

As gods, and by their own recovered strength,   20
Not by the sufferance of supernal power.
     "Is this the region, this the soil, the clime,"
Said then the lost Archangel, "this the seat
That we must change for heav'n, this mournful gloom
For that celestial light? Be it so, since he   25
Who now is sovran can dispose and bid
What shall be right: farthest from him is best
Whom reason hath equaled, force hath made supreme
Above his equals. Farewell, happy fields,
Where joy for over dwells: hail horrors, hail,   30
Infernal world, and thou, profoundest hell
Receive thy new possessor: one who brings
A mind not to be changed by place or time.
The mind is its own place, and in itself
Can make a heav'n of hell, a hell of heav'n.   35
What matter where, if I be still the same,
And what I should be, all but less than he
Whom thunder hath made greater? Here at least
We shall be free; th' Almighty hath not built
Here for his envy, will not drive us hence: 40
Here may we reign secure, and in my choice
To reign is worth ambition though in hell:
Better to reign in hell, than serve in heav'n."

In dealing with the loss of humankind's spiritual innocence, Milton paints Satan larger than life and gives him a central place in the drama. He describes in vivid detail Satan's passage from Hell to Earth, his demon armies, and the fall of the rebel angels—a lengthy account that was likely inspired by the English civil wars. The following lines from Book I relate how Satan tears himself from the burning lake on which he is chained in Hell and continues to manipulate his fallen legions:

Forthwith upright he rears from off the pool   1
His mighty stature; on each hand the flames
Driv'n backward slope their pointing spires, and rolled
In billows, leave i' th' midst a horrid vale.
Then with expanded wings he steers his flight   5
Aloft, incumbent on the dusty air
That felt unusual weight, till on dry land
He lights, if it were land that ever burned
With solid, as the lake with liquid fire,
And such appeared in hue; as when the force   10
Of subterranean wind transports a hill
Torn from Pelorus,⁵ or the shattered side
Of thund'ring Etna, whose combustible
And fuelled entrails thence conceiving fire,
Sublimed with mineral fury, aid the winds,   15
And leave a singèd bottom all involved
With stench and smoke: such resting found the sole
Of unblest feet. Him followed his next mate,
Both glorying to have scaped the Stygian flood

---

⁵A promontory near the volcanic Mount Etna in Sicily.

The titanic Satan of Milton's *Paradise Lost* is a metaphor for the Puritan conception of evil in the world. Less vividly drawn, Adam is an expression of Protestant pessimism—a figure who, for all his majesty, is incapable of holding onto Paradise. *Paradise Lost* may be considered a Christian parable of the human condition. In its cosmic scope and imaginative exuberance, it is also a mirror of the baroque imagination.

The London of Christopher Wren

The London of Donne and Milton was a city of vast extremes. England's commercial activities in India and the Americas made London a center for stock exchanges, insurance firms, and joint-stock companies, but great numbers of Londoners (among a population of a quarter of a million people) remained poor. While one-fourth of London's inhabitants could neither read nor write, intellectuals advanced scientific learning by founding, in 1645, the Royal Society of London for Improving Natural Knowledge. Londoners enjoyed some of the finest libraries and theaters in Western Europe, but, under the Puritan-dominated Parliament of the 1640s, stage plays were suppressed, and many old theaters, including Shakespeare's Globe, were torn down. The restoration of the monarchy in 1658 brought with it a revived interest in drama and in the construction of indoor theaters (as opposed to the open-air theaters of Shakespeare's time).

In 1666, a devastating fire tore through London and destroyed over thirteen thousand homes, eighty-seven parish churches, and the cathedral church of Saint Paul's. Following the fire, there was an upsurge of large-scale building activity and a general effort to "modernize" London. The architect Christopher Wren (d. 1723) played a leading role in this effort. An inventor, experimental scientist, and professor of astronomy at London and Oxford, Wren was one of the founding fathers of the Royal Society. Following the Great Fire, Wren prepared designs for the reconstruction of London. Although his plans for new city streets (based on the model of Rome) were ignored, he was commissioned to rebuild more than fifty churches, including Saint Paul's—the first church in Christendom to be completed in the lifetime of its architect. Wren's early designs for Saint Paul's featured the Greek cross plan that Michelangelo favored for Saint Peter's in Rome (figure 17.29A). However, the clergy of Saint Paul's preferred a Latin cross structure. The final church was a compromise that combined classical, Gothic, Renaissance, and baroque architectural features. Saint Paul's dramatic two-story facade, with its ornate twin clock towers and its strong contrasts of light and dark (figure 21.1), looks back to Borromini (figure 20.14), but its massive scale and overall design—a large dome set upon a Latin cross basilica—reveal Wren's high regard for Saint Peter's (figures 17.29B and 20.10). As at Saint Peter's, Wren's dome, which physically resembles Bramante's *Tempietto* (figure 17.24), is equal in its diameter to the combined width of the nave and side aisles. And like Saint Peter's, the dimensions of Saint Paul's are colossal: 366 feet from ground level to the top of the lantern cross (Saint Peter's reaches 405 feet).

Wren envisioned a dome that was both impressive from the outside and easily visible from the inside. He came up with an inventive and complex device: two domes, one exterior (made of timber covered with lead) and the other interior (made of light brick), are supported by a third, cone-shaped, middle dome, which is hidden between the other two (figure 21.2). The monumental silhouette of Wren's exterior dome, some 102 feet in diameter, remains an impressive presence on the London skyline. From within the church, there is the equally impressive illusionism of the *trompe l'oeil* heavens painted on the inner surface of the central cupola. Like Milton's *Paradise Lost,* Wren's Saint Paul's is a majestic synthesis of classical and Christian traditions, while its huge size, dramatic exterior, and light-filled interior are baroque in conception and effect.

FIGURE 21.2 Cutaway drawing of Saint Paul's showing Wren's three domes.

Rembrandt and Protestant Devotionalism

In the Netherlands, developments in painting rivaled those in English architecture. Among the great artists of the Protestant North, Rembrandt van Rijn (d. 1669) stands out. A man of towering stature and talent, his contribution to the humanistic tradition is better understood in the context of his time and place.

Since 1560, when Spain had invaded the Dutch Lowlands, the seventeen provinces of the Netherlands had been engaged in a bitter struggle against the Catholic forces of the Spanish king Philip II. In 1579, after years of bloodshed, Philip's armies were forced to withdraw. In 1581, the seven hearty provinces of the North Netherlands declared their independence. By the end of the century the predominantly Calvinist Dutch Republic (also called "Holland") was a self-governing state and one of the most commercially active territories in Western Europe. Dutch shipbuilders produced some of the finest trading vessels on the high seas, while Dutch sailors, aided by skilled navigators, brought those vessels to all parts of the world. In Amsterdam, as in

FIGURE 21.3 *The Return of the Prodigal Son*, **Rembrandt van Rijn, ca. 1662–68. Oil on canvas, 8 ft. 8 in. × 6 ft. 8 in. Hermitage Museum, Leningrad.**

hundreds of other Dutch towns, merchants and crafts-people shared the responsibilities of local government, profiting handsomely from the smooth-running, primarily maritime economy.

The autonomous towns of the North Netherlands, many of which supported fine universities, fostered freedom of thought and a high rate of literacy. Hard-working, thrifty, and independent minded, the seventeenth-century Dutch enjoyed a degree of freedom and material prosperity unmatched elsewhere in the world. Their proletarian tastes, along with a profound appreciation for the physical comforts of home and hearth, inspired their call for such secular subjects as portraits, still lifes, landscapes, and scenes of domestic life (chapter 22). While the arts in Italy reflected the Mediterranean love for outdoor display, in the North, where a harsher climate prevailed, artistic expression centered on the domestic interior. And, in the North, where vestiges of ancient Greece and Rome were fewer, the classical heritage figured less visibly in the arts.

Since Calvinism strongly discouraged the use of religious icons, sculpture was uncommon in the Protestant North. But paintings, especially those

with scriptural subjects, were favored sources of seventeenth-century moral knowledge and instruction. The Old Testament was especially popular among the Dutch, who viewed themselves God's "chosen" people, elected to triumph over Spain. Amsterdam's leading painter, Rembrandt van Rijn, preferred biblical subjects that were uncommon in Catholic art. His moving representation of *The Return of the Prodigal Son* (Luke 15: 11–32), for instance, shows the moment when the wayward son in Jesus' parable returns home in rags and, humbly kneeling before his father, receives forgiveness (figure 21.3). The figures of father and son, bathed in golden light, form an off-center triangle balanced by the sharply lit vertical figure to the right. The composition is thus "open" and asymmetrical, rather than "closed" and symmetrical in the manner of High Renaissance art (figures 17.3, 17.16, and 17.23). As if to symbolize spiritual revelation itself, Rembrandt "pulls" figures out of the shadowy depths of the background. His rich contrasts between bright **impasto** areas (produced by building up thick layers of paint) and dark, brooding passages work to increase the dramatic impact of the composition. Rembrandt learned much about theatrical staging from Caravaggio, but, if one compares the works of the Italian baroque master (figures 20.7 and 20.8) with those by Rembrandt, it is evident that Rembrandt has reached further below surface appearances to explore the psychological depths of his subjects.

Rembrandt's un-idealized treatment of sacred subject matter belonged to a long tradition of Northern European medieval devotionalism (see figure 15.8), but his sympathetic depiction of the poor and the persecuted was uniquely Protestant. His Anabaptist upbringing, with its fundamentalist approach to Scripture and its solemn attention to the role of individual conscience in daily life, surely contributed to Rembrandt's habit of portraying biblical subjects in literal, human terms. The people of the streets provided him with a cast of characters, and his biblical scenes abound with the faces of Spanish and Jewish refugees, whom he regularly sketched in the ghettos of Amsterdam.

Rembrandt's technical virtuosity as a draftsman made him more famous in his own time as a print-maker than as a painter. Like the woodcuts and engravings of his Northern Renaissance predecessors, Dürer and Holbein (figures 18.6 and 18.7), Rembrandt's **etchings** met the demands of middle-class patrons who sought private devotional images that—by comparison with paintings—were inexpensive. A consummate printmaker, Rembrandt used the **burin** (a steel cutting tool) to develop dramatic contrasts of deep, rich darks and theatrically emphatic lights

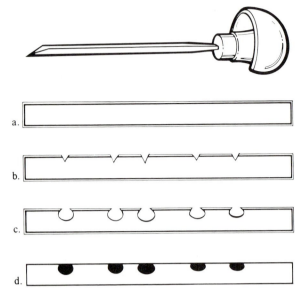

FIGURE 21.4 Etching is an intaglio printing process. A metal plate is coated with resin (*a*) then images are scratched through the coating with a burin, or graver (*b*). Acid is applied, which "eats" or etches the metal exposed by the scratches (*c*). The resin is then removed and ink is rubbed into the etched lines on the metal plate (*d*). After the plate is wiped clean, it is pressed onto paper and the ink-filled lines are deposited on the paper surface. Other intaglio processes include engraving and aquatint.

(figure 21.4). *Christ Preaching* (also known as *The Hundred Guilder Print,* because it sold for one hundred Dutch guilders in a seventeenth-century auction) illustrates parts of the Gospel of Matthew (figure 21.5). In the etching, Rembrandt depicts Jesus addressing the members of the Jewish community—the sick and the lame (*foreground*), "the little children" (*middle left*), the ill and infirm (*right*), and an assembly of Pharisees (*far left*). With an extraordinary economy of line—no more than a few deft strokes of the pen—the artist brings to life the woes of the poor, the downtrodden, and the aged (figure 21.6). So colloquial is Rembrandt's handling of the biblical story that it seems familiar and immediate.

The Music of the Protestant North

Handel and the English Oratorio

In the same way that the Protestant North produced memorable works of religious literature and art, it also produced great works of music. The careers of two extraordinary German composers, George Frederick Handel (d. 1756) and Johann Sebastian Bach (d. 1750), represent the culmination of the baroque style in Northern European music.

FIGURE 21.5 *Christ Preaching,* ("The Hundred Guilder Print"), Rembrandt van Rijn, ca. 1648–50. Etching. Rijksmuseum, Amsterdam. Art Resource, New York.

Born in the Lutheran trading city of Halle, Germany, George Frederick Handel was determined to pursue his childhood musical talents. When his father, who intended for him a career in law, refused to provide him with a musical instrument, he smuggled a small clavichord into the attic. After proving himself at the keyboard and as a successful violinist and composer in the courts of Hamburg, Rome, Paris, Naples, and Venice, he migrated to London in 1710 and became an English citizen in 1726. Like many of his contemporaries, Handel began his career as a student of Italian opera. He composed forty-six operas in Italian and four in his native German. He also produced a prodigious number of instrumental works. But it was for his development of the **oratorio** that he earned fame among the English, who called him "England's greatest composer."

An oratorio is the musical setting of a long text that is performed in concert by a narrator, soloists, chorus, and orchestra (figure 21.7). Like operas, oratorios are large in scale and dramatic in intent, but unlike opera, they are performed without scenery, costumes, or dramatic action. Soloists and chorus assume the roles of the main characters in the narrative. The word "oratorio" refers to a church chapel, and most oratorios were religious in content; however, they were never intended for church services.

FIGURE 21.6 Detail of figure 21.5. The Metropolitan Museum of Art (29.107.35).

FIGURE 21.7 Performance of an oratorio. Handel is conducting. Woodcut. The Bettmann Archive.

Rather, they were performed in public concert halls. With the oratorio, we see an example of the shift from music written and performed for church or court to music played in concert halls (or opera houses) and enjoyed—as is usually the case today—by the general public. Appropriately, in the late seventeenth century, public concerts (and entrance fees) made their first appearance in the social history of music.

In his lifetime, Handel composed more than thirty oratorios. Like Rembrandt and Milton (whose verses he borrowed for the oratorio *Samson*), Handel brought Scripture to life. The most famous of Handel's oratorios is *Messiah*, which was written in the English of the King James Bible. Composed, remarkably enough, in twenty-four days, it was performed for the first time in Dublin in 1742. It received instant acclaim. One of the most moving pieces of choral music ever written, *Messiah* celebrates the birth, death, and resurrection of Jesus. Unlike most of Handel's oratorios, *Messiah* is not a biblical dramatization but rather a collection of verses from the Old and New Testaments. The first part of the piece recounts Old Testament prophecies of a Savior, the second relates the suffering and death of Jesus, and the third rejoices in the redemption of humankind through Christ's rebirth. In many Christian communities, it has become traditional to perform Handel's *Messiah* during both the Christmas and Easter seasons.

Messiah is typical of the baroque sensibility: indeed, the epic proportions of its score and *libretto* call to mind Milton's *Paradise Lost*. It is also baroque in its style, which features vigorous contrasts of tempo and dynamics and dramatic interaction between participating ensembles—solo voices, chorus, and instruments. A master of theatrical effects, Handel employed word painting and other affective devices throughout the piece. For example, the music for the last words of the sentence, "All we, like sheep, have gone astray," consists of deliberately divergent melodic lines. The best-loved choral work in the English language, and one of the musical masterpieces of all time, *Messiah* has outlasted its age. The jubilant Hallelujah Chorus⁵ (which ends the second of the three parts of the oratorio) still brings audiences to their feet, even as it did King George II of England, who introduced this tradition by rising from his seat when he first heard it performed in London in 1743.

Handel's *Messiah* features occasional polyphonic phrases and embellishments such as the melismas at the last word of the line, "Unto us, a Child is born." Nevertheless, like Handel's other oratorios, *Messiah* is essentially **homophonic**, that is, its musical organization depends on the use of a dominant melody

FIGURE 21.8 *Johann Sebastian Bach*, **Elias Gottlob Haussman, 1746. Oil on canvas. William H. Scheide Library, Princeton University.**

supported by chordal accompaniment. The homophonic organization of melody and chords differed dramatically from the polyphonic interweaving of voices that characterized most music prior to the seventeenth century. The chords in a homophonic composition served to support—or, in the visual sense, to "spotlight"—a primary melody. In the seventeenth century, there evolved a form of musical shorthand that allowed musicians to fill in the harmony for a principal melody. The **figured bass**, as this shorthand was called, consisted of a line of music with numbers written below it to indicate the harmony accompanying the primary melody. The use of the figured bass (also called the "continuous bass," since it played throughout the duration of the piece) was one of the main features of baroque music.

Bach and Religious Music

Johann Sebastian Bach (d. 1750, figure 21.8) was born in the small town of Eisenach, very near the castle in which Martin Luther—hiding from the wrath of the Roman papacy—had first translated the Bible into German. Unlike the cosmopolitan Handel, Bach never strayed more than a couple of hundred miles from his birthplace. Nor did he depart from his Protestant roots: Luther's teachings and Lutheran hymn tunes were

FIGURE 21.9 Organ, Joseph Gabler, 1729–33. Benedictine Abbey Church, Ochsenhausen, Germany. © 1984, Office du Livre, S.A.

Bach's major sources of religious inspiration, and the organ, the principal instrument of Protestant church music, was one of his favorite instruments. The Germans were the masters of the organ, and Bach was acknowledged to be the finest of organ virtuosi. He served as a consultant in the construction of baroque organs, whose ornately embellished casings made them the glory of many Protestant churches (figure 21.9). As organ master and choir director of the Lutheran Church of Saint Thomas in Leipzig, Bach assumed the responsibility of composing music for each of the Sunday services and for holidays. A pious Lutheran and the father of twenty children from two marriages (five of whom became notable musicians), Bach humbly dedicated his compositions "to the glory of God."

Bach's religious vocal music included such forms as the oratorio, the Mass, and the **cantata**. The cantata is a multi-movement work sung in verse by chorus and soloists and accompanied by a musical instrument or instruments. Like the oratorio, the cantata may be sacred or secular in subject matter and lyric or dramatic in style. Bach composed cantatas as musical commentaries on the daily scriptural lessons of the Lutheran church service. Extraordinary in their florid counterpoint, Bach's 195 surviving cantatas were usually inspired by the simple melodies of Lutheran cho-

rales. The *Cantata No. 80*♭ is based on Luther's *A Mighty Fortress is our God,* the most important hymn of the Lutheran church (chapter 18). Bach used Protestant chorales, with their regular rhythms and rugged melodies, not only for his cantatas but as the basis for many of his instrumental compositions (see chapter 22), including the 170 organ **preludes** that he composed to precede and set the mood for congregational singing.

At the apex of Bach's achievement in vocal music is the *Passion According to Saint Matthew,* an oratorio written for the Good Friday service at Saint Thomas Church in Leipzig. This majestic piece of religious music consists of the sung texts of chapters 26 and 27 of Saint Matthew's Gospel, which describe Christ's Passion: the events between the Last Supper and the Resurrection. The biblical verses alternate with narrative commentary from a text written by a local German poet. Bach's combination of Bible and moral commentary dramatize Scripture with an eloquence and expressive power comparable to that of Rembrandt's *Prodigal Son* or his *Christ Preaching.*

The *Passion According to Saint Matthew* was sung by a double chorus whose members took the parts of the disciples, the Pharisees, and other characters in the biblical account. The chorus alternated with soloists (representing Matthew, Jesus, Judas, and others) who sang the arias and recitatives. Two orchestras accompanied the voices. The three-and-a-half-hour-long piece consisted of two parts: the first to be sung before the Vespers sermon and the second after. In Bach's time, the church congregation participated in the performance of the choral portions—thus adding to the sheer volume of sound produced by choir and orchestra. Performed today in the church or in the concert hall, Bach's masterpiece still conveys the devotional spirit of the Protestant North. In its imaginative use of Scripture, as well as in its vivid tonal color and dramatic force, the *Passion According to Saint Matthew* compares with the best of Rembrandt's Bible narratives, Handel's *Messiah,* and Milton's *Paradise Lost.*

Summary

In seventeenth-century Northern Europe, a unique set of circumstances shaped the progress of the baroque style. These circumstances included the dominance of Protestantism, with its strong scriptural and devotional emphasis, rising commercialism, and—especially in England and Holland—passionate, antiauthoritarian efforts to sustain personal rights and political liberties. The study of sacred Scripture was central to the ideals of Pietism and Protestant belief. Consequently, northern baroque artistic expression

---

♭See Music Listening Selections at end of chapter.

turned inward to the personal and subjective, rather than outward to spectacular forms of religious display.

In the literary domain, the King James translation of the Bible brought the English language to new heights of eloquence. The Anglican John Donne and the Puritan John Milton produced poetry that reflected Protestant perspectives of morality, evil, and death. Donne's metaphysical poetry featured ingenious conceits and paradoxes. Milton's *Paradise Lost,* the last great epic poem in Western literature, recast the heritage of the Hebrew Bible according to Puritan views of sin and salvation. The poem's cosmic scope, colossal proportions, and majestic language exemplify the baroque spirit in the Protestant North.

The religious works of the Dutch master Rembrandt van Rijn present a visual parallel to these literary landmarks. Rembrandt illustrated the contents of Holy Scripture in paintings, drawings, and etchings that were at once realistic, theatrical, and psychologically profound. With bold compositions and an inventive use of light, he described sacred events as though they had occurred in his own time and place.

The genius of Rembrandt was matched in music by the German masters Johann Sebastian Bach and George Frederick Handel. Handel dramatized scriptural narrative by means of the oratorio, a new musical form that typified the baroque taste for rich color and dramatic effect. Handel's *Messiah,* an early landmark in homophonic composition, remains one of the most stirring examples of baroque music. Handel's Lutheran contemporary, Johann Sebastian Bach, dedicated much of his life to creating musical compositions that honored God. His cantatas and his preludes employ melodies borrowed from Lutheran hymns. In the *Passion According to Saint Matthew,* Bach brought polyphonic choral music to new heights of dramatic grandeur. Like Milton's *Paradise Lost* and the paintings of Rembrandt, Bach's music invested Protestant Christianity with a sublime and deeply personal sense of human tragedy. In all, the contributions of Milton, Rembrandt, Handel, and Bach constitute the crowning achievements of the baroque style in the Protestant North.

GLOSSARY

burin   a steel tool used for engraving and incising
cantata   (Italian, *cantare* = "to sing") a multi-movement composition for voices and instrumental accompaniment; smaller in scale than the *oratorio*

etching   a kind of engraving in which a metal plate is covered with resin, then incised with a *burin*; acid is applied to "eat" away the exposed lines, which are inked before the plate is wiped clean and printed; figure 21.4
figured bass   in baroque music, the line of music with numbers written below (or above) it to indicate the required harmonies, usually improvised in the form of keyboard chords accompanying the melody; also called *continuous bass*
homophony   a musical texture consisting of a dominant melody supported by chordal accompaniment that is far less important than the melody; compare *monophony* (chapter 6) and *polyphony* (chapter 13)
impasto   a style in painting in which the paint is applied thickly or heavily
oratorio   (Latin, *oratory* = "church chapel") a musical setting of a long text, either religious or secular, for soloists, chorus, narrator, and orchestra; usually performed without scenery, costumes, or dramatic action
prelude   a piece of instrumental music that introduces either a church service or another piece of music; see also chapter 29

SUGGESTIONS FOR READING

Arnold, Denis. *Bach.* New York: Oxford University Press, 1984.
Bukofzer, Manfred. *Music in the Baroque Era.* New York: Norton, 1947.
Clark, Kenneth. *An Introduction to Rembrandt.* New York: Harper, 1978.
Kahr, Madlyn M. *Dutch Painting in the Seventeenth Century.* New York: Harper, 1978.
Palisca, C. V. *Baroque Music.* Englewood Cliffs, N.J.: Prentice-Hall, 1968.
Price, J. L. *Culture and Society in the Dutch Republic during the Seventeenth Century.* New York: Scribners, 1974.
Schama, Simon. *An Embarrassment of Riches: An Interpretation of Dutch Art.* New York: Knopf, 1987.
Schwendowius, Barbara, and Wolfgang Dömling, eds. *Johann Sebastian Bach: Life, Times, Influence.* Basel: Bärenreiter Kassel, 1977.
Wallace, Robert. *The World of Rembrandt 1606–1669.* Library of Art Series. New York: Time-Life Books, 1968.

MUSIC LISTENING SELECTIONS

Cassette II Selection 3. Handel, Messiah, "Hallelujah Chorus," 1742.
Cassette II Selection 4. Bach, *Cantata,* No. 80, "Ein Feste Burg ist unser Gott" ("A Mighty Fortress is Our God."), Chorale, 1724.

22

THE SCIENTIFIC REVOLUTION AND THE NEW LEARNING

While the seventeenth century was a period of religious turbulence and heightened spirituality, it was also an age of scientific discovery and development. The Scientific Revolution that occurred in Europe between approximately 1600 and 1750 was not entirely sudden, nor were its foundations exclusively European. It owed much to a long history of science and technology that reached back to ancient Egypt, China, and Islam, to the construction of pyramids and cathedrals, the formulation of Euclidian geometry, and the invention of the windmill, the magnetic compass, and the printing press. As Renaissance artist-scientists diligently investigated the visible world, efforts to control nature by means of practical knowledge gained impetus in the West. Following the pioneering efforts of Leonardo da Vinci, the Dutch physician Andreas Vesalius (d. 1574) dissected cadavers to make an accurate record of the human anatomy. The Swiss alchemist Philippus Ambrosius Paracelsus (d. 1541) compounded curatives from minerals rather than from the older, botanical substances. And the Polish humanist, physician, and astronomer Nicolas Copernicus (d. 1543) opposed the traditional **geocentric** (earth-centered) explanation of the cosmos with the **heliocentric** (sun-centered) theory according to which the earth and all the other planets circled around the sun.

The Scientific Revolution

Those who launched the Scientific Revolution differed from their Asian and European predecessors in effectively combining the tools of mathematics and experimentation. They invented new instruments with which to measure more precisely natural phenomena, to test scientific hypotheses, and to predict the operations of nature (figure 22.1). They also differed from their predecessors in asserting that *scientia* (the Latin word for "knowledge") existed separate and apart from divine power and authority. If medieval intellectuals viewed the universe as the extension of an absolute and eternal God, modern scientists regarded it as a mechanism that operated according to its own laws. Modern scientists took nature out of the hands of poets and priests and put it inside the laboratory.

Kepler and Galileo

Even before the second century A.D., when the Greek geographer Ptolemy published his theory of a geocentric universe, learned individuals regarded the earth as fixed in space and spherical in shape. They envisioned the earth at the center of a series of endlessly turning crystalline spheres, one for each of the celestial bodies: the Moon, Mercury, Venus, the Sun,

FIGURE 22.1 *The Astronomer,* Jan Vermeer, ca. 1662. Oil on canvas, 20 7/8 in. × 18 1/4 in. Stadelsches Kunstinstitut, Frankfurt. Bildarchiv Foto Marburg/Art Resource, New York.

Mars, Jupiter, and Saturn—a cosmology enshrined in Dante's *Divine Comedy* (see figure 12.4). According to Aristotle, movement in nature was the work of a *prime mover* or, in the later, Christian view, of some supernatural force. During the one hundred years following the publication of Copernicus' *Six Books Concerning the Revolution of the Heavenly Spheres* in 1543, such speculations came under scrutiny. Early in the seventeenth century, the German mathematician Johann Kepler (d. 1630) made detailed records of the planets' movements to substantiate the heliocentric theory. Challenging the conventional assumption that the planetary orbits had to be perfectly circular, Kepler showed that the five known planets moved around the sun in elliptical paths. He argued that the magnetic force emitted by the sun determined the movements of the planets and their distances from the sun. Kepler's new physics, which advanced the idea of a universe in motion, contradicted the Aristotelian notion of a fixed and unchanging cosmos. It also stood in opposition to the Bible—where, for example, the Hebrew hero Joshua is described as making the sun stand still, a miraculous event that could have occurred only if the sun normally moved around the earth. Although Catholics and Protestants were at odds on many theological matters, in defending the inviolable truth of Scripture against the claims of the new science, they were one.

While Kepler was hard at work in Germany, in Italy, his contemporary Galileo Galilei (d. 1642) was experimenting with matters of terrestrial motion. Whether or not Galileo actually dropped different-sized weights from the top of the Leaning Tower of Pisa—as legend has it—in an effort to determine rates of speed relative to mass, the Florentine astronomer did arrive at the *law of falling bodies,* which proclaimed that the earth's gravity attracts all objects—regardless of shape, size, or density—at the same rate of acceleration. In 1608, shortly after the publication of this theorem, a Dutch lensmaker invented an instrument that magnified objects seen at a great distance. Galileo perfected the telescope so that it literally revealed new worlds. Through its lens, one could see the craters of the moon, the rings of Saturn, and the moons of Jupiter, which, Galileo observed, operated exactly like Earth's moon. The telescope turned the heliocentric theory into fact.

Galileo's discoveries immediately aroused opposition from Catholics and Protestants committed to maintaining orthodox Christian beliefs, especially as set forth in Scripture. Not only did the theory of a heliocentric universe contradict God's word and challenge the Christian concept of a stable and finite universe, it also deprived human beings of their central place in that universe. The heliocentric theory made humanity seem incidental to God's plan and the heavens seem material and "corruptible." But such discoveries did not go unchallenged. The first institutional attack on "the new science" occurred in 1600, when the Catholic Inquisition tried, condemned, and publicly executed the Italian astronomer Giordano Bruno, who had asserted that the universe was infinite and without center. Bruno also suggested that other solar systems might exist in space. Sixteen years after Bruno was burned at the stake, Copernicus' writings were put on the Catholic *Index of Forbidden Books.* Galileo added to the controversy by making his own findings public; and all the more public because he wrote in every day Italian rather than in Latin—the traditional language of Western authority.

More inflammatory still in the eyes of the Church was the publication of Galileo's *Dialogue Concerning the Two Principal Systems of the World* (1632), a fictional conversation between a Copernican and the defenders of the old order, one of whom resembled the pope. Earlier in his career, when it had become evident that his gravitational theories contradicted Aristotle, Galileo had been forced to give up his position as mathematics professor at the University of Pisa. Now, he was brought before the Inquisition, and after a long and unpleasant trial, Church officials, threatening torture, forced the aging astronomer to "admit his errors"—legend has it that after denying that the earth moved around the sun, he muttered under his breath, "*Eppur si muove*" ("But it *does*

MAP 22.1 Western Europe: The intellectual revolution of the seventeenth and eighteenth centuries.

move!''). Though condemned to indefinite imprisonment, Galileo was permitted to reside—under "house arrest"—in a villa outside of Florence.

Despite Church opposition, scientists pressed on to devise new instruments for measurement and new procedures for experimentation and analysis. The slide rule, the magnet, the microscope, the mercury barometer, and the air pump were among the many products of the European quest to calculate, investigate, predict, and ultimately master nature. Seventeenth-century Western scientists investigated the workings of the human eye and explored the properties of light, thus advancing the science of optics beyond the frontiers of Islamic and Renaissance inquiry. They accurately described the action of gases and the circulation of the blood. And, they devised the branches of higher mathematics known as coordinate geometry, trigonometry, and infinitesimal calculus, by means of which modern scientists might analyze matters of space and motion.

The New Learning

Bacon and the Empirical Method

One of the most characteristic features of the Scientific Revolution was its glorification of the empirical method, a manner of inquiry that depended on direct observation and experimentation. Natural phenomena, argued seventeenth-century scientists, provided evidence from which one might draw general conclusions or axioms, according to a process known as **inductive reasoning**. The leading spokesman for the new learning was the English scientist and politician Francis Bacon (d. 1626). In 1620, Bacon published his *Novum Organum (New Method),* an impassioned plea for objectivity and clear thinking and the strongest defense of the empirical method ever written. "Man, being the servant and interpreter of Nature," wrote Bacon, "can do and understand so much and so much only as he has observed in fact or in thought of the course of nature: beyond this he neither knows anything nor can do anything."

Bacon argued that human beings must be aided by scientific instruments and human perception guided by precise methods. He promoted an objective system of experimentation, tabulation, and record keeping that became the touchstone of modern scientific inquiry. In an era dominated by fervent spirituality, Bacon demanded a separation of religion and science. "In every age," observed Bacon, "Natural Philosophy has had a troublesome adversary . . . namely, superstition, and the blind and immoderate zeal of religion." Unlike earlier humanists, Bacon turned his back on Aristotle and classical science. A prophet of the new learning, he sought to eliminate errors in reasoning derived from blind adherence to traditional sources of authority and religious belief. He condemned such obstacles to the progress of science as the sentiment of despair and the conviction that material achievement was impossible. And, with astonishing insight, he warned against four "false notions," or Idols, which, as the following excerpts from his *Novum Organum* illustrate, he perceived as hindrances to clear and objective thinking.

READING 78 From Bacon's *Novum Organum*

36

One method of delivery alone remains to us; which is simply this: we must lead men to the particulars themselves, and their series and order; while men on their side must force themselves for awhile to lay their notions by and begin to familiarize themselves with facts.

The idols and false notions which are now in possession of the human understanding, and have taken deep root therein, not only so beset men's minds that truth can hardly find entrance, but even after entrance obtained, they will again in the very instauration[1] of the sciences meet and trouble us, unless men being forewarned of danger fortify themselves as far as may be against their assaults.

39

There are four classes of Idols which beset men's minds. To these for distinction's sake I have assigned names,—calling the first class *Idols of the Tribe;* the second, *Idols of the Cave;* the third, *Idols of the Marketplace;* the fourth, *Idols of the Theatre.*

41

The Idols of the Tribe have their foundation in human nature itself, and in the tribe or race of men. For it is a false assertion that the sense of man is the measure of things. On the contrary, all perceptions as well of the sense as of the mind are according to the measure of the individual and not according to the measure of the universe. And the human understanding is like a false mirror, which, receiving rays irregularly, distorts and discolors the nature of things by mingling its own nature with it.

42

The Idols of the Cave are the idols of the individual man. For every one (besides the errors common to human nature in general) has a cave or den of his own, which refracts and discolors the light of nature; owing either to his own proper and peculiar nature; or to his education and conversation with others; or to the reading of books, and the authority of those whom he esteems and admires; or to the differences of impressions, accordingly as they take place in a mind preoccupied and predisposed or in a mind indifferent and settled; or the like. So that the spirit of man (according as it is meted out to different individuals) is in fact a thing variable and full of perturbation, and governed as it were by chance. Whence it was well observed by Heraclitus[2] that men look for sciences in their own lesser worlds, and not in the greater or common world.

---

[1]Reorganization or renewal.

[2]A Greek philosopher of ca. 500 B.C., who taught that all of nature was in a state of flux.

43

There are also Idols formed by the intercourse and association of men with each other, which I call Idols of the Market place, on account of the commerce and consort of men there. For it is by discourse that men associate; and words are imposed according to the apprehension of the vulgar. And therefore the ill and unfit choice of words wonderfully obstructs the understanding. Nor do the definitions or explanations wherewith in some things learned men are wont to guard and defend themselves, by any means set the matter right. But words plainly force and overrule the understanding, and throw all into confusion, and lead men away into numberless empty controversies and idle fancies.

44

Lastly, there are Idols which have immigrated into men's minds from the various dogmas of philosophies, and also from wrong laws of demonstration. These I call Idols of the Theatre; because in my judgment all the received systems are but so many stage-plays, representing worlds of their own creation after an unreal and scenic fashion. Nor is it only of the systems now in vogue, or only of the ancient sects and philosophies, that I speak; for many more plays of the same kind may yet be composed and in like artificial manner set forth; seeing that errors the most widely different have nevertheless causes for the most part alike. Neither again do I mean this only of entire systems, but also of many principles and axioms in science, which by tradition, credulity, and negligence have come to be received.

———————————◆———————————

Bacon observes that every culture and every age has "worshiped" the Idols. In describing the fallacies that have their foundations in human nature (*Idols of the Tribe*), he points to the fact that human understanding is self-reflective; it functions like a "false mirror," distorting universal truth. Privately held fallacies (*Idols of the Cave*), on the other hand, derive from individual educations and backgrounds. An individual may assert, for instance, that one or another religion is "the true faith," that certain racial or ethnic groups are superior to others, or that women should be judged by a different set of standards than those applied to men. The errors resulting from human association and communication, the *Idols of the Market place*, arise, according to Bacon, from a "ill or unfit choice of words." To offer a modern-day example: the use of the noun "mankind" to designate all human beings and the pronouns "she" and "her" to refer to countries and nation-states may work to cultivate a sexist bias in thinking about human history. Finally, Bacon attacks the *Idols of the Theater*—false dogmas perpetuated by philosophies and institutions in antiquity and in his own time, as well as those that "may

yet be composed." It seems likely that Bacon would have regarded the modern doctrines of "divine right monarchy" (see chapter 24) and "separate but equal education" as examples of this category of Idols.

Bacon's clarion call for intellectual objectivity and experimentation inspired the founding (in 1645) of the Royal Society of London for Improving Natural Knowledge. The first of many such European and American societies for scientific advancement, the Royal Society has attracted, over the centuries, thousands of members. Their achievements have confirmed one nineteenth-century historian's assessment of Bacon as "the man that moved the minds that moved the world."

While Bacon wrote his scientific treatises in Latin, he used English for essays designed to instruct the average reader. In *The Advancement of Learning* (1605), a sketch of his key ideas concerning methods for acquiring and classifying knowledge, and in such essays as *Of Studies*, Bacon demonstrated the masterful use of prose as a tool for theorizing. Written in the "poetic" prose of the early seventeenth century, *Of Studies* describes the ways in which books and book learning serve the individual and society at large. In the excerpt that follows, Bacon eloquently defends reading as a source of pleasure, but equally important, as a source of practical knowledge and power.

READING 79 From Bacon's *Of Studies*

Studies serve for delight, for ornament, and for ability. 1
Their chief use for delight is in privateness and retiring;
for ornament, is in discourse; and for ability, is in the
judgment and disposition of business. For expert men
can execute, and perhaps judge of particulars, one by
one; but the general counsels and the plots and
marshalling of affairs come best from those that are
learned. To spend too much time in studies is sloth; to
use them too much for ornament is affectation; to make
judgment wholly by their rules is the humor of a scholar. 10
They perfect nature, and are perfected by experience:
for natural abilities are like natural plants, that need
pruning by study; . . . Read not to contradict and
confute; nor to believe and take for granted; nor to find
talk and discourse, but to weigh and consider. Some
books are to be tasted, others to be swallowed, and
some few to be chewed and digested; that is, some
books are to be read only in parts; others to be read,
but not curiously; and some few to be read wholly, and
with diligence and attention. . . . Reading maketh a full 20
man; conference a ready man; and writing an exact
man. And therefore, if a man write little, he had need
have a great memory; if he confer little, he had need
have a present wit; and if he read little, he had need
have much cunning, to seem to know that he does not.

Histories make men wise; poets witty; mathematics subtile; natural philosophy deep; moral [philosophy] grave; logic and rhetoric able to contend. . . .

---◆---

Descartes and the Birth of Modern Philosophy

Bacon was thirty-five years old when, across the English Channel in France, René Descartes was born. Descartes (d. 1650, figure 22.2) is usually regarded as the founder of modern Western philosophy and the father of analytic geometry. His writings revived the ancient Greek quest to discover how one knows what one knows, and his methods made the discipline of philosophy wholly independent of theology.

Whereas Bacon gave priority to knowledge gained through the senses, Descartes, the supreme rationalist, valued abstract reasoning and mathematical speculation. Descartes did not deny the importance of the senses in the search for truth, but he observed that our senses might deceive us. As an alternative to induction, he championed a procedure for investigation called **deductive reasoning**. The reverse of the inductive method, the deductive process began with clearly established general premises and moved toward the establishment of particular truths. Among the rules Descartes set forth were the following: never accept anything as true that you do not clearly know to be true; dissect a problem into as many parts as possible, reason from simple to complex knowledge, and finally, draw complete and exhaustive conclusions. In the *Discourse on the Method of Rightly Conducting the Reason and Seeking for Truth in the Sciences,* perhaps the most important of all his philosophic works, Descartes began by systematically calling everything into doubt. He then proceeded to identify the first thing that he could not doubt—his existence as a thinking individual. This one clear and distinct idea of himself as a "thinking thing," expressed in the proposition "*Cogito, ergo sum*" ("I think, therefore I am"), became Descartes' "first principle" and the premise for all of his major arguments.

For Descartes, the human mind was the source of all natural understanding. "Except [for] our own thoughts," he insisted, "there is nothing absolutely in our power." Having established the mind as the only sure point of departure for knowledge, Descartes proceeded to examine the world. He made a clear distinction between physical and psychical phenomena, that is, between matter and mind, and between body and soul. According to this dualistic model, the human body operated much like a computer, with the immaterial mind (the software) "informing" the physical components of the body (the hardware). The

FIGURE 22.2 *Portrait of René Descartes,* **Frans Hals, 1649. Oil on panel. Royal Museum of Fine Arts, Copenhagen, Denmark.**

Cartesian view of the human mind as a thinking substance distinct from the human body dominated European philosophic thought until the end of the nineteenth century and still has some strong adherents today.

READING 80   From Descartes' *Discourse on Method* (Part IV)

I do not know that I ought to tell you of the first   1
meditations there made by me, for they are so
metaphysical and so unusual that they may perhaps not
be acceptable to everyone. And yet at the same time, in
order that one may judge whether the foundations
which I have laid are sufficiently secure, I find myself
constrained in some measure to refer to them. For a
long time I had remarked that it is sometimes requisite
in common life to follow opinions which one knows to be
most uncertain, exactly as though they were   10
indisputable, as has been said above. But because in
this case I wished to give myself entirely to the search
after Truth, I thought that it was necessary for me to
take an apparently opposite course, and to reject as
absolutely false everything as to which I could imagine
the least ground of doubt, in order to see if afterwards
there remained anything in my belief that was entirely

certain. Thus, because our senses sometimes deceive us, I wished to suppose that nothing is just as they cause us to imagine it to be; and because there are men who deceive themselves in their reasoning and fall into paralogisms,[3] even concerning the simplest matters of geometry, and judging that I was as subject to error as was any other, I rejected as false all the reasons formerly accepted by me as demonstrations. And since all the same thoughts and conceptions which we have while awake may also come to us in sleep, without any of them being at that time true, I resolved to assume that everything that ever entered into my mind was no more true than the illusions of my dreams. But immediately afterwards I noticed that whilst I thus wished to think all things false, it was absolutely essential that the 'I' who thought this should be somewhat, and remarking that this truth *'I think, therefore I am'* was so certain and so assured that all the most extravagant suppositions brought forward by the sceptics were incapable of shaking it, I came to the conclusion that I could receive it without scruple as the first principle of the Philosophy for which I was seeking.

And then, examining attentively that which I was, I saw that I could conceive that I had no body, and that there was no world nor place where I might be; but yet that I could not for all that conceive that I was not. On the contrary, I saw from the very fact that I thought of doubting the truth of other things, it very evidently and certainly followed that I was; on the other hand if I had only ceased from thinking, even if all the rest of what I had ever imagined had really existed, I should have no reason for thinking that I had existed. From that I knew that I was a substance the whole essence or nature of which is to think, and that for its existence there is no need of any place, nor does it depend on any material thing; so that this 'me,' that is to say, the soul by which I am what I am, is entirely distinct from body, and is even more easy to know than is the latter; and even if body were not, the soul would not cease to be what it is.

After this I considered generally what in a proposition is requisite in order to be true and certain; for since I had just discovered one which I knew to be such, I thought that I ought also to know in what this certainty consisted. And having remarked that there was nothing at all in the statement *'I think, therefore I am'* which assures me of having thereby made a true assertion, excepting that I see very clearly that to think it is necessary to be, I came to the conclusion that I might assume, as a general rule, that the things which we conceive very clearly and distinctly are all true—remembering, however, that there is some difficulty in ascertaining which are those that we distinctly conceive.

Following upon this, and reflecting on the fact that I doubted, and that consequently my existence was not quite perfect (for I saw clearly that it was a greater perfection to know than to doubt), I resolved to inquire whence I had learnt to think of anything more perfect than myself was; and I recognised very clearly that this conception must proceed from some nature which was really more perfect. As to the thoughts which I had of

many other things outside of me, like the heavens, the earth, light, heat, and a thousand others, I had not so much difficulty in knowing whence they came, because, remarking nothing in them which seemed to render them superior to me, I could believe that, if they were true, they were dependencies upon my nature, in so far as it possessed some perfection; and if they were not true, that I held them from nought, that is to say, that they were in me because I had something lacking in my nature. But this could not apply to the idea of a Being more perfect than my own, for to hold it from nought would be manifestly impossible; and because it is no less contradictory to say of the more perfect that it is what results from and depends on the less perfect, than to say that there is something which proceeds from nothing, it was equally impossible that I should hold it from myself. In this way it could but follow that it had been placed in me by a Nature which was really more perfect than mine could be, and which even had within itself all the perfections of which I could form any idea— that is to say, to put it in a word, which was God. . . .

———◆———

Religion and the New Learning

The new learning, a composite of scientific method and rational inquiry, presented its own challenge to traditional religion. From "self-evident" propositions, Descartes arrived at conclusions to which empirical confirmation was irrelevant. His rationalism— like Plato's—involved a process of the mind independent of the senses. Reasoning that the concept of perfection ("something more perfect than myself") had to proceed from "some Nature which in reality was more perfect," Descartes "proved" the existence of God. Since something cannot proceed from nothing, argued Descartes, the idea of god held by human beings must come from God. Moreover, the idea of Perfection (God) embraces the idea of existence, for, if something is perfect, it must exist. Raised by Jesuits, Descartes believed in the existence of a Supreme Creator, but he shared with many seventeenth-century intellectuals the view that God was neither Caretaker nor Redeemer. The idea that God did not interfere with the laws of man and nature was central to **deism**, a system of thought advocating a "natural" religion based on human reason rather than revelation. Deists minimized superstition, mythology, and ritual. They viewed God as a master mechanic who had created the universe and then stepped aside and allowed his World-Machine to run unattended.

Unlike Bacon, Descartes did not envision any conflict between science and religion. He optimistically concluded that "all our ideas or notions contain in them some truth; for otherwise it could not be that God, who is wholly perfect and veracious, should have placed them in us." Like other deists of his time, Descartes held that to follow reason was to follow God.

In Amsterdam, a city whose reputation for freedom of thought attracted Descartes—he lived there between 1628 and 1649—the Jewish philosopher Baruch Spinoza (d. 1677) addressed the question of the new science versus the old faith. Stripping God of his traditional role as Creator (and consequently finding himself ousted from the synagogue), Spinoza claimed that God was neither behind, nor beyond, nor separate from nature but rather, identical with nature. Every physical thing, including the human being, was an expression of God in some variation of mind combined with matter. In a pantheistic spirit reminiscent of Hinduism and Taoism, Spinoza held that the greatest good was the union of the human mind with the whole of nature.

For the French physicist-mathematician Blaise Pascal (d. 1662), on the other hand, science and religion were irreconcilable. Having undergone a mystical experience that converted him to devout Roman Catholicism, he believed that the path to God was through the heart rather than through the head. Although reason might yield a true understanding of nature, it could in no way prove God's existence. We are capable, wrote Pascal, of "certain knowledge and of absolute ignorance." In his collected meditations on human nature, called simply *Pensées (Thoughts)*, Pascal proposed a wager that challenged the indifference of skeptics: If God does *not* exist, skeptics lose nothing by believing in him, but if God *does* exist, they reap eternal life. The spiritual quest for purpose and value in a vast, impersonal universe moved the precision-minded Pascal—inventor of a machine that anticipated the digital calculator—to confess: "The eternal silence of these infinite spaces frightens me."

Locke and the Culmination of the Empirical Tradition

The writings of the English philosopher and physician John Locke (d. 1704) firmly defended the empirical tradition in seventeenth-century thought and provided the basis for centuries of philosophic debate. Written seventy years after Bacon's *Novum Organum,* Locke's *Essay Concerning Human Understanding* (1690) confirmed his predecessor's thesis that everything one knows derives from sensory experience. According to Locke, the human mind at birth is a *tabula rasa* ("blank slate") upon which

experience—consisting of sensation, followed by reflection—writes the script. No innate moral principles or ideas exist; rather, human knowledge consists of the progressive accumulation of the evidence of the senses.

The implications of Locke's principles of knowledge strongly affected European and (later) American thought and helped to shape an optimistic view of human destiny. For, if experience influenced human knowledge and behavior, argued the empiricists, then, surely, improving the social environment would work to perfect the human condition. Locke's ideas became basic to eighteenth-century liberalism, as well as to all political ideologies that held that human knowledge, if properly applied, would produce happiness for humankind (see chapter 24).

READING 81 From John Locke's *Essay Concerning Human Understanding*

Idea is the Object of Thinking.—Every man being 1
conscious to himself that he thinks, and that which his
mind is applied about whilst thinking, being the ideas
that are there, it is past doubt that men have in their
minds several ideas, such as are those expressed by
the words whiteness, hardness, sweetness, thinking,
motion, man, elephant, army, drunkenness, and others.
It is in the first place then to be inquired how he comes
by them. I know it is a received doctrine that men have
native ideas and original characters stamped upon their 10
minds in their very first being. This opinion I have at
large examined already; and I suppose what I have
[already] said . . . will be much more easily admitted
when I have shown whence the understanding may get
all the ideas it has, and by what ways and degrees they
may come into the mind; for which I shall appeal to
every one's own observation and experience.

All Ideas come from Sensation or Reflection.—Let us
then suppose the mind to be, as we say, white paper,
void of all characters, without any ideas; how comes it 20
to be furnished? Whence comes it by that vast store
which the busy and boundless fancy of man has
painted on it with an almost endless variety? Whence
has it all the materials of reason and knowledge? To this
I answer in one word, from experience; in that all our
knowledge is founded, and from that it ultimately
derives itself. Our observation employed either about
external sensible objects, or about the internal

operations of our minds, perceived and reflected on by ourselves, is that which supplies our understandings with all the materials of thinking. These two are the fountains of knowledge from whence all the ideas we have or can naturally have do spring.

The Objects of Sensation one Source of Ideas.— First, our senses, conversant about particular sensible objects, do convey into the mind several distinct perceptions of things, according to those various ways wherein those objects do affect them: and thus we come by those ideas we have, of yellow, white, heat, cold, soft, hard, bitter, sweet, and all those which we call sensible qualities; which when I say the senses convey into the mind, I mean, they from external objects convey into the mind what produces there those perceptions. This great source of most of the ideas we have, depending wholly upon our senses, and derived by them to the understanding, I call Sensation.

The Operations of our Minds, the other Source of them.—Secondly, the other fountain, from which experience furnishes the understanding with ideas, is the perception of the operations of our own mind within us, as it is employed about the ideas it has got; which operations, when the soul comes to reflect on and consider, do furnish the understanding with another set of ideas, which could not be had from things without; and such are perception, thinking, doubting, believing, reasoning, knowing, willing, and all the different actings of our own minds; which we being conscious of, and observing in ourselves, do from these receive into our understandings as distinct ideas, as we do from bodies affecting our senses. This source of ideas every man has wholly in himself; and though it be not sense, as having nothing to do with external objects, yet it is very like it, and might properly enough be called internal sense. But as I call the other Sensation, so I call this Reflection, the ideas it affords being such only as the mind gets by reflecting on its own operations within itself. By reflection then, in the following part of this discourse, I would be understood to mean that notice which the mind takes of its own operations, and the manner of them; by reason whereof there come to be ideas of these operations in the understanding. These two, I say, *viz.,* external material things, as the objects of sensation; and the operations of our own minds within, as the objects of reflection; are to me the only originals from whence all our ideas take their beginnings. . . .

All our Ideas are of the one or the other of these.— The understanding seems to me not to have the least glimmering of any ideas which it doth not receive from one of these two. External objects furnish the mind with the ideas of sensible qualities, which are all those different perceptions they produce in us; and the mind furnishes the understanding with ideas of its own operations.

These, when we have taken a full survey of them, and their several modes, combinations, and relations, we shall find to contain all our whole stock of ideas; and that we have nothing in our minds, which did not come in one of these two ways. Let any one examine his own thoughts, and thoroughly search into his understanding; and then let him tell me, whether all the original ideas he has there, are any other than of the objects of his senses, or of the operations of his mind, considered as objects of his reflection: and how great a mass of knowledge soever he imagines to be lodged there, he will, upon taking a strict view, see that he has not any idea in his mind, but what one of these two have imprinted. . . .

———————————◆———————————

Newton's Scientific Synthesis

The work of the great English astronomer and mathematician Isaac Newton (d. 1727) represents a practical synthesis of seventeenth-century physics and mathematics and the union of the inductive and deductive methods. Newton advanced the new science from its speculative and empirical phases (represented by Copernicus and Galileo, respectively) to the stage of codification. He combined Kepler's laws of celestial mechanics and Galileo's terrestrial law of falling bodies into an all-embracing theory of universal gravitation that described every physical movement in the universe—from the operation of the tides to the effects of a planet upon its moons. In 1687 Newton published his monumental treatise on the laws of motion: the *Philosophiae Naturalis Principia Mathematica (Mathematical Principles of Natural Philosophy).* Newton's *Principia,* the fundamentals of which went unchallenged until the late nineteenth century, promoted the idea of a uniform and intelligible universe that operated as systematically as a well-oiled machine. Newton desanctified nature; his universal laws applied equally to terrestrial and celestial matter. Morever, Newton showed that by means of mathematical analysis and scientific observation, enlightened individuals might comprehend and control their world more completely than had ever before been possible.

FIGURE 22.3 *Still Life with View of the Sea,* Jan Davidsz de Heem, 1646. Oil on canvas, 23 3/8 in. × 36 1/2 in. Courtesy of the Toledo Museum of Art. Gift of Edward Drummond Libbey.

The Impact of the Scientific Revolution on Art

Northern Baroque Painting

If the new science engendered a spirit of objective inquiry in literature, it also had a profound influence on the visual arts. In the cities of seventeenth-century Holland, where Dutch lensmakers had produced the first telescopes and microscopes, there evolved a style of painting that reflected an obsessive attention to the natural world. In still lifes, portraits, landscapes, and scenes of everyday life—all secular subjects—Dutch masters practiced the "art of describing."[4] The almost photographic realism of such paintings as *Still Life with View of the Sea* by Jan Davidsz de Heem (d. 1684) is typical of the new "Baconian" attention to nature in baroque art (figure 22.3). A distant view

of the sea and a storm-tossed vessel in the background of the painting are less than subtle reminders that Dutch maritime activity financed the bounties of the dinner table.

While de Heem's fruits and meats celebrate the robust pleasures of life, the objects in Maria van Oosterwyck's realistic *Still Life* of 1668—a skull, insects, a tiny mouse nibbling at some grain—make cloaked reference to decay and death (figure 22.4). Van Oosterwyck's *Still Life* belongs to a large group of European *vanitas* paintings, the contents of which suggest the corruptibility of worldly goods and the inevitability of death. Such paintings look back upon a long tradition, common among such Netherlanders as Jan van Eyck (figure 17.9) and Hieronymus Bosch (figure 18.9), that favored hidden or secondary meanings in realistically depicted imagery. Van Oosterwyck brings the naturalist's passion for detail to every item in the painting: the radiant flowers (which include a mag-

---

[4]See Svetlana Alpers, *The Art of Describing: Dutch Painting in the Seventeenth Century* (New York: Knopf, 1987).

FIGURE 22.4 *Vanitas Still Life*, Maria Van Oosterwyck, 1668. Oil on canvas, 29 in. × 35 in. Kunsthistorische Museum, Vienna.

nificent Dutch tulip), the microscopically precise fly, the worn book, the meticulously detailed globe, and the minute self-portrait (reflected in the carafe at the left).

In seventeenth-century Holland, genre paintings, packed with images of everyday life, were in high demand. The domestic scenes painted by Pieter de Hooch (d. 1683) show Dutch art to be societal—an art concerned with conviviality and companionship. In one painting, de Hooch uses a spacious courtyard filled with cool, bright light as the setting for such ordinary pleasures as pipe smoking and beer drinking (figure 22.5). He captures a mood of domestic inti-

macy in his loving attention to humble fact: the crumbling brick wall, the gleaming tankard, the homely matron, and the pudgy child. The strict verticals and horizontals of the composition—established with Cartesian clarity and precision—create a sense of tranquility and order.

Music making, one of the major domestic entertainments of the seventeenth century, is the subject of many northern baroque paintings, including de Hooch's *The Music Party* (figure 22.6). Holland was a center for the manufacture of musical instruments, and the Dutch household, here seen with a variety of stringed instruments, fondly engaged in amateur mu-

FIGURE 22.5 *A Dutch Courtyard*, Pieter de Hooch, ca. 1660. Oil on linen canvas, 26 3/4 in. × 23 in. National Gallery of Art, Washington, D.C. Andrew W. Mellon Collection.

FIGURE 22.6 *The Music Party*, Pieter de Hooch, 1663. Oil on canvas. Cleveland Museum of Art. Gift of the Hanna Fund (51.355).

PART I: THE AGE OF THE BAROQUE

FIGURE 22.7 *The Suitor's Visit,* **Gerard ter Borch, 1658–70. Oil on linen canvas, 31 1/2 in. × 29 5/8 in. National Gallery of Art, Washington, D.C., Andrew Mellon Collection.**

sical performance. Such cities as Amsterdam and Leyden vied with London and Venice in the publication of printed scores. The popularity of music in Holland followed closely upon the proliferation of amateur music societies. Music making also figures in the delightful painting called *The Suitor's Visit,* by Gerard ter Borch (d. 1681). The narrative is staged like a scene from a play: a well-dressed gentleman, who who has just entered the parlor of a well-to-do middle-class family, bows before a young woman whose coy apprehension suggests that she is the object of courtship (figure 22.7). The father and the family dog take note of the tense moment, while a younger woman, absorbed in playing the lute, ignores the interruption. Ter Borch was famous for his virtuosity in

painting gleaming silk fabrics that subtly illuminate the shadowy depths of domestic interiors. Equally impressive, however, was his ability to dignify an inconsequential event with profound human meaning.

Vermeer and Dutch Painting

In landscape painting as in still life, Dutch artists described nature with an attention to detail and a sensitivity to atmosphere unmatched even in the landscapes of Dürer and Brueghel (chapter 18). Holland's leading artists were familiar with the optical experiments of Dutch scientists: the Delft artist Jan Vermeer (d. 1675) is thought to have conceived his paintings with the use of the *camera obscura* (figure

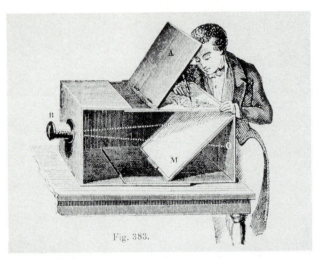

FIGURE 22.8 A camera obscura; the image formed by the lens and reflected by the mirror on the ground glass is traced by the artist. Photo courtesy Beaumont Newhall.

22.8), an optical device that anticipated the modern pinhole camera (though it lacked the means of capturing the image on film). Vermeer's *View of Delft,* a topographical study of the artist's native city, reveals a typically Dutch affection for the visible world and its all-embracing light (figure 22.9). Vermeer lowers the horizon line of the painting to give increased attention to the sky—a reflection perhaps of his interest in the new astronomy. Unlike the great landscape painters of China (chapter 14), whose multifocused vistas unfold only gradually, Vermeer fixes a single point of view at a single moment in time. Yet his broad horizon seems to reach beyond the limits of the frame to embrace a world that exceeds the mundane boundaries of seventeenth-century Delft. Dwarfed by their setting, two tiny figures (artfully placed in the left foreground) behold the landscape from within the painting as we do from without.

The exemplar of an age of observation, Vermeer brought to his compositions a keen sensitivity to light. Small beads of light, an effect produced by the *camera obscura,* twinkle on the surface of his canvases. In *The Astronomer,* a warm golden light highlights the scientist's face and hands, while it creates a unifying atmosphere for the scholarly tools and instruments of his studio-laboratory (figure 22.1). In *The Goldweigher* (figure 22.10), light transforms a mundane subject—the weighing of gold—into an allegory illustrating the balance between material prosperity (symbolized by the jewels on the table) and spiritual

destiny (represented by the painting of the Last Judgment that hangs on the wall). With cool intellectualism, Vermeer balances the negative space of the background against the positive figure of the pregnant woman. He weighs light against dark as he sets realistic details against broadly generalized shapes. These formal devices seem to reinforce the allegorical theme of balance. But whether or not Vermeer intended the painting as an allegory, the affective power of *The Goldweigher* lies in its intimacy and in the meditative mood created by light, which, entering from a nearby window, subtly illuminates the face and body of the young woman. (Vermeer's Netherlandish ancestor, Jan van Eyck, had captured a similar mood in the Arnolfini marriage portrait executed two centuries earlier—figure 17.9). Women, usually self-contained and self-possessed, and always without children, were one of Vermeer's favorite subjects. He pictured them playing musical instruments, reading letters, and enjoying the company of men.

Dutch Portraiture

The vogue of portraiture in northern baroque art reflected the self-conscious materialism of a rising middle class. Like the portraits of wealthy Renaissance aristocrats (figures 17.10, 17.11, and 17.12), the painted likenesses of seventeenth-century Dutch burghers fulfilled the desire to immortalize one's worldly image. But in contrast to Italian portraits, the painted images of middle-class Dutch men and women are usually unidealized and often even unflattering.

Two contemporaries, Frans Hals (d. 1666) and Rembrandt van Rijn (the latter discussed in chapter 21 in the context of religious art), dominated the genre of portraiture in seventeenth-century Dutch painting. Hals was the leading painter of Haarlem and one of the great realists of the Western portrait tradition. His talent lay in capturing the fleeting expressions that characterized the personality and physical presence of his sitters. Hals rendered the jaunty self-confidence of a Dutch officer (figure 22.11) with the same fidelity to nature that he used to convey the dour solemnity of the scholar-philosopher Descartes (figure 22.2). A master of the brush, Hals brought his forms to life by means of quick, loose, staccato brushstrokes and impasto highlights. Immediacy, spontaneity, and impulsive movement, features typical of baroque art, are captured in Hals's vigorous portraits.

FIGURE 22.9 *View of Delft,* Jan Vermeer, 1658. Oil on canvas, 38 3/4 in. × 46 in. The Hague, Mauritshuis. Scala/Art Resource, New York.

These qualities also appear in the work of Judith Leyster (d. 1660), an artist from the Netherlands province of Utrecht, whose canvases until this century were usually attributed to Hals. Leyster's *Self-Portrait* achieves a sense of informality through the casual manner in which the artist turns away from her canvas to greet the viewer (figure 22.12). The laughing violinist that is the subject of the "painting within the painting" provides an exuberant counterpoint to Leyster's self-confident visage. Leyster's portrait is a personal comment on the role of the artist as muse and artisan.

Hals' and Leyster's portraits were astute records of surface appearance and the social milieu. By comparision, Rembrandt's portraits are studies of the inner life of his sitters. A keen observer of human nature and a master technician, Rembrandt became the leading portrait painter in the city of Amsterdam. The commissions he received at the beginning of his career exceeded his ability to fill them. But after a meteoric rise to fame, his fortunes declined. Accumulated debts led to poverty, bankruptcy, and depression—the last compounded by the loss of his beloved wife. Rembrandt's self-portraits, over sixty of

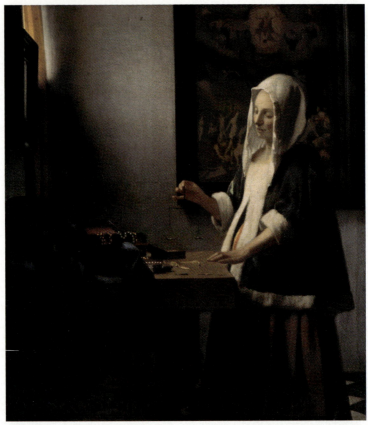

FIGURE 22.10 *The Goldweigher,* Jan Vermeer, ca. 1657. Oil on canvas, 16 3/4 in. × 15 in. The Widener Collection, National Gallery of Art, Washington, D.C.

FIGURE 22.11 *Portrait of an Officer,* Frans Hals, 1635–48. Oil on canvas, 33 3/4 in. × 27 in. Andrew Mellon Collection, 1937. National Gallery of Art, Washington, D.C.

FIGURE 22.12 *Self-Portrait,* Judith Leyster, ca. 1634. Oil on canvas, 29 3/8 in. × 25 5/8 in. National Gallery of Art, Washington, D.C. Gift of Mr. and Mrs. Robert Woods Bliss.

FIGURE 22.13 *Self-Portrait,* Rembrandt van Rijn, 1659. Oil on canvas, 33 1/4 in. × 26 in. National Gallery of Art, Washington, D.C. Andrew W. Mellon Collection.

which survive, are a kind of visual diary, a lifetime record of the artist's passionate effort to document the interior life. His self-portrait of 1659, with its slackened facial muscles and worried brow, reveals a noble and yet vulnerable personality (figure 22.13).

Among the most lucrative of Rembrandt's commissions was the group portrait, a uniquely Dutch genre that commemorated the achievements of wealthy families, guild members, and militia officers. In paintings whose sizes (some over 12 by 14 feet) exemplify the baroque love for colossal proportions, Rembrandt combined theatrical effects with sober, unidealized characterization. These features are especially obvious in *The Anatomy Lesson of Dr. Nicolaes Tulp* (1632), the painting that established Rembrandt's reputation as a master portraitist (figure 22.14). Rembrandt eliminated the posed look of the conventional group portrait by staging the scene as a dissection in progress. Here, as in his religious compositions (compare figure 21.3), he manipulates light for dramatic purposes: he spotlights the dissected corpse in the foreground and balances the darker area on the right, dominated by the figure of the doctor, with a triangle formed by the illuminated heads of the students (whose names appear on the piece of paper held by the central figure). The faces of Tulp's students carry the force of individual personalities and capture the spirit of inquisitiveness peculiar to the Age of Science.

Baroque Instrumental Music

Until the sixteenth century, almost all music was written for the human voice rather than for musical instruments. Even during the Renaissance, instrumental music was, for the most part, the result of substituting an instrument for a voice in music written for singing or dancing. The seventeenth century marked the rise of music that lacked extramusical meaning. Like a mathematical equation or a geometric formula, the instrumental music of the early modern era carried no explicit narrative content—it was neither a vehicle of religious expression nor a means of supporting a secular vocalized text. Such music was written without consideration for the associational content traditionally provided by a set of sung lyrics. The idea of music as an aesthetic exercise, composed for its own sake rather than to serve a religious or communal purpose, was a notable feature of the seventeenth century and one that distinguished modern Western European music from the musical traditions of Asia and Africa.

Not surprisingly, the rise of instrumental music was accompanied by improvements in instruments and refinements in tuning. Indeed, instrumental music came to dominate musical composition at the very moment that Western musicians were perfecting such stringed instruments as the violin, viola, and cello (figure 22.7) and such keyboard instruments as the organ and harpsichord (figure 22.15). By the early eighteenth century, musicians were adopting the system of tuning known as **equal temperament**, whereby the octave was divided into twelve half steps of equal size. Equal temperament made the chromatic scale uniform among instruments. J. S. Bach's *Well-Tempered Keyboard* (1722) was an attempt to popularize this system to a skeptical musical public. The new attention to improving instruments and systemizing key mirrored the efforts of scientists and philosophers to establish uniform tools and precise methods for scientific inquiry.

In the seventeenth-century, northern Italy was the center for the manufacture of violins. The Amati, Guarneri, and Stradivari families of Cremona, Italy, established the techniques of making quality violins, which they transmitted from father to son. Some of those techniques were guarded so secretly that modern violin makers have never successfully imitated them. Elsewhere, around 1650, earlier instruments were standardized and refined. The ancient

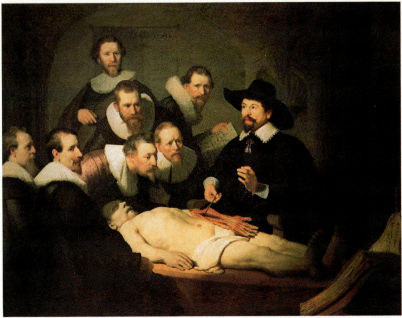

FIGURE 22.14 *The Anatomy Lesson of Dr. Nicolaes Tulp,* Rembrandt van Rijn, 1632. Oil on canvas, 5 ft. 3 3/8 in. × 7 ft. 1 1/4 in. The Hague, Mauritshuis. Scala/Art Resource, New York.

FIGURE 22.15 Seventeenth century Flemish Harpsichord-double-banked; Compass, four octaves, and a fifth F to C (each keyboard); Maker: Johannes Couchet, ca. 1650. Case decorated with carving and gilt gesso work. The Metropolitan Museum of Art, The Crosby Brown Collection of Musical Instruments, 1889 (89.4.2363).

double reed wind instrument known as the shawm, for instance, developed into the modern oboe. While amateur music making was widespread (figure 22.6), professional performance also took a great leap forward, as a new breed of virtuosos inspired the writing of treatises on performance techniques.

Three main types of composition—the sonata, the suite, and the concerto—dominated seventeenth-century instrumental music. All three reflect the baroque taste for dramatic contrasts in tempo and texture. The **sonata** (from the Italian word for "sounded," that is, music played and not sung) was a piece written for a few instruments—often no more than one or two. It usually consisted of three **movements** of contrasting tempo—fast/slow/fast—each based on a song or dance form of the time. The **suite**, written for any combination of instruments, was a sequence or series of movements derived from various European court or folk dances—for example, the sarabande, the pavane, the minuet, and the gigue, or jig. Henry Purcell (d. 1695) in England, François Couperin (d. 1733) in France (chapter 26), and J. S. Bach (d. 1750) in Germany all contributed to the development of the suite as a musical genre. Finally, the **concerto** (from the same root as *concertato,* which describes opposing or contrasting bodies of sound, see chapter 20) was a composition consisting of two groups of instruments, one small and the other large, playing in "dialogue." The typical baroque concerto, the **concerto grosso** ("large concerto") featured several movements, whose number and kind varied considerably.

The leading Italian instrumental composer of the baroque era was Antonio Vivaldi (d. 1741), a Roman Catholic priest and the son of a prominent violinist at Saint Mark's Cathedral. Vivaldi wrote some 450 concertos. He systematized the concerto grosso into a three-movement form (fast/slow/fast) and increased the distinctions between solo and ensemble groups in each movement. Of the many exciting compositions Vivaldi wrote for solo violin and ensemble, the most glorious is *The Four Seasons,* a group of four violin concertos, each of which musically describes a single season. Vivaldi intended that this piece be "programmatic," that is, that it carry meaning outside of the music itself. As if to ensure that the music duplicate the descriptive power of the traditional vocal lines, he added poems at appropriate passages in the score for the instruction of the performers. At the section called "Spring," for instance, Vivaldi's verses describe "flowing streams" and "singing birds." And while one may enjoy detecting such sounds in the music of Vivaldi's *The Four Seasons,* the brilliance of this instrumental masterpiece lies not in its programmatic innovations, but, rather, in its vibrant rhythms, its lyrical solos, and its exuberant "dialogues" between violin and small orchestra.

Rivaling Vivaldi's *The Four Seasons* in their spiraling melodies and expansive rhythms are Johann Sebastian Bach's *Brandenburg Concertos*. Bach dedicated the six concertos to Christian Ludwig, who, as Margrave of Brandenberg, had commissioned Bach to write music for his court orchestra. The *Brandenburg Concertos* employ most of the principal instruments of Bach's time: violin, oboe, recorder, trumpet, and harpsichord (figure 22.15). Totally unconcerned with extramusical meaning, Bach applied himself to developing rich contrasts of tone and texture between the two "contending" groups of instruments—note especially the massive sound of the entire ensemble versus the lighter sounds of the small sections in the first movement of the fourth Concerto. Here, tightly drawn webs of counterpoint are spun between upper and lower instrumental parts, while musical lines, driven by an unflagging rhythm and energy, seem to unfold majestically.

In one of the most compelling examples of baroque instrumental music, *The Art of the Fugue,* Bach wedded the scientific rationalism of his day to the art of musical composition. The **fugue** (literally "flight") is a polyphonic composition in which a single musical theme (or subject) is restated in sequential phrases. In composing the religious music that had occupied most of his career (chapter 21), Bach had used a fugue based on a chorale melody to introduce and set the mood for each of his 170 chorale preludes. Only one year before he died, in 1749, he undertook the monumental work on the art and science of fugal counterpoint that came to be called *The Art of the Fugue*. Unfinished at the time of his death, *The Art of the Fugue* systematically explored the vast potential of fugal composition. With mathematical precision, Bach arranged the musical subject so that it might appear backwards or inverted (or both), augmented (the time value of the notes doubled, so that the melody moves twice as slowly), or diminished (note values halved, so that the melody moves twice as fast). In the incomplete final fugue, he even "signed" his name with a musical motif made up of the letters of his name—B flat, A, C, and B natural. Even the listener who cannot read music or analyze the intricacies of Bach's inventions is struck by the concentrated brillance of a Bach fugue. No less than Newton's codification of the laws of nature, *The Art of the Fugue* was the triumphant expression of the Age of Science.

Summary

During the seventeenth century, European scientists advanced a new picture of the cosmos. They showed that earth, like the other planets, followed an elliptical and therefore irregular path around the sun, which was the center of the solar system. Clearly, the planet earth and its human inhabitants could no longer be regarded as the center of a motionless universe. The progress of the Scientific Revolution moved from the stage of methodical speculation (represented by Copernicus and Kepler) to that of empirical confirmation (provided by Galileo's telescope) and, ultimately with Newton's *Principia,* to codification. Between 1600 and 1750, many new scientific instruments were invented, and the sciences of physics and astronomy, along with the language of higher mathematics, were firmly established.

While the new science demystified nature, the new learning pursued a methodology for more accurately describing and predicting the operations of nature. Francis Bacon championed induction and the empirical method, which gave priority to knowledge gained through the senses. John Locke, the most influential philosopher of the age, defended the empirical tradition by claiming that all ideas came from sensation and reflection. René Descartes opposed such views; he gave priority to deductive reasoning and mathematical analysis. Despite their differences, seventeenth-century intellectuals shared the deist notions of God as a master mechanic and the universe as a great machine that operated independent of divine intervention.

The Scientific Revolution and the new learning ushered in a phase of the baroque style marked by an empirical attention to detail, a fascination with light and space, and an increased demand for such subjects as still life, landscape, portraiture, and genre painting. The many examples of each produced in this era testify to the secular preoccupations of middle-class patrons. In seventeenth-century art, cosmic landscapes such as Vermeer's *View of Delft* are balanced by the genre paintings of de Hooch and ter Borch, which explore the intimate pleasures of house and home, and by the portraits of Hals, Leyster, and Rembrandt, which give clear evidence of the robust confidence of the age.

Modern science also touched the art of music. During the seventeenth century, the violin and the organ were perfected, and keyboard instruments (and musical performance in general) benefited from the development of a uniform system of tuning. Treatises on the art of instrumental performance became popular. The seventeenth century saw the rise of wholly instrumental music and of such instrumental forms as the sonata, the suite, and the concerto. Vivaldi and Bach perfected the concerto grosso, a multi-movement form characterized by vivid contrasts between small and large instrumental groups. Bach exploited the art of the fugue in musical compositions whose complexity and intricacy remain unrivaled. These instrumental forms captured the exuberance of the baroque spirit, even as they summed up the dynamic intellectualism of the age.

GLOSSARY

Cartesian   of or relating to René Descartes or his philosophy

concerto   (Italian, "opposing" or "competing") an instrumental composition consisting of one or more solo instruments and a larger group of instruments playing in "dialogue"

concerto grosso   a "large concerto," the typical kind of baroque concerto, consisting of several movements

deductive reasoning   a method of inquiry that begins with clearly established general premises and moves toward the establishment of particular truths

deism   a movement or system of thought advocating natural religion based on human reason rather than revelation; deists described God as Creator, but denied that God interfered with the laws of the universe

equal temperament   a system of tuning that originated in the seventeenth century, whereby the octave was divided into twelve half steps of equal size; since intervals have the same value in all keys, music may be played in any key, and a musician may change from one key to another with complete freedom

fugue   ("flight") a polyphonic composition in which a theme (or subject) is imitated, restated, and developed by successively entering voice parts

geocentric   earth-centered

heliocentric   sun-centered

inductive reasoning   a method of inquiry that begins with direct observation and experimentation and moves toward the establishment of general conclusions or axioms

movement   a major section in a long instrumental composition

sonata   an instrumental composition consisting of three movements of contrasting tempo, usually fast/slow/fast; see also Glossary, chapter 26

suite   an instrumental composition consisting of a sequence or series of movements derived from court or folk dances

vanitas   (Latin, "vanity") a type of still life consisting of objects that symbolize the brevity of life and the transience of earthly pleasures and achievements

SUGGESTIONS FOR READING

Alpers, Svetlana. *The Art of Describing: Dutch Art in the Seventeenth Century.* Chicago: University of Chicago Press, 1983.

———. *Rembrandt's Enterprise: The Studio and the Market.* Chicago: University of Chicago Press, 1990.

Donington, Robert. *Baroque Music: Style and Performance.* New York: Norton, 1982.

Hall, A. Rupert. *The Revolution in Science: 1500–1750.* New York: Longman, 1983.

Havens, George R. *The Age of Ideas.* New York: Holt, 1955.

Jacob, Margaret C. *The Cultural Meaning of the Scientific Revolution.* New York: Knopf, 1988.

Montias, John M. *Vermeer and His Milieu.* Princeton, N.J.: Princeton University Press, 1991.

Nussbaum, Frederick L. *The Triumph of Science and Reason.* New York: Harper, 1953.

Rossi, Paolo. *Francis Bacon: From Magic to Science.* Chicago: University of Chicago Press, 1968.

Stechow, Wolfgang. *Dutch Landscape Painting of the Seventeenth Century.* London: Phaidon, 1966.

MUSIC LISTENING SELECTIONS

Cassette II Selection 5. Vivaldi, *The Four Seasons,* "Spring," Concerto in E Major, Op. 8, No. 1; first movement, 1725.

Cassette II Selection 6. Bach, Brandenburg *Concerto* No. 4 in G Major, first movement, 1721.

Cassette II Selection 7. Bach, *The Art of the Fugue,* Canon in the 12th, 1749–50.

23

ABSOLUTE POWER AND THE ARISTOCRATIC STYLE

The early modern era in the West is sometimes called the Age of Absolutism. During the seventeenth and into the eighteenth century, divine right kings, that is, rulers who were believed to hold their power directly from God, exercised unlimited power over various European nation-states. But the term "Age of Absolutism" is equally appropriate to the period as it unfolded in the lands beyond Europe, for in China, India, and elsewhere, divine right monarchs also held unlimited control over their own vast states and empires (Map 23.1).

Absolute rulers maintained their authority by controlling a centralized bureaucracy and a standing army, and by pursuing economic policies designed to maximize the wealth of the state. In Western Europe, the mightiest of such potentates was King Louis XIV of France. During the nearly three-quarters of a century that Louis occupied the French throne (1643–1715), he dictated the political, economic, and cultural policies of the country. Under his guidance, France assumed a position of political and military leadership in Western Europe. As cultural arbiter, Louis helped to bring about a phase of the baroque called the *classical baroque.* This style pervaded the arts of seventeenth-century France and became one of the hallmarks of French absolutism. It also impressed its stamp on the rest of Europe and, somewhat later, on an emergent American culture.

Outside of Europe, monarchs as "absolute" as Louis XIV held sway: Suleiman the Magnificent—grand vizier of the Ottoman Turks, the Safavids of Persia in the Middle East, the Moguls in India, and the Ming and Ch'ing emperors in China. Within each of these territories, as within the European nation-states, the arts flourished as an expression of the majesty of the ruler and of the wealth and strength of his domain.

Louis XIV and French Absolutism

Like the pharoahs of ancient Egypt and in the tradition of his medieval ancestors, Louis XIV (d. 1715) governed France as the direct representative of God on earth (figure 23.1). Neither the Church, nor the nobility, nor the will of his subjects limited his power. During his seventy-two years on the throne, the Estates General, France's moribund representative assembly, was never once called into session. As absolute monarch, Louis brought France to a position of political and military preeminence among the European nation-states. He challenged the power of the feudal nobility and placed the Church under the authority of the state, thus centralizing all authority in his own hands. By exempting the nobility and upper middle class from taxation and offering them important positions at court, he turned potential opponents

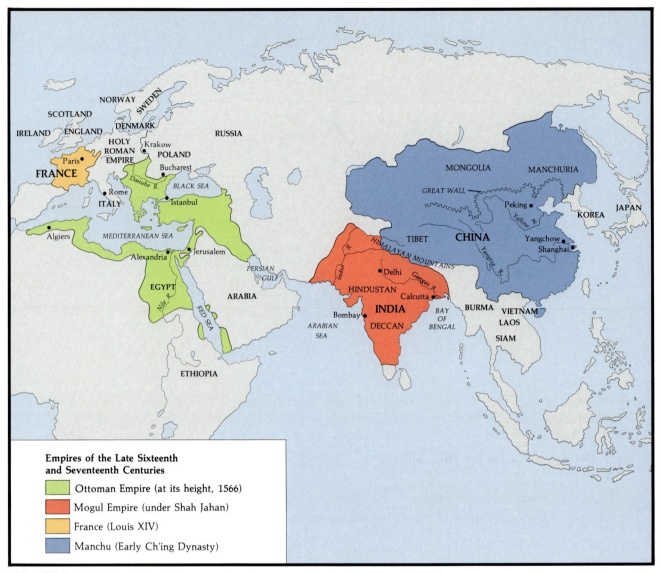

Empires of the Late Sixteenth and Seventeenth Centuries

- 🟩 Ottoman Empire (at its height, 1566)
- 🟥 Mogul Empire (under Shah Jahan)
- 🟧 France (Louis XIV)
- 🟦 Manchu (Early Ch'ing Dynasty)

MAP 23.1   Empires of the Late Sixteenth and Seventeenth Centuries

into supporters. Even if Louis never uttered the famous words attributed to him, "I am the state," he surely operated according to that precept. Indeed, as an expression of his unrivaled authority, he took as his official insignia the image of the classical sun god Apollo (figure 23.2) and referred to himself as *le roi soleil* (the Sun King).

As ruler of France, Louis was one of the world's most influential figures. Under his leadership, the center of artistic patronage and productivity shifted from Italy to France, French culture in all of its forms—from art and architecture to fashions and fine *cuisine*—came to dominate European tastes, a condition that prevailed until well into the early twentieth century. Although Louis was not an intellectual, he was both shrewd and ambitious. He chose first-rate advisers to execute his policies and financed those policies with money from taxes that fell primarily

upon the backs of French peasants. Vast amounts of money were spent to make France the undisputed military leader of Western Europe. But Louis, who instinctively recognized the propaganda value of the arts, also used the French treasury to glorify himself and his office. His extravagances left France in woeful financial condition, a circumstance that contributed to the outbreak of revolution at the end of the eighteenth century. Incapable of foreseeing these circumstances, Louis cultivated the arts as an adjunct to majesty.

Versailles: Symbol of Royal Absolutism

The French royal family traditionally resided in Paris, at the palace known as the Louvre. But Louis, who detested Paris, moved his capital to a spot from which he might more directly control the nobility and keep them dependent upon him for honors and financial favors. Early in his career he commissioned a massive

FIGURE 23.1 *Portrait of Louis XIV*, Hyacinthe Rigaud, 1701. Oil on canvas. Approx. 9 ft. 2 in. × 6 ft. 3 in. Louvre, Paris. Giraudon/Art Resource, New York.

renovation of his father's hunting lodge at the village of Versailles, some twelve miles from Paris. It took thirty-six thousand workers and nearly twenty years to build Versailles, but, in 1682, the French court finally established itself in the apartments of this magnificent unfortified *chateau* (castle). More than a royal residence, Versailles was—in its size and splendor—the symbol of Louis' absolute supremacy over the landed aristocracy, the provincial governments, the urban councils, and the Estates General.

The wooded site that constituted the village of Versailles, almost half the size of Paris, was connected to the old capital by a grand boulevard that (following the path of the sun) ran from the king's bedroom—where most state business was transacted—to the Avenue de Paris. Even a cursory examination of the plan of Versailles, laid out by the French architect Louis le Vau (d. 1670), reveals Vau's esteem for the rules of symmetry, clarity, and geometric regularity (figure 23.3). These principles, in combination with a taste for spatial grandeur, dramatic contrast, and theatrical display, were the distinguishing features of the classical baroque style.

Shaped like a winged horseshoe, the almost two-thousand-foot-long royal residence—best viewed in its entirety from the air—was the focus of an immense complex of parks, lakes, and forest (figure 23.4). The central building of the palace was designed by le Vau, while two additional wings were added by Jules Hardouin Mansart (d. 1708). Three levels of vertically aligned windows march across the palace facade like soldiers in a formal procession (figure 23.5). Porches bearing freestanding Corinthian columns accent the second level, and ornamental statues at the roofline help to relieve the monotonous horizontality of the structure. In its total effect, the palace is dignified and commanding, a grand synthesis of classical and Palladian elements. Its calm nobility provides a striking contrast to the robust theatricality of Italian baroque architecture (figures 20.12 and 20.14).

The grandeur and majesty of Versailles made it the model for hundreds of palace-estates and city planning projects in both Europe and America for the next two centuries. Le Vau's facade became the prototype for the remodeled royal palace in Paris, the Louvre. Designed by Claude Perrault (d. 1688), the east facade of the Louvre echoes the basic classical baroque features of Louis' residence at Versailles: a strong rectilinear organization, paired Corinthian columns, and a gabled entrance that provides dramatic focus (figure 23.6).

The palace at Versailles housed Louis' family, his royal mistresses (one of whom bore him nine children), and hundreds of members of the French nobility whose presence was politically useful to Louis.

FIGURE 23.2 Emblem of the Sun King. Detail from a door in the Salon of Apollo in the Grand Apartement de Versailles. Musée de la Marine, Paris.

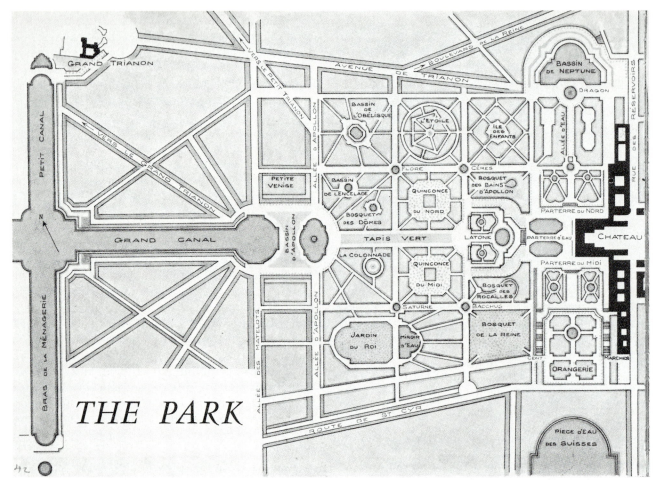

FIGURE 23.3 Plan of Versailles. Musée de Versailles.

FIGURE 23.4 Anonymous seventeenth-century painting of Versailles. © The Bettmann Archive.

FIGURE 23.5   Versailles, the north flower bed. Giraudon/Art Resource, New York.

FIGURE 23.6   Facade of the Louvre, Paris, Claude Perrault, Louis le Vau, and Charles le Brun, 1667–70. Cliché des Musées Nationaux, Paris.

FIGURE 23.7 Versailles, Ornamental Lake and Fountain of Latone. Musée de Versailles. Photo courtesy of Gloria Fiero.

Life at the court of the Sun King was both formal and public—a small army of servants, courtiers, ministers, and pet animals constantly surrounded Louis. All forms of behavior were fixed by protocol. Rank at court determined where one sat at the dinner table and whether one or both panels of Versailles' "French doors" were to be opened upon entering.

Flanking the palace were barracks for honor guards, lodgings for over fifteen hundred servants, kennels, greenhouses, an orangery with over two thousand orange trees, and over seven miles of gardens. André Le Nôtre (d. 1700) designed the formal gardens with the same compelling sense of order that le Vau brought to the architecture. The great park featured an array of hedges clipped into geometric shapes, sparkling fountains (that favorite of all baroque mechanical devices), artificial lakes, grottoes, a zoo, theaters, and outdoor "rooms" for private gatherings and clandestine meetings (figure 26.11). The gardens, planted with over four million tulip bulbs, which Louis imported annually from Holland, were a spectacular sight. They framed and embellished the long walkways that radiated purposefully from the central building. On the garden side of the palace, artificial pools reflected sculptures whose subject matter glorified the majesty of the king (figure 23.7). Itself a kind of outdoor theater, the royal palace pro-

vided the ideal backdrop for the ballets, operas, and plays that were regular features of court life (figure 23.8).

If the exterior of Versailles symbolized the grandeur of the king, the interior was a monument to princely self-indulgence (figure 23.9). Though now shorn of many of their original furnishings, Versailles' sumptuous *salons* (drawing rooms) still testify to Louis' success at cultivating French trades in such luxury items as crafted silver, clocks, lace, brocades, porcelain, and fine glass. During the seventeenth century, the silk industry reached its peak, French carpets competed with those of Turkey and Persia, the art of **marquetry** (inlaid wood) rivaled that of Italy, and the tapestries produced at the Gobelin factory in Paris outclassed those woven in Flanders. Versailles' salons were adorned with illusionistic frescoes, gilded stucco moldings, crystal chandeliers, and huge, ornate mirrors. The rooms housed some of the most lavish *objets d'art* (art objects) in Western history, all of which, it is sobering to recall, were enjoyed at a time when the peasant majority of the French population lived in one-room, thatch-roofed houses filled with rough wooden furniture. Equally sobering is the fact that despite its splendor, the palace lacked any kind of indoor plumbing. Servants carried out the slops, but

FIGURE 23.8 Marble Court, Versailles Palace, Louis Le Vau. Engraving by Lepautre showing a performance of Lully's *Alceste,* 1674. The Metropolitan Museum of Art, New York City, Harris Brisbane Dick Fund, 1930. 30–22.32[53]

FIGURE 23.9 Versailles, Apartment of the Queen—Salon of the Nobles. Musée de Versailles. Giraudon/Art Resource, New York.

FIGURE 23.10 Versailles, *Salon de Guerre* (Drawing Room of War). Musée de Versailles. Giraudon/Art Resource, New York.

the unpleasant odor of human waste was difficult to mask, even with French perfumes.

Each of Versailles' rooms illustrated a specific theme: the *Salon de Venus* was decorated by Charles le Brun (d. 1690) with ceiling paintings portraying the influence of love on various kings in history. In the *Salon de Guerre* (Drawing Room of War), an idealized, equestrian Louis, carved in low-relief marble, is shown receiving the victor's crown (figure 23.10)—though Louis himself rarely took part in combat. The most splendid room at Versailles, however, is the 240-foot-long Hall of Mirrors, which once connected the royal apartments with the chapel (figure 23.11). Embellished with glorious frescoes, marble pilasters, and gilded bronze capitals, and furnished with ornate candelabra and bejeweled trees (the latter have since disappeared), the hall features a wall of seventeen mirrored arcades that face an equal number of high-arched windows opening onto the garden. Framing this opulent royal passageway, mirrors and windows set up a brilliant counterpoint of image and reflection. Mirrors were to Versailles what fountains were to Rome: vehicles for the theatrical display of changing light in unbounded space.

Louis as Patron of the Arts

At Versailles, Louis was the arbiter of fashion and manners. Within his dining salons, linen napkins came into use, forks replaced fingers for eating, and elaborate dishes were served to suit the royal palate. Graced with an eye for beauty and a passion for aggrandizement, Louis increased the number of paintings in the French royal collection from the two hundred he inherited upon his accession to the throne to the two thousand he left at his death. These paintings formed the basis of the permanent collection at the Louvre, now a world-renowned art museum.

As Louis dictated the table manners and even the menus of the French court, so on a grander scale he dictated the standards of artistic production. Following in the tradition of his father, Louis XIII, who had instituted the French Royal Academy of Language and Literature in 1635, he created and subsidized government-sponsored institutions in the arts, appointing his personal favorites to oversee each. In 1648, Louis founded the Academy of Painting and Sculpture; in 1661 he established the Academy of Dance; in 1666, the Academy of Sciences; in 1669, the Academy of Music, and in 1671, the Academy of Architecture. The creation of the academies was a

FIGURE 23.11 *Galerie des palace* (Hall of Mirrors), Versailles, Jules Hardouin Mansart and Charles le Brun, ca. 1680. Musée de Versailles. Giraudon/Art Resource, New York.

symptom of royal efforts to fix standards, but Louis had something more personal in mind: he is said to have told a group of academicians, "Gentlemen, I entrust to you the most precious thing on earth—my fame." His trust was well placed, for the academies brought glory to the king and set standards that would govern the arts for at least two centuries. These standards were enshrined in "rules" inspired by the legacy of ancient Greece and Rome, thus *neoclassicism*—the revival of classical style and subject matter—became the accepted style of academic art.

In the early days of his reign, when Italy was the leader in artistic style, Louis invited Italian artists to execute royal commissions. Among the artists whom Louis brought to France was the master architect-sculptor Gianlorenzo Bernini (chapter 20). Bernini had submitted designs for a remodeled Louvre, and although his plans were rejected ultimately in favor of Perrault's, his vigorous style survives in such works as the life-size marble portrait bust of Louis completed in 1665 (figure 23.12). Originally designed to stand on a gilded enamel globe inscribed with a message celebrating the king's lofty position, this sculp-

ture—with its billowing draperies, elaborate coiffure, and idealized features—glorifies the ruler in typically baroque fashion. Bernini's theatrical exuberance contrasts sharply with the sober neoclassicism of the French academician François Girardon (d. 1715). Girardon drew on Hellenistic models for the ideally proportioned statues that he arranged in graceful tableaux for the gardens of Versailles. In one such tableau, Girardon's neoclassical nymphs are seen entertaining the sun god Apollo—an obvious reference to Louis as *roi soleil* (figure 23.13).

Poussin and the Academic Style in Painting

Girardon's compositions owed much to the paintings of the leading exponent of French academic art, Nicolas Poussin (d. 1665). Poussin spent most of his life in Rome, absorbing the rich heritage of the classical and Renaissance past. He revered Raphael as master of the High Renaissance and heir to the classical style, and, like many neoclassicists to come, he shared Raphael's esteem for lofty subjects drawn from classical mythology and Christian legend. In an influential treatise on painting, Poussin formalized the rules that would become the basis for neoclassical art: He advised that artists choose only grandiose subjects, "such as battles, heroic actions, and religious themes," and reject crude, bizarre, and ordinary subject matter. As to the manner of representation, artists should make the physical action suit the mood of the narrative, avoiding, at all cost, any type of exaggeration. They should present their subjects clearly and evenly in harmonious compositions that were free of irrelevant details. Restraint, moderation, and decorum—(that is, propriety and good taste)—should govern all aspects of pictorial representation.

Poussin faithfully followed the rules that he himself outlined. His *Arcadian Shepherds,* completed in 1639, transports us to the idyllic region in ancient Greece known as Arcadia, a place where men and women were said to live in harmony with nature (figure 23.14). Three shepherds have come upon an ancient tomb, a symbol of death, which—as the allegorical Muse of History (*right*) confirms—reigns even in the most perfect of places. Cool, bright colors and even lighting enhance the elegaic mood, while sharp contours and the sure use of line provide absolute clarity of design. But the real power of the

FIGURE 23.12 *Louis XIV,* Gianlorenzo Bernini, 1665. Marble, height 33 1/8 in. Musée de Versailles. Alinari/Art Resource, New York.

FIGURE 23.13 *Apollo Attended by the Nymphs,* François Girardon, ca. 1666–72. Marble, life-size. Park of Versailles. Giraudon/Art Resource, New York.

painting lies in its rigorous composition. Poussin arrived at this composition by arranging and rearranging miniature wax models of his figures within a small rectangular box. He then posed these figures—statuesque, heroically proportioned, and idealized—so that their every gesture helped to narrate the story. Indeed, all of the elements in the painting, from the Muse's feet (which parallel the horizontal picture plane) to the trees in the landscape and right edge of the tomb (which parallel the vertical picture plane) contribute to the perfect geometry of the pictorial structure.

Despite the grand theatricality of Poussin's paintings, order always dominates over spontaneity. Both in form and in content, Poussin's canvases are intellectual; that is, they appeal to the mind rather than to the senses. In contrast to such Italian baroque painters as Caravaggio, whose works he detested, Poussin soberly advanced the aesthetics of neoclassicism.

Poussin and his contemporary, Claude Gellée (d. 1682), known as Lorrain, were responsible for creating the genre known as the "ideal landscape," a landscape painted in the rational and high-minded style that characterized favorite moral subjects. For such paintings, academic artists made sketches of the countryside around Rome and then deliberately reordered the natural elements according to the rules of balance and clarity. Lorrain's landscapes became noble settings for lofty mythological or biblical subjects (figure 23.15). Unlike the Dutch landscape painters, who rendered nature with forthright realism, (figure 22.9), academic artists imposed a preconceived order upon the natural world.

The Aristocratic Portrait

The Age of the Baroque was the great period of aristocratic portraiture. Commissioned by the hundreds by Louis XIV and the members of his court, aristocratic portraits differ dramatically from the portraits of such artists as Hals, Leyster, and Rembrandt (figures 22.11, 22.12, and 22.13). Whereas Dutch artists investigated the personalities of their sitters, French artists were concerned primarily with outward appearance.

FIGURE 23.14 *Arcadian Shepherds,* Nicolas Poussin, 1638–39. Oil on canvas, 33 1/2 in. × 47 5/8 in. Louvre, Paris. Scala/Art Resource, New York.

FIGURE 23.15 *The Marriage of Isaac and Rebekah (The Mill)*, Claude Lorrain (Claude Gellée), 1642. Oil on canvas, 59 in. × 77 in. National Gallery, London.

The classic example of French aristocratic portraiture is the regal image of Louis XIV painted in 1701 by Hyacinthe Rigaud (d. 1743, figure 23.1). Rigaud shows the aging king adorned with ermine-lined coronation robes, silk stockings, lace cravat, high-heeled shoes, and a well-manicured wig—all but the first were fashionable hallmarks of upper-class wealth. Louis' mannered pose, which harks back to classical models, reflects self-conscious pride in status. Rigaud employed special devices to enhance the theme of authority and regality: satin curtains theatrically dignify the king and a lone column compositionally and metaphorically underscores his rectitude. Such devices would become standard conventions in European and American portraits of the eighteenth century (figure 26.26).

The Aristocratic Style Outside of France: Velásquez, Rubens, and van Dyck

In Spain, Diego Velásquez (d. 1660), court painter to King Philip IV, became that country's most prestigious artist. A master of the brush, Velásquez excelled at modeling forms so that they conveyed the powerful presence of real objects in atmospheric space. For the Spanish court, Velásquez painted a variety of classical and Christian subjects, but his masterpiece was the informal group portrait known as *Las Meninas* (*The Maids of Honor*, figure 23.16). In this painting, Velásquez depicted himself at his easel, alongside the members of the royal court: the *infanta* (the five-year-old daughter of the king), her maids of honor, her dwarf, her dog, and the royal escorts. In the background is a mirror that reflects the images of the king and queen of Spain—presumably the subjects of the large canvas Velásquez shows himself painting in the

FIGURE 23.16 *The Maids of Honor (Las Meninas),* Diego Velásquez, 1656. Oil on canvas, 10 ft. 5 in. × 9 ft. Prado Museum, Madrid. Giraudon/Art Resource, New York.

left foreground. Superficially, this is a group portrait of the kind we have already encountered in the art of Rembrandt (figure 22.14), but it is also an intriguing comment on the relationship between the perceived and the perceiver. Almost all of the characters in the painting, including the painter himself, are shown gazing at the royal couple, who must be standing outside of the picture space in the very spot occupied by the viewer. With baroque inventiveness, Velásquez expands the spatial field to include the beholder; at the same time he cunningly contrasts different points of view. The painting becomes a visual "conceit" that provokes a dialogue between viewer and viewed and between patron and artist.

Like Velásquez, the internationally renowned Flemish painter Peter Paul Rubens (d. 1640) established his reputation in the courts of Europe. The well-educated Rubens, who spoke six languages fluently, traveled widely as a diplomat and art dealer for royal patrons in Italy, England, and France. He also headed a large studio workshop that trained scores of assistants to help fill his many commissions. For the Luxembourg Palace of Paris, Rubens and his studio executed twenty-one monumental canvases that glorified Marie de' Medici, Louis XIV's grandmother, and her late husband, King Henry IV of France. Like Poussin, Rubens studied in Italy and was familiar with both classical and High Renaissance art. But Rubens deeply admired the flamboyant colorists Titian and Tintoretto, and he developed a style that, by comparison with Poussin's, was painterly in technique and dynamic in composition.

One of Rubens' most memorable canvases, *The Rape of the Daughters of Leucippus,* depicts the abduction of two mortal women by the Roman gods

FIGURE 23.17 *Rape of the Daughters of Leucippus,* Peter Paul Rubens, ca. 1618. Oil on canvas, 7 ft. 3 in. × 6 ft. 10 in. Alte Pinakothek, Munich.

Castor and Pollux (figure 23.17). Rubens illustrated the classical story with vigor and imagination, pressing the fleshy bodies of the maidens against the picture plane and arranging their limbs in the pattern of a slowly revolving pinwheel. His masterful paint-strokes exploited sensuous contrasts of luminous flesh, burnished armor, gleaming satins, and dense horsehide. Probably commissioned to commemorate the double marriage of Louis XIII of France to a Spanish princess and Philip IV of Spain to a French princess (and, thus, to celebrate the diplomatic alliance of France and Spain), the painting communicates a message of (male) power over (female) privilege—and, by extension, of political absolutism. Images of subjugation by force, whether in the form of lion hunts (as in ancient Assyrian reliefs, figure 3.11) or in paintings and sculptures depicting mythological stories of rape, were metaphors for the sovereign authority of the ruler over his subjects.

In England, the most accomplished seventeenth-century portraitist was the Flemish master Anthony van Dyck (d. 1641). Van Dyck had been an assistant to Rubens and may have worked with him on the *Rape of the Daughters of Leucippus.* Unwilling to compete with Rubens, van Dyck moved to Genoa and then to London, where he became court painter to King Charles I of England (chapter 21). Van Dyck's many commissioned portraits of Italian and English aristocrats are striking for their polished elegance and idealized grandeur, features that are especially evident in his equestrian portrait of King Charles I (figure 23.18). In this painting, which revives the traditional motif of ruler-on-horseback (figures 7.20, 11.2, 17.13), van Dyck shows the king, who was actually short and undistinguished looking, as handsome and regal. The fluid composition and the shimmering vitality of the brushwork make this one of the most memorable examples of aristocratic baroque portraiture.

FIGURE 23.18 *Charles I on Horseback*, Anthony van Dyck, ca. 1638. Oil on canvas, 12 ft. × 9 ft. 7 in. National Gallery, London.

FIGURE 23.19 King Louis XIV as the sun in the 1653 *Ballet de la Nuit.* Bibliothèque Nationale, Paris.

Music and Dance at the Court of Louis XIV

In France, the court at Versailles was the setting for an extraordinary outpouring of music, theater, and dance (figure 23.8). In order to provide musical entertainments for state dinners, balls, and operatic performances, Louis established a permanent orchestra, the first in European history. Its director, the Italian-born (but French-educated) Jean Baptiste Lully (d. 1687), also headed the French Academy of Music. Often called the father of French opera, Lully oversaw all phases of musical performance, from writing scores and conducting the orchestra to training the chorus and staging operatic productions. Many of Lully's operas were based on themes from classical mythology. Their semidivine heroes, models of Louis himself, flattered his image as absolute ruler.

Lully's operas shared the pomp and splendor of le Brun's frescoes, the strict clarity of Poussin's paintings, and the formal correctness of classical drama. Though Lully's music was generally lacking in spontaneity and warmth of feeling, it was faithful to the neoclassical unity of words and music. Lully modified the music of the recitative to follow precisely and with great clarity the inflections of the spoken word. Lully introduced to opera the "French overture," an instrumental form that featured contrasts between a slow first part in homophonic texture with a fast, contrapuntal second part. Under Lully's leadership, French opera also developed its characteristic feature: the inclusion of formal dance.

At the court of Louis XIV, dancing and fencing were the touchstones of aristocratic grace. All members of the upper class were expected to perform the basic court dances, including the very popular *minuet,* and the courtier who could not dance was judged rude and inept. Accordingly, in Molière's comedy-ballet *Le Bourgeois Gentilhomme,* the dancing master insists that the ills of humankind arise from lack of skill in dancing. Like his father, Louis XIII, who had commissioned and participated in extravagantly expensive ballets, Louis XIV was a superb dancer. Dressed as the sun, he danced the lead in the 1653 performance of the *Ballet de la Nuit* (figure 23.19). Still more significant was Louis' contribution to the birth of professional dance: he helped to transform court dance into an independent art form. During the late seventeenth century, French ballet masters of the Royal Academy of Music and the Dance established rules for five positions that have become the basis for classical dance. Clarity, balance, and proportion, along with studied technique—elements characteristic of classicism in general—became the informing ideals of the classical ballet.

By 1685 female dancers joined the previously all-male French dance ensembles in staged performances. And in 1700 Raoul Auget Feuillet published a system of abstract symbols for recording specific dance steps and movements, thus facilitating **choreography**. Ballet, itself a metaphor for the strict etiquette and ceremony of court life, enriched all aspects of the French theater. However, since classical ballet demanded a rigorous attention to proper form, it soon became too specialized for any but professionals to perform, hence there developed the gap between performer and audience that exists to this day in the art of dance.

Neoclassicism and French Literature

As with other forms of artistic expression in seventeenth-century France, in literature neoclassical precepts of form and content held sway. French writers addressed questions of human dignity and morality in a language that was clear, polished, and precise. Their prose is marked by refinement, good taste, and the concentrated presentation of ideas.

One literary genre that typified the neoclassical spirit was the **maxim**. A maxim is a short, concise, and often witty saying, usually drawn from experience and offering some practical advice. Witty sayings that distilled wisdom into a few words were popular in many cultures, including those of the Hebrews, the Greeks, and the Africans. But in seventeenth-century France, the cautionary or moralizing aphorism was acknowledged as the ideal means of teaching good sense and decorum. Terse and lean, the maxim exalted precision of language and thought. France's greatest maxim writer was François de La Rochefoucauld (d. 1680), a nobleman who had participated in a revolt against Louis XIV early in his reign. Withdrawing from court society, La Rochefoucauld wrote with a cynicism that reflected his conviction that self-interest, hypocrisy, and greed motivated the behavior of most human beings—including and especially the aristocrats of his day. As the following maxims illustrate, however, La Rochefoucauld's insights into human behavior apply equally well to individuals of all social classes and to any age.

READING 82 From La Rochefoucauld's *Maxims*

Truth does less good in the world than its appearances do harm.

* * * *

Love of justice in most men is only a fear of encountering injustice.

* * * *

We often do good that we may do harm with impunity.

* * * *

As it is the mark of great minds to convey much in few words, so small minds are skilled at talking at length and saying little.

* * * *

Virtue would not go nearly so far if vanity did not keep her company.

* * * *

We confess to small faults to create the impression that we have no great ones.

* * * *

To be rational is not to use reason by chance, but to recognize it, distinguish it, appreciate it.

———————————◆———————————

Like La Rochefoucauld's maxims, but on a larger scale, French drama reflected the neoclassical effort to restrain passionate feeling by means of cool objectivity and common sense. The leading French tragedian of the seventeenth century, Jean Racine (d. 1699) wrote plays that treated high-minded themes in an elevated language. Racine amended Aristotle's "unities" of action and time (chapter 6) to include a strict unity of place. In the play *Phaedra,* itself based on Greek models, Racine explored the conflict between human passions (Phaedra's "unnatural" infatuation with her stepson) and human reason (Phaedra's duty as the wife of Theseus, king of Athens). The subject matter of Racine's plays addresses the disasterous consequences of emotional indulgence—a weakness especially peculiar to Racine's female characters. Likewise, the structure of Racine's plays manifests his abiding commitment to intellectual control.

Molière's Human Comedy

Jean Baptiste Poquelin (d. 1673), whose stage name was Molière, was France's leading comic dramatist. Like all great humorists, Molière played upon the incongruities between the ideal and the real, between fact and pretense, and between inner conviction and outward behavior. In bringing to life specific incidents of hypocrisy, pomposity, and other human foibles, Molière illustrated the essentially neoclassical conviction that excesses of human passion and vanity enfeeble human dignity.

Molière, the son of a wealthy upholsterer, abandoned a career in law in favor of acting and play writing. He learned much from the *commedia del arte,* a form of improvised Italian street theater that depended on buffoonery, slapstick humour, and pantomine. Molière's plays involved simple story lines that brought to life the comic foibles of such stock characters as the miser, the hypochondriac, the hypocrite, the misanthrope, and the would-be gentleman. The last of these, a character whose attempts to assume the trappings of upper-class respectability turn him into a dupe, is the subject of one of Molière's last plays, *Le Bourgeois Gentilhomme (The Tradesman Turned Gentleman). Le Bourgeois Gentilhomme* was designed as a *comédie-ballet,* a dramatic performance that incorporated interludes of song and dance (in a manner similar to modern musical comedy). Lully provided the music, choreographed the ballet, and directed the entire production, which, like many other Molière's plays, was well-received by the king and his court.

But even beyond Versailles, Molière's hilarious comedy, the tale of a prosaic Parisian who tries to buy "class," had wide appeal. French aristocrats, who saw themselves as above imitation, heartily enjoyed the play. So did upper-middle-class patrons who, while claiming an increasingly prominent place in the social order, refused to see themselves as "tradesmen turned gentlemen." Women found themselves endowed in Molière's play with confidence and guile, while servants discovered themselves invested with admirable common sense. The play reflected the clearly defined class structure of early modern European society, with its firmly drawn lines between the sexes. In a single stroke, *Bourgeois Gentilhomme* captured the spirit of the seventeenth century—its class tensions and social contradictions, along with its ambitions and high expectations. The play is universal and timeless, however, as a rollicking exposition of human nature.

READING 83 From Molière's *Bourgeois Gentilhomme*

Characters
Mr. Jourdain
Mrs. Jourdain, his wife
Lucile, his daughter
Cléonte, suitor of Lucile
Dorimene, a marquise
Dorante, a count, in love with Dorimene
Nicole, servant to Mr. Jourdain
Covielle, valet to Clèonte
A Music-Master
His Scholar
A Dancing-Master
A Fencing-Master
A Philosophy-Master
A Master Tailor
A Journeyman Tailor
Two Lackeys
Musicians, Dancers, Cooks, Journeymen Tailors, and other characters to dance in the interludes

The scene is at Paris

Act I

Overture, played by a full orchestra; in the middle of the stage the Music-Master's Scholar, seated at a table, is composing the air for a serenade which Mr. Jourdain has ordered.

Scene I

Music-Master, Dancing-Master, Three Singers, Two Violinists, Four Dancers

Music-Master, *to the singers:* Here, step inside, and wait until he comes.   1

Dancing-Master, *to the dancers:* And you too, this way.

Music-Master, *to his scholar:* Is it finished?

Scholar: Yes.

Music-Master: Let's see . . . That's good.

Dancing-Master: Is it something new?

Music-Master: Yes, 'tis the air for a serenade which I have had him compose, while waiting for our gentleman to wake up.   10

Dancing-Master: May I see it?

Music-Master: You shall hear it, with the words, when he comes. He won't be long.

Dancing-Master: You and I have no lack of occupation now.

Music-Master: That's true. We have found a man here who is just what we both needed. He's a nice little source of income for us, this Mr. Jourdain, with his   20 visions of nobility and gallantry that he has got into his noddle. And 't would be a fine thing for your dancing and my music if everybody were like him.

Dancing-Master: No, no, not quite; I could wish, for his sake, that he had some true understanding of the good things we bring him.

Music-Master: 'Tis true he understands them ill, but he pays for them well; and that is what the arts need most nowadays.

Dancing-Master: For my part, I'll own, I must be fed somewhat on fame. I am sensitive to applause, and I feel that in all the fine arts 'tis a grievous torture to show one's talents before fools, and to endure the barbarous judgments of a dunce upon our compositions. There's great pleasure, I tell you, in working for people who are capable of feeling the refinements of art, who know how to give a flattering reception to the beauties of your work, and recompense your toil by titillating praise. Yes, the most agreeable reward possible for what we do, is to see it understood, to see it caressed by applause that honors us. Nothing else, methinks, can pay us so well for all our labors; and enlightened praise gives exquisite delight.

Music-Master: I grant you that, and I relish it as you do. There is surely nothing more gratifying than such praise as you speak of; but man cannot live on applause. Mere praise won't buy you an estate; it takes something more solid. And the best way to praise, is to praise with open hands. Our fellow, to be sure, is a man of little wit, who discourses at random about anything and everything, and never applauds but at the wrong time. But his money sets right the errors of his mind; there is judgment in his purse; his praises pass current; and this ignorant shopkeeper is worth more to us, as you very well see, than the enlightened lord who introduced us to his house.

Dancing-Master: There is some truth in what you say; but methinks you set too much store by money; and self-interest is something so base that no gentleman should ever show a leaning towards it.

Music-Master: Yet I haven't seen you refuse the money our fellow offers you.

Dancing-Master: Certainly not; but neither do I find therein all my happiness; and I could still wish that with his wealth he had good taste to boot.

Music-Master: I could wish so too; and 'tis to that end that we are both working, as best we may. But in any case, he gives us the means to make ourselves known in the world; he shall pay for others, and others shall praise for him.

Dancing-Master: Here he comes

[Act I, Scene II: Mr. Jourdain converses with his music- and dancing-masters, who dispute as to which is the more important art: music or dance. A dialogue in music, written by the music-master, follows, then a ballet choreographed by the dancing-master.

Act II, Scene I: Mr. Jourdain dances the minuet for the dancing-master, and then learns how to make a "proper" bow.]

Act II, Scene II

Mr. Jourdain, Music-Master, Dancing-Master, Lackey

Lackey: Sir, here is your fencing-master.

Mr. Jourdain: Tell him to come in and give me my lesson here. *(To the music-master and dancing-master)* I want you to see me perform.

Scene III

Mr. Jourdain, Fencing-Master, Music-Master, Dancing-Master, a Lackey *with two foils*

Fencing-Master, *taking the two foils from the lackey and giving one of them to Mr. Jourdain:* Now, sir, your salute. The body erect. The weight slightly on the left thigh. The legs not so far apart. The feet in line. The wrist in line with the thigh. The point of your sword in line with your shoulder. The arm not quite so far extended. The left hand on a level with the eye. The left shoulder farther back. Head up. A bold look. Advance. The body steady. Engage my sword in quart[1] and finish the thrust. One two. Recover. Again, your feet firm. One, two. Retreat. When you thrust, sir, your sword must move first, and your body be held well back, and sideways. One, two. Now, engage my sword in tierce,[2] and finish the thrust. Advance. Your body steady. Advance. Now, from that position. One, two. Recover. Again. One, two. Retreat. On guard, sir, on guard *(the fencing-master gives him several thrusts)*, on guard.

Mr. Jourdain: Well?

Music-Master: You do wonders.

Fencing-Master: I've told you already: the whole secret of arms consists in two things only: hitting and not being hit. And as I proved to you the other day by demonstrative logic, it is impossible that you should be hit if you know how to turn aside your adversary's sword from the line of your body; and that depends merely on a slight movement of the wrist, inwards or outwards.

Mr. Jourdain: So, then, without any courage, one may be sure of killing his man and not being killed?

Fencing-Master: Certainly. Didn't you see the demonstration of it?

Mr. Jourdain: Yes.

Fencing-Master: And by this you may see how highly our profession should be esteemed in the State; and how far the science of arms excels all other sciences that are of no use, like dancing, music . . .

Dancing-Master: Softly, Mr. Swordsman; don't speak disrespectfully of dancing.

Music-Master: Learn, pray, to appreciate better the excellences of music.

Fencing-Master: You are absurd fellows, to think of comparing your sciences with mine.

Music-Master: Just see the man of consequence!

Dancing-Master: The ridiculous animal, with his padded stomacher![3]

---

[1]A defensive posture in the art of fencing.

[2]Another fencing posture.

[3]Protection used in fencing.

Fencing-Master: My little dancing-master, I will make you dance to a tune of my own, and you, little songster, I will make you sing out lustily.

Dancing-Master: Mr. Ironmonger, I'll teach you your own trade.

Mr. Jourdain, *to the dancing-master:* Are you mad, to pick a quarrel with him, when he knows tierce and quart and can kill a man by demonstrative logic?

Dancing-Master: A fig for his demonstrative logic, and his tierce and his quart.

Mr. Jourdain, *to the dancing-master:* Softly, I tell you.

Fencing-Master, *to the dancing-master:* What, little Master Impudence!

Mr. Jourdain: Hey! my dear fencing-master.

Dancing-Master, *to the fencing-master:* What, you great cart-horse!

Mr. Jourdain: Hey! my dear dancing-master.

Fencing-Master: If I once fall upon you . . .

Mr. Jourdain, *to the fencing-master:* Gently.

Dancing-Master: If I once lay hands on you . . .

Mr. Jourdain, *to the dancing-master:* So, so.

Fencing-Master: I will give you such a dressing . . .

Mr. Jourdain, *to the fencing-master:* I beg you.

Dancing-Master: I will give you such a drubbing . . .

Mr. Jourdain, *to the dancing-master:* I beseech you . . .

Music-Master: Let us teach him manners a little.

Mr. Jourdain: Good Heavens! do stop.

Scene IV

Professor of Philosophy, Mr. Jourdain, Music-Master, Dancing-Master, Fencing-Master, Lackey

Mr. Jourdain Oho! Mr. Philosopher, you've arrived in the nick of time with your philosophy. Do come and set these people here at peace.

The Philosopher How now? What is the matter, gentlemen?

Mr. Jourdain: They have put themselves in a passion about the precedence of their professions, and even insulted each other and almost come to blows.

The Philosopher: O fie, gentlemen! Should a man so lose his self-control? Have you not read the learned treatise which Seneca composed, *Of Anger?*[4] Is there anything more base or shameful than this passion, which of a man makes a savage beast? Should not reason be mistress of all our emotions?

Dancing-Master: How, how, sir! Here he comes and insults us both, by condemning dancing, which I practise, and music, which is his profession.

The Philosopher: A wise man is above all the insults that can be offered him; and the chief answer which we should make to all offences, is calmness and patience.

---

[4] A treatise by the first-century Roman stoic, Lucius Annaeus Seneca (see chapter 7).

Fencing-Master: They both have the insolence to think of comparing their professions with mine!

The Philosopher: Should that move you? 'Tis not for vain glory and precedence that men should contend; what really distinguishes us from each other is wisdom and virtue.

Dancing-Master: I maintain to his face that dancing is a science which cannot be too highly honored.

Music-Master: And I, that music is a science which all ages have reverenced.

Fencing-Master: And I maintain, against both of them, that the science of fencing is the finest and most indispensable of all sciences.

The Philosopher: But what then becomes of philosophy? I think you are all three mighty impertinent to speak with such arrogance before me, and impudently to give the name of science to things which ought not even to be honored with the name of art, and which may best be classed together as pitiful trades, whether of prize-fighters, ballad-mongers, or mountebanks.[5]

Fencing-Master: Go to, dog of a philosopher.

Music-Master: Go to, beggarly pedagogue.

Dancing-Master: Go to, past master pedant.

The Philosopher: What, you rascally knaves! . . . *(He falls upon them, and they all three belabor him with blows.)*

Mr. Jourdain: Mr. Philosopher!

The Philosopher: Villains! varlets! insolent vermin!

Mr. Jourdain: Mr. Philosopher!

Fencing-Master: Plague take the beast!

Mr. Jourdain: Gentlemen!

The Philospher: Brazen-faced ruffians!

Mr. Jourdain: Mr. Philosopher!

Dancing-Master: Deuce take the old pack-mule!

Mr. Jourdain: Gentlemen!

The Philosopher: Scoundrels!

Mr. Jourdain: Mr. Philosopher!

Music-Master: Devil take the impertinent puppy!

Mr. Jourdain: Gentlemen!

The Philosopher: Thieves! vagabonds! rogues! imposters!

Mr. Jourdain: Mr. Philosopher! Gentlemen! Mr. Philosopher! Gentlemen! Mr. Philosopher! *(Exit fighting.)*

Scene V

Mr. Jourdain, Lackey

Mr. Jourdain: Oh! fight as much as you please; I can't help it, and I won't go spoil my gown trying to part you. I should be mad to thrust myself among them and get some blow that might do me a mischief.

Scene VI

The Philosopher, Mr. Jourdain, Lackey

The Philosopher, *straightening his collar:* Now for our lesson.

Mr. Jourdain: Oh! sir, I am sorry for the blows you got.

---

[5] Charlatans or quacks.

The Philosopher: That's nothing. A philosopher kows how to take things aright; and I shall compose a satire against them in Juvenal's manner,[6] which will cut them up properly. But let that pass. What do you want to learn? 150

Mr. Jourdain: Everything I can; for I have the greatest desire conceivable to be learned; it throws me in a rage to think that my father and mother did not make me study all the sciences when I was young.

The Philosopher: That is a reasonable sentiment; *nam, sine doctrina, vita est quasi mortis imago.* You understand that, for of course you know Latin. 160

Mr. Jourdain: Yes; but play that I don't know it; and explain what it means.

The Philosopher: It means that, *without learning, life is almost an image of death.*

Mr. Jourdain: That same Latin's in the right.

The Philosopher: Have you not some foundations, some rudiments of knowledge?

Mr. Jourdain: Oh! yes, I can read and write.

The Philosopher: Where will you please to have us begin? Shall I teach you logic? 170

Mr. Jourdain: What may that same logic be?

The Philosopher: 'Tis the science that teaches the three operations of the mind.

Mr. Jourdain: And who are they, these three operations of the mind?

The Philosopher: The first, the second, and the third. The first is to conceive aright, by means of universals; the second, to judge aright, by means of the categories; and the third, to draw deductions aright, by means of the figures: *Barbara, Celarent, Darii, Ferio, Baralipton.*[7] 180

Mr. Jourdain: There's a pack of crabbed words. This logic doesn't suit me at all. Let's learn something else that's prettier.

The Philosopher: Will you learn ethics?

Mr. Jourdain: Ethics?

The Philosopher: Yes.

Mr. Jourdain: What is your ethics about?

The Philosopher: It treats of happiness, teaches men to moderate their passions, and . . . 190

Mr. Jourdain: No; no more of that. I am choleric as the whole pack of devils, ethics or no ethics; no, sir, I'll be angry to my heart's content, whenever I have a mind to it.

The Philospher: Is it physics you want to learn?

Mr. Jourdain: And what has this physics to say for itself?

The Philosopher: Physics is the science which explains the principles of natural phenomena, and the properties of bodies; which treats of the nature of the elements, metals, minerals, stones, plants, and animals, and teaches us the causes of all such things as 200

meteors, the rainbow, St. Elmo's fire,[8] comets, lightning, thunder, thunderbolts, rain, snow, hail, winds, and whirlwinds.

Mr. Jourdain: There's too much jingle-jangle in that, too much hurly-burly.

The Philosopher: Then what do you want me to teach you? 210

Mr. Jourdain: Teach me spelling.

The Philosopher: With all my heart.

Mr. Jourdain: And afterward, you shall teach me the almanac, so as to know when there's a moon, and when there isn't.

The Philosopher: Very well. To follow up your line of thought logically, and treat this matter in true philosophic fashion, we must begin, according to the proper order of things, by an exact knowledge of the nature of the letters, and the different method of 220 pronouncing each one. And on that head I must tell you that the letters are divided into vowels, so called— *vowels*— because they express the sounds of the *voice* alone; and consonants, so called—*con-sonants*— because they *sound with* the vowels, and only mark the different articulations of the voice. There are five vowels, or voices: A, E, I, O, U.

Mr. Jourdain: I understand all that.

The Philosopher: The vowel A is formed by opening the mouth wide: A. 230

Mr. Jourdain: A,A. Yes.

The Philsoper: The vowel E is formed by lifting the lower jaw nearer to the upper: A, E.

Mr. Jourdain: A,E; A,E. On my word, 'tis so. Ah! how fine!

The Philosopher: And the vowel I, by bringing the jaws still nearer together, and stretching the corners of the mouth toward the ears; A, E, I.

Mr. Jourdain: A, E, I, I, I, I. That is true. Science forever! 240

The Philosopher: The vowel O is formed by opening the jaws, and drawing in the lips at the corners: O.

Mr. Jourdain: O, O. Nothing could be more correct: A, E, I, O, I, O. 'Tis admirable! I, O; I, O.

The Philosopher: The opening of the mouth looks exactly like a little circle, representing an O.

Mr. Jourdain: O, O, O. You are right. O. Ah! What a fine thing it is to know something!

The Philosopher: The vowel U is formed by bringing the teeth together without letting them quite touch, and thrusting out the lips, at the same time bringing them together without quite shutting them: U. 250

Mr. Jourdain: U, U. Nothing could be truer: U.

The Philosopher: Your lips are extended as if you were pouting; therefore if you wish to make a face at anyone, and mock at him, you have only to say U.

Mr. Jourdain: U, U. ''Tis true. Ah! would I had studied sooner, to know all that!

The Philosopher: To-morrow, we will consider the other letters, namely the consonants. 260

---

[6] A Roman satirist of the early second century (see chapter 7).

[7] Part of a series of Latin names used by medieval logicians to help remember the valid forms of syllogisms.

---

[8] Electrical discharges seen by sailors before and after storms at sea and named after the patron saint of sailors.

Mr. Jourdain: Are there just as curious things about them as about these?

The Philsopher: Certainly. The consonant D, for instance, is pronounced by clapping the tip of the tongue just above the upper teeth: D.

Mr. Jourdain: D, D. Yes! Oh! what fine things! what fine things!

The Philosopher: The F, by resting the upper teeth on the lower lip: F. 270

Mr. Jourdain: F, F. 'Tis the very truth. Oh! father and mother of me, what a grudge I owe you!

The Philosopher: And the R by lifting the tip of the tongue to the roof of the mouth; so that being grazed by the air, which comes out sharply, it yields to it, yet keeps returning to the same point, and so makes a sort of trilling: R, Ra.

Mr. Jourdain: R, R, Ra, R, R, R, R, R, Ra. That is fine. Oh! what a learned man you are, and how much time I've lost! R, R, R, Ra. 280

The Philosopher: I will explain all these curious things to you thoroughly.

Mr. Jourdain: Do, I beg you. But now, I must tell you a great secret. I am in love with a person of very high rank, and I wish you would help me to write her something in a little love note which I'll drop at her feet.

The Philosopher: Excellent!

Mr. Jourdain: 'Twill be very gallant, will it not?

The Philosopher: Surely. Do you want to write to her in verse? 290

Mr. Jourdain: No, no; none of your verse.

The Philosopher: You want mere prose?

Mr. Jourdain: No, I will have neither prose nor verse.

The Philosopher: It must needs be one or the other.

Mr. Jourdain: Why?

The Philosopher: For this reason, that there is nothing but prose or verse to express oneself by.

Mr. Jourdain: There is nothing but prose or verse? 300

The Philosopher: No, sir. All that is not prose is verse, and all that is not verse is prose.

Mr. Jourdain: But when we talk, what is that, say?

The Philosopher: Prose.

Mr. Jourdain: What! When I say: "Nicole, bring me my slippers and give me my nightcap," that's prose?

The Philosopher: Yes, sir.

Mr. Jourdain: On my word, I've been speaking prose these forty years, and never knew it; I am infinitely obliged to you for having informed me of this. Now I 310 want to write to her in a note: *Fair Marquise,[9] your fair eyes make me die of love;* but I want it to be put in gallant fashion, and neatly turned.

The Philosopher: Say that the fires of her eyes reduce your heart to ashes; that night and day you suffer for her all the tortures of a . . .

Mr. Jourdain: No, no, no, I want none of all that. I will have nothing but what I told you: *Fair Marquise, your fair eyes make me die of love.*

The Philosopher: You must enlarge upon the 320 matter a little.

Mr. Jourdain: No, I tell you. I'll have none but those very words in the note, but put in a fashionable way, arranged as they should be. Pray tell me over the different ways they can be put, so that I may see.

The Philosopher: You can first of all put them as you said: *Fair Marquise, your fair eyes make me die of love.* Or else: *Of love to die me make, fair Marquise, your fair eyes.* Or else: *Your fair eyes of love me make, fair Marquise, to die.* Or else: *To die your fair eyes, fair* 330 *Marquise, of love me make.* Or else: *Me make your fair eyes die, fair Marquise, of love.*

Mr. Jourdain: But which of all these ways is the best?

The Philosopher: The way you said it: *Fair Marquise, your fair eyes make me die of love.*

Mr. Jourdain: And yet I never studied, and I did it at the first try. I thank you with all my heart, and beg you to come again to-morrow early.

The Philosopher: I shall not fail to. 340

Scene VII

Mr. Jourdain, Lackey

Mr. Jourdain, *to the lackey:* What! Haven't my clothes come yet?

Lackey: No, sir.

Mr. Jourdain That cursed tailor makes me wait a long while, on a day when I'm so busy. I am furious. May the quartan ague[10] wring this villain of a tailor unmercifully! To the devil with the tailor! Plague choke the tailor! If I had him here now, that wretch of a tailor, that dog of a tailor, that scoundrel of a tailor, I'd . . .

Scene VIII

Mr. Jourdain, A Master-Tailor; A Journeyman-Tailor, *carrying Mr. Jourdain's suit;* Lackey

Mr. Jourdain: Ah! so there you are! I was just going 350 to get angry with you.

Master-Tailor: I could not come sooner, I had twenty men at work on your clothes.

Mr. Jourdain: You sent me some silk stockings so tight that I had dreadful work getting them on, and there are two stitches broke in them already.

Master-Tailor: If anything, they will grow only too loose.

Mr. Jourdain: Yes, if I keep on breaking out stitches. And you made me some shoes that pinch 360 horribly.

Master-Tailor: Not at all, sir.

Mr. Jourdain: What! Not at all?

Master-Tailor: No, they do not pinch you.

Mr. Jourdain: I tell you they do pinch me.

Master-Tailor: You imagine it.

Mr. Jourdain: I imagine it because I feel it. A fine way of talking!

_____
[10]An intermittant fever.

_____
[9]The wife of a nobleman ranking below a duke and above an earl or count.

Master-Tailor: There, this is one of the very handsomest and best matched of court costumes. 'Tis a 370 masterpiece to have invented a suit that is dignified, yet not of black; and I'd give the most cultured tailors six trials and defy them to equal it.

Mr. Jourdain: What's this? You have put the flowers upside down.

Master-Tailor: You didn't tell me you wanted them right end up.

Mr. Jourdain: Was there any need to tell you that?

Master-Tailor: Why, of course. All persons of quality wear them this way. 380

Mr. Jourdain: Persons of quality wear the flowers upside down?

Master-Tailor: Yes, sir.

Mr. Jourdain: Oh! that's all right then.

Master-Tailor If you wish, I will put them right end up.

Mr. Jourdain: No, no.

Master-Tailor: You have only to say the word.

Mr. Jourdain: No, I tell you; you did rightly. Do you think the clothes will fit me? 390

Master-Tailor: A pretty question! I defy any painter, with his brush, to make you a closer fit. I have in my shop a fellow that is the greatest genius in the world for setting up a pair of German breeches; and another who is the hero of our age for the cut of a doublet.[11]

Mr. Jourdain: Are the wig and the feathers just as they should be?

Master-Tailor: Everything is just right.

Mr. Jourdain, *looking at the tailor's suit*: Ah! ah! Mr. Tailor here is some of the cloth from my last suit you 400 made me. I know it perfectly.

Master-Tailor: The cloth seemed to me so fine that I thought well to cut a suit for myself out of it.

Mr. Jourdain: Yes; but you ought not to have cabbaged[12] it out of mine.

Master-Tailor: Will you put on your suit?

Mr. Jourdain: Yes; let me have it.

Master-Tailor: Wait. That is not the way to do things. I have brought my men with me to dress you to music; clothes such as these must be put on with 410 ceremony. Ho! enter, you fellows.

Scene IX

Mr. Jourdain, Master-Tailor, Journeyman-Tailor; Dancers, *in the costume of journeymen-tailors*; Lackey.

Master-Tailor, *to his journeymen*: Put on the gentleman's suit, in the style you use for persons of quality.

First Ballet

Enter four journeymen-tailors, two of whom pull off Mr. Jourdain's breeches that he has on for his exercise, and the other two his jacket; then they put on his new suit; and Mr. Jourdain walks about among them, showing off his suit, to see if it is all right. All this to the accompaniment of full orchestra. 420

---

[11]A man's close-fitting jacket.

[12]Stolen or filched.

Journeyman-Tailor: Noble Sir, please give the tailor's men something to drink.

Mr. Jourdain: What did you call me?

Journeyman-Tailor: Noble Sir.

Mr. Jourdain: Noble Sir! That is what it to dress as a person of quality! You may go clothed as a tradesman all your days, and nobody will call you Noble Sir. (*Giving him money*) There, that's for Noble Sir.

Journeyman-Tailor: My Lord, we are greatly obliged to you. 430

Mr. Jourdain: My Lord! Oh! oh! My Lord! Wait, friend; My Lord deserves something, 'tis no mean word, My Lord! There, there's what His Lordship gives you.

Journeyman-Tailor: My Lord, we will all go and drink Your Grace's health.

Mr. Jourdain: Your Grace! Oh! oh! oh! wait; don't go. Your Grace, to me! (*Aside*) Faith, if he goes as far as Your Highness he'll empty my purse. (*Aloud*) There, there's for Your Grace.

Journeyman-Tailor: My Lord, we thank you most 440 humbly for your generosity.

Mr. Jourdain: He did well to stop. I was just going to give it all to him.

Second Ballet

The four journeymen-tailors celebrate Mr. Jourdain's liberality with a dance, which forms the second interlude.

[Act III, Scenes I through XI: The servant Nicole and Mrs. Jourdain mock Mr. Jourdain's efforts to become a gentleman. The count Dorante comes to borrow money from Mr. Jourdain and to arrange a clandestine meeting between Jourdain and the latest object of his attention, Dorimene, whom he presumes to be a marquise. Cléonte expresses his love for Mr. Jourdain's daughter, Lucile. With Mrs. Jourdain's encouragement, he approaches Mr. Jourdain to ask for Lucile's hand in marriage.]

Scene XII

Cléonte, Mr.Jourdain, Mrs. Jourdain, Lucile, Covielle, Nicole

Cléonte: Sir, I would let no one speak for me, to make of you a request that I have long had in my thoughts. It concerns me so closely that I must do it myself, and without further circumlocution I will inform 450 you that the honor of being your son-in-law is a proud favor which I beg you to grant me.

Mr. Jourdain: Before giving you your answer, sir, I beg you to tell me whether you are a gentleman.

Cléonte: Sir, on this point most people would not hesitate long; the word is easily spoken. People have no scruple about assuming the title, and common custom nowadays seems to authorise the theft. But I must own that I feel somewhat more delicately upon this subject. I think any imposture is unworthy of a true man, and 460 there is a baseness in disguising that birth which Heaven chose for us, in tricking oneself out before the world in a stolen title, and trying to pass for what one is not. My forbears did indeed hold honorable employments; I have won for myself the honor of six years' service under arms; and I am rich enough to keep up a fair rank in society; but for all that I do not choose to give myself a name which others in my place might think they could lay claim to, and I will tell you frankly that I am not of gentle birth.   470

Mr. Jourdain: Your hand on it, sir; my daughter is not for you.

Cléonte: What?

Mr. Jourdain: You are not a gentleman born, you shall not have my daughter.

Mrs. Jourdain: What d'ye mean with your gentleman born? Are we of the rib of St. Louis[13] ourselves?

Mr. Jourdain: Hold your tongue, wife; I see what you're coming at.   480

Mrs. Jourdain: Did either of us come of any but honest tradesmen?

Mr. Jourdain: Just listen to her, will you!

Mrs. Jourdain: And wasn't your father a shopkeeper as well as mine?

Mr. Jourdain: Plague take the woman! she always does it. If your father was a shopkeeper, so much the worse for him; but as for mine, they're malaperts[14] who say so. All I have to say to you, is that I mean to have a gentleman for a son-in-law.   490

Mrs. Jourdain: Your daughter should have a husband that is a proper match for her; and she'd be better off with a good honest fellow, rich and handsome, than with a beggarly broken-down nobleman.

Nicole: That's so; there's the Squire's son in our village, who's the greatest lout and the silliest noodle I ever set eyes on.

Mr. Jourdain, *to Nicole:* Hold your prate, Mistress Impertinence. You're always thrusting yourself into the conversation. I have riches enough for my daughter; all I   500 need is honors, so I shall make her a marquise.

Mrs. Jourdain: A marquise?

Mr. Jourdain: Yes, a marquise.

Mrs. Jourdain: Ah! Heaven save us from that!

Mr. Jourdain: 'Tis a thing I am resolved on.

Mrs. Jourdain: 'Tis a thing to which I shall never consent. Your marriages with people above you are always subject to wretched vexations. I don't want my daughter to have a husband that can reproach her with her parents and children that will be ashamed to call me   510 grandma. If she should come to call on me in her fine lady's equipage, and fail by chance to bow to any of the neighbors, they would be sure to say a hundred ill-natured things. "D'ye see," they'd say, "this marquise that gives herself such airs? She's the daughter of Mr. Jourdain, and she was only too happy, when she was little, to play at My Lady[15] with us. She hasn't always been so high and mighty as all that and her grandfathers were both drapers beside St. Innocent's Gate.[16] They piled up a good fortune for their children,   520

[13]Descendants of the medieval king of France, Louis IX (d. 1270).

[14]Impudent fellows.

[15]Pretend to be titled.

[16]Dealers in textile fabrics located at one of the markets in Paris.

which they're paying mighty dear for now, may be, in another world; riches like that aren't got by honest practices." I don't want all this cackle, and, in a word, I want a man who shall be beholden to me for my daughter, and to whom I can say: "Sit down there, son-in-law, and have dinner with me."

Mr. Jourdain: Those are the sentiments of a petty soul, willing to stay forever in a mean station. Don't talk back to me any more. My daughter shall be a marquise, in spite of all the world, and if you provoke me I'll make   530 her a duchess.

Scene XIII

Mrs. Jourdain, Lucile, Cléonte, Nicole, Covielle

Mrs. Jourdain: Cléonte, don't lose heart yet. (*To Lucile*) Follow me, daughter, come and tell your father boldly that if you cannot have him, you won't marry anybody.

Scene XIV

Cléonte, Covielle

Covielle: You've made fine work of it, with your lofty sentiments.

Cléonte: What can I do? I have scruples in this matter which the example of others cannot overcome.

Covielle: What nonsense, to take things seriously   540 with such a man! Don't you see he is off his head? Would it have cost you anything to have accommodated yourself to his chimeras?

Cléonte: You are right; but I didn't suppose one had to bring his proofs of nobility in order to become Mr. Jourdain's son-in-law.

Covielle, *laughing:* Ha! ha! ha!

Cléonte: What are you laughing at?

Covielle: At an idea that has come into my head to trick the fellow, and get you what you want.   550

Cléonte: How?

Covielle: The idea is altogether comical.

Cleonte: But what is it?

Covielle: There was a certain masquerade performed not long ago, which fits in here excellently, and which I mean to work into a burlesque that I'll play upon our coxcomb.[17] The thing borders on farce; but with him, we can venture anything; we needn't be too particular, for he is a man to play his rôle in it to a marvel, and swallow greedily all the absurdities we take   560 it into our heads to tell him. I have the actors and costumes all ready; just let me alone for it.

Cléonte: But tell me . . .

Covielle: I will let you know all about it. But let's get away; here he is, coming back.

[Act III, Scenes XV through XIX: Mr. Jourdain continues to woo Dorimene, unaware that Dorante is also pursuing her. Act IV, Scenes I through IV: Mr. Jourdain entertains Dorante and Dorimene. Mrs. Jourdain returns home unexpectedly.]

[17]A fool.

Scene V

Mr. Jourdain; Covielle, *in disguise*

Covielle: Sir, I am not sure whether I have the honor to be known to you.

Mr. Jourdain: No, sir.

Covielle, *holding out his hand about a foot from the ground:* I saw you when you were no bigger than that. 570

Mr. Jourdain: Me?

Covielle: Yes. You were the prettiest child in the world, and all the ladies used to take you in their arms to kiss you.

Mr. Jourdain: To kiss me?

Covielle: Yes. I was a great friend of your late father.

Mr. Jourdain: Of my late father?

Covielle: Yes. He was a very worthy gentleman. 580

Mr. Jourdain: What do you say?

Covielle: I say he was a very worthy gentleman.

Mr. Jourdain: My father?

Covielle: Yes.

Mr. Jourdain: You knew him well?

Covielle: Indeed I did.

Mr. Jourdain: And you knew him for a gentleman?

Covielle: Beyond doubt.

Mr. Jourdain: Then I don't know what to make of the world. 590

Covielle: Why?

Mr. Jourdain: There are silly people who insist on telling me that he was a shopkeeper.

Covielle: He, a shopkeeper! It is pure slander; he never was. All he did was this: he used to be very obliging, very polite, and since he was a connoisseur in cloth, he used to go about choosing it everywhere, and had it brought to his house, and gave it to his friends, for money.

Mr. Jourdain: I am charmed to know you, and to have you bear witness that my father was a gentleman. 600

Covielle: I will maintain it to all comers.

Mr. Jourdain: I shall be obliged to you. What business brings you here?

Covielle: Since my acquaintance with the worthy gentleman, your late father, which I told you of, I have travelled round the whole world.

Mr. Jourdain: The whole world?

Covielle: Yes.

Mr. Jourdain: It must be a long way to that country. 610

Covielle: Indeed it is. I came back from my far travels only four days ago; and on account of the interest I take in all that concerns you, I have come to bring you the best piece of news in the world.

Mr. Jourdain: What news?

Covielle: You know the son of the Grand Turk is here?

Mr. Jourdain: I? No.

Covielle: What! He has an absolutely magnificent retinue; people are all flocking to see him, and he has been received here as a very great lord. 620

Mr. Jourdain: On my word, I didn't know it.

Covielle: The point of advantage for you in all this, is that he's in love with your daughter.

Mr. Jourdain: The son of the Grand Turk?

Covielle: Yes; and he wants to be your son-in-law.

Mr. Jourdain: My son-in-law, the son of the Grand Turk?

Covielle: The son of the Grand Turk, your son-in-law. I went at once to see him, and since I understand 630 his language perfectly, he conversed at length with me; and after some other talk, he said: *Acciam croc soler ouch allah moustaph gidelum amanahem varahini oussere carbulath?* which is to say: Have you seen a handsome young lady, the daughter of Mr. Jourdain, a gentleman of Paris?

Mr. Jourdain: The son of the Grand Turk said that of me?

Covielle: Yes. When I told him I knew you especially well, and that I had seen your daughter: Ah! said he, 640 *marababa sahem!* which is to say: Ah! how deeply am I enamored of her!

Mr. Jourdain: *Marababa sahem* means, Ah! how deeply am I enamored of her?

Covielle: Yes.

Mr. Jourdain: Marry, you do well to tell me so; for I never would have thought that *marababa sahem* could mean, Ah! how deeply am I enamored of her! 'Tis an admirable language, this Turkish.

Covielle: More than you have any idea of. Do you 650 know what *cacaracamouchen* means?

Mr. Jourdain: *Cacaracamouchen?* No.

Covielle: It means: My dear soul.

Mr. Jourdain: *Cacaracamouchen* means, My dear soul?

Covielle: Yes.

Mr. Jourdain: That is something marvellous. *Cacaracamouchen,* My dear soul. Who would have thought it? It quite astounds me.

Covielle: In short, to complete my embassy, he is 660 coming to ask you for your daughter in marriage; and that his father-in-law may be worthy of him, he means to make you *mamamouchi,* which is a certain dignity in his country.

Mr. Jourdain: *Mamamouchi?*

Covielle: Yes. *Mamamouchi,* which means, in our language, paladin.[18] Paladin, that is, one of those ancient . . . in short, a paladin. There is nothing more noble on earth, and you will rank equal with the greatest lords in the world. 670

Mr. Jourdain: The son of the Grand Turk does me great honor; I beg you to take me to him, to pay him my thanks.

Covielle: What! he is just coming here.

Mr. Jourdain: He is coming here?

Covielle: Yes; and he is bringing everything needful for your installation.

Mr. Jourdain: That is doing things mighty sudden.

Covielle: His love can endure no delay.

---

[18]One who fights to defend his lord.

Mr. Jourdain: What troubles me is, that my daughter is an obstinate wench, and has taken to fancy to a certain Cléonte, and swears she'll never marry any one else. 680

Covielle: She will change her mind when she sees the son of the Grand Turk; besides the singular thing about it is, that the son of the Grand Turk looks like this Cléonte, or very nearly so. I have just seen him, he was pointed out to me. The love she bears to the one may easily pass to the other, and . . . But I hear him coming; here he is. 690

Scene VI

Cléonte, *disguised as a Turk;* Three Pages, *bearing his long tunic;* Mr. Jourdain, Covielle

Cléonte: *Ambousahim oqui boraf, Giourdina salamalequi!*

Covielle, *to Mr. Jourdain* Which is to say: Mr. Jourdain, may your heart be all the year round like a rose-tree in bloom. These are polite forms of expression in his country.

Mr. Jourdain: I am his Turkish Highness's most humble servant.

Covielle: *Carigar camboto oustin moraf.*

Cléonte: *Oustin yoc catamalequi basum base alla moran!* 700

Covielle: He says: May Heaven give you the strength of lions and the cunning of serpents.

Mr. Jourdain: His Turkish Highness honors me too much, and I wish him all manner of prosperity.

Covielle: *Ossa binamen sadoc babally oracaf ouram.*

Cléonte: *Bel-men.*

Covielle: He says you must go with him at once to get ready for the ceremony, so that he may then see your daughter and conclude the marriage. 710

Mr. Jourdain: All that in two words?

Covielle: That is the way with the Turkish tongue; it says much in few words. Go with him at once.

Scene VII

Covielle, *laughing:* Ho! ho! ho! Faith, 'tis altogether comical. What a dupe! If he had learnt his rôle by heart, he could not play it better. Ha! ha!

[*Scene VIII: A farciful ceremony, complete with music and dance, prepares Mr. Jourdain to receive the title of a Turkish nobleman. Dressed in Turkish style, Jourdain is presented with a turban and cudgeled with a sword (a satire on the European ritual of knighthood). Act V, Scenes I through IV: Now a nobleman, Mr. Jourdain proudly confronts Mrs. Jourdain, Dorante, and Dorimene.*]

Scene VI

Lucile, Cléonte, Mr. Jourdain, Dorimene, Dorante, Covielle

Mr. Jourdain: Come, daughter; come here, come and give your hand to the gentleman who does you the honor to ask for you in marriage. 720

Lucile: Why, father, what a guy you are! Are you acting a play?

Mr. Jourdain: No, no, 'tis no play; 'tis a very serious matter, and the most honorable for you that heart could wish. (*Pointing to Cléonte*) Here is the husband I bestow on you.

Lucile: On me, father?

Mr. Jourdain: Yes, on you. Come, put your hand in his, and thank Heaven for your good fortune.

Lucile: I don't want to be married. 730

Mr. Jourdain: I want you married, and I'm your father.

Lucile: I'll do nothing of the kind.

Mr. Jourdain: Oh! what a to-do! Come, I tell you, Here, your hand.

Lucile: No, father; I have told you, no power can force me to accept any husband but Cléonte; and I will sooner go to all extremities than . . . (*Recognizing Cléonte*) To be sure, you are my father; I owe you entire obedience; and it is for you to dispose of me according to your pleasure. 740

Mr. Jourdain: Ah! I am charmed to see you return so quickly to a sense of your duty; I like to have an obedient daughter.

Scene VII

Mrs. Jourdain, Cléonte, Mr. Jourdain, Lucile, Dorante, Dorimene, Covielle

Mrs. Jourdain: How now? What't all this? I hear you're set on marrying your daughter to a mummer.[19]

Mr. Jourdain: Will you be still, foolish woman? You always come and thrust in your impertinence everywhere. 'Tis impossible to teach you common-sense. 750

Mrs. Jourdain: You are the one 'tis impossible to teach any sense to; you go from folly to folly. What are you driving at now, and what do you mean with this crazy match?

Mr. Jourdain: I am going to wed my daughter to the son of the Grand Turk.

Mrs. Jourdain: To the son of the Grand Turk?

Mr. Jourdain, *pointing to Covielle:* Yes. Make your compliments to him by the dragoman[20] there.

Mrs. Jourdain: I've no use for any dragonman; I'll tell him for myself, to his face, that he sha'n't have my daughter. 760

Mr. Jourdain: Will you hold your tongue, I say again?

Dorante: What! Mrs. Jourdain you set yourself in opposition to an honor such as this? You refuse His Turkish Highness for son-in-law?

Mrs. Jourdain: Bless me, sir! Mind your own business.

Dorante: 'Tis a great honor and not to be refused. 770

Mrs. Jourdain: Madam, I beg you likewise not to trouble yourself about what doesn't concern you.

---

[19]An actor.

[20]An interpreter of Arabic, Turkish, or Persian.

Dorante: It is our friendship for you that makes us take an interest in your welfare.

Mrs. Jourdain: I'll get along without your friendship.

Dorante: Your daughter here submits to her father's wishes.

Mrs. Jourdain: My daughter consents to marry a Turk?

Dorante: Certainly.　　　　　　　　　　　780

Mrs. Jourdain: Can she forget Cléonte?

Dorante: What will one not do to be a great lady?

Mrs. Jourdain: I'd strangle her with my own hands if she played a trick like that.

Mr. Jourdain: This is too much prate. I tell you this marriage shall be.

Mrs. Jourdain: And I tell you it shall not be.

Mr. Jourdain: Oh! what a to-do.

Lucile: Mother!

Mrs. Jourdain: Go to, you're a pitiful hussy.　　790

Mr. Jourdain: What, you scold her for obeying me.

Mrs. Jourdain: Yes. She is as much mine as yours.

Covielle, to Mrs. Jourdain: Madam!

Mrs. Jourdain: What have you go to say about it?

Covielle: One word.

Mrs. Jourdain: I've no use for your word.

Covielle, to Mr. Jourdain: Sir, if she will listen to a word in private, I promise to make her consent to everything you wish.

Mrs. Jourdain: I shall not consent.　　　　800

Covielle: Only listen to me.

Mrs. Jourdain: No.

Mr. Jourdain, to Mrs. Jourdain: Listen to him.

Mrs. Jourdain: No; I will not listen.

Mr. Jourdain: He will tell you . . .

Mrs. Jourdain: I won't be told.

Mr. Jourdain: Just like a woman's obstinacy! Will it do you any harm to hear him?

Covielle: Only hear me; then you shall do as you please.　　　　　　　　　　　　810

Mrs. Jourdain: Well! What?

Covielle, aside to Mrs. Jourdain: We've been making signs to you, madam, this hour or more. Don't you see that all this is only done to humor your husband's whimsies; that we are tricking him by this disguise, and that the son of the Grand Turk is Cléonte himself?

Mrs. Jourdain, aside to Covielle: Oho!

Covielle, aside to Mrs. Jourdain: And I, Covielle, am the dragoman.　　　　　　　　820

Mrs. Jourdain, aside to Covielle: Ah! in that case I give in.

Covielle, aside to Mrs. Jourdain: Don't let the cat out of the bag.

Mrs. Jourdain, aloud: Yes, it is all right, I consent to the marriage.

Mr. Jourdain: Ah! now everybody submits to reason. (To Mrs. Jourdain) You wouldn't listen to him. I was sure he'd explain to you about the son of the Grand Turk.　　　　　　　　830

Mrs. Jourdain: He has explained it to me properly, and I am satisfied. Let us send for the notary.

Dorante: Well said. And, Mrs. Jourdain, that your mind may be perfectly at rest, and that you may abandon at once all jealousy of your husband, this lady and I will make use of the same notary for our marriage.

Mrs. Jourdain: I give my consent to that, too.

Mr. Jourdain, aside to Dorante: So, you'll hoodwink her.

Dorante, aside to Mr. Jourdain: We must needs　840 put her off with this pretence.

Mr. Jourdain, aside: Good, good. (Aloud) Go fetch the notary.

Dorante: While he is coming, and drawing up his writings, let us see our ballet, and offer His Turkish Highness the diversion of it.

Mr. Jourdain: A good idea. Let's take our places.

Mrs. Jourdain: And Nicole?

Mr. Jourdain: I give her to the dragoman; and my　850 wife, to anybody that will have her.

Covielle: Sir, I thank you. (Aside) If 'tis possible to find a madder felow, I'll go tell it at Rome.

The comedy ends with the ballet which had been prepared.

---◆---

Absolute Power and the Aristocratic Style Beyond Europe

It was not by chance that Molière wove a Turkish theme into the fabric of *Le Bourgeois Gentilhomme.* Asian and Oriental potentates, whose embassies visited Louis' court regularly, were—as Molière implies—the functional equivalents of the Sun King and his heirs—hence Mr. Jourdain's desire to see his daughter wed to one of them. France had long maintained diplomatic ties with the Ottoman Turks, the Muslim rulers of the Near East, North Africa, and parts of southeastern Europe (Map 23.1). Indeed, so powerful were the Ottoman forces and so vast were their territories that one of Louis' ancestors, Francis I, had attempted to tip the balance of power in Western Europe by forming, in 1536, an "unholy" alliance with the great Muslim leader Suleiman (d. 1566).

Under Suleiman, known for his military and cultural leadership as "the Magnificent," the Ottoman Empire became a model of Muslim absolutism. Unlimited power, including the power to interpret the Koran and to issue new decrees, lay in Suleiman's hands: when his son and grandson rose against him, he promptly had them executed. A goldsmith and a poet of some esteem, Suleiman initiated a golden age of literature and art. Pomp and luxury characterized Suleiman's court, and the arts that flourished under his patronage shared with those of seventeenth-century France a taste for the ornate and a high degree of technical skill (figure 23.20). Suleiman personally oversaw the activities of official court poets, painters,

FIGURE 23.20 Gold ceremonial canteen decorated with jade plaques and gems, Ottoman Empire, second half of sixteenth century. Topkapi Sarayi Museum, Istanbul, Turkey.

architects, and musicians. He established a model for imperial patronage that ensured the triumph of the aristocratic style not only in Turkish lands but in all parts of his empire.

Neither absolutism nor its manifestation in the arts were the invention of Suleiman, any more than they were the creation of Louis XIV. Suleiman's ancestors, as well as his successors and their rivals, were equally autocratic. During the seventeenth century, as the Ottoman Empire declined, Persian Muslims of the Safavid dynasty rose to power under the leadership of Shah (the word means "king") Abbas (d. 1629). Shah Abbas was ruthless in war, astute in politics, and unbending in his desire to make Persia (present-day Iran) the political, economic, and cultural leader of Asia. By the year 1600, Persian silk rivaled that of China at European markets. Carpet weaving became a national industry that employed over twenty-five thousand people in the capital city of Isfahan alone. Persian tapestries (figure 23.21) and ceramics were avidly sought throughout the world, and Persian manuscripts, embellished with brightly printed illustrations came to be imitated throughout Asia. The arts were as much an adjunct to the majesty of Shah Abbas as they had been to Suleiman and would be to Louis XIV.

In the field of architecture, the outstanding monument to Safavid wealth and power was the Imperial Mosque, commissioned by Shah Abbas for the city of

FIGURE 23.21 Safavid carpet, Persia, seventeenth century. Silk and wool, 24 ft. 11 in. × 10 ft. 8 in. Austrian Museum for Applied Art, Vienna.

Isfahan (figure 23.22). Completed in 1637, this magnificent structure, flanked by two minarets, encloses a square main hall covered by a dome that rises to 177 feet. The surfaces of the mosque, both inside and out, are covered with colored glazed tiles (compare figure 2.15) ornamented with delicate blue and yellow blossoms. French aristocrats in the service of Louis XIV brought back to France enthusiastic reports of the Imperial Mosque—a fact that has led scholars to detect the influence of Persian art on some of Louis' more splendid enterprises at Versailles.

FIGURE 23.22   Imperial Mosque, 1637, Isfahan, Iran. Photo: Jean Mazenod. Editions Citadelles & Mazenod, Paris.

Akbar and the Imperial Moguls of India

While India had been the object of Muslim conquest for almost a thousand years, it was not until the sixteenth century that the Moguls (the name derives from "Mongol") actually united all of India (Map 23.1). Distant cousins of the Persian princes, the Moguls ruled India as absolute monarchs from 1526 to 1707. They imported Persian culture and language into India in much the same way that Louis XIV brought Italian culture into France, and they encouraged the development of an aristocratic style, which—like that of the Sun King—served as an adjunct to majesty.

The Mogul ruler Akbar (d. 1605) came to the throne at the age of thirteen and laid the foundations for a luxurious court style that his son and grandson would perpetuate. A ruthless warrior and a devout Muslim, Akbar ruled over a court consisting of thousands of courtiers, servants, wives, and concubines. He centralized his control over the feudal nobility and court officials who, unlike their French counterparts, received paid salaries. Amidst the primarily Hindu population, Akbar pursued a policy of religious toleration and rid India of such outmoded traditions as the immolation of wives on their husband's funeral pyres. Despite Akbar's reforms, however, the lower classes and especially the peasants were taxed heavily (as were the French peasants under Louis) to finance the luxuries of the upper-class elite.

In the seventeenth century, the Moguls governed the wealthiest state in the world, a state whose revenues were ten times greater than those of France. Akbar commissioned magnificent works of music, poetry, painting, and architecture—the tangible expression of princely affluence and taste. As was the case in Louis' court, most of these exquisite objects were designed for domestic, not liturgical, use. A state studio of over one hundred artists working under Persian masters created a library of over twenty-four-thousand illuminated manuscripts, the contents of which ranged from love poetry to Hindu epics and religious tales. Mogul paintings reveal the brilliant union of delicate line, vivid color, and strong surface patterns—features that also appear in Asian carpets (figure 23.21). In a miniature illustrating the "heav-

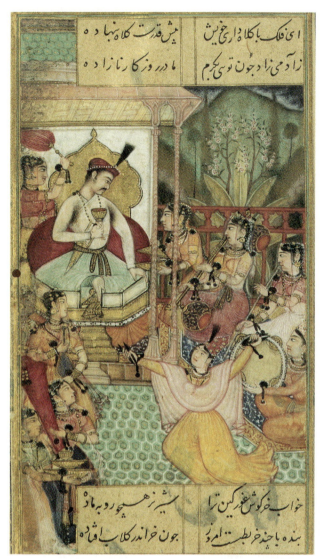

FIGURE 23.23 *Heavenly Joys Come to Earth for Akbar*, painted miniature in Mogul manuscript of 1588. Opaque watercolor on paper, 5 1/2 × 3 in. The Harvard University Art Museums, Gift of John Goelet.

enly joys" of Akbar, the ruler, holding a gold goblet, sits on a cushioned throne beneath an elegant canopy, while female dancers and musicians entertain him with flutes, sitars, castenets, and cymbals (figure 23.23). Bright colors and the absence of Western perspective give the scene a strong decorative quality.

FIGURE 23.24 *Jahangir Preferring a Sufi Shaikh to Kings,* from the Leningrad Album by Bichitr, Indian painting school of Jahangir, seventeenth century. Color and gold, 10 × 7 1/8 in. Courtesy of the Freer Gallery of Art, Smithsonian Institution, Washington, D.C., 42.15A.

The Patronage of Jahangir and Shah Jahan

Under Akbar's son, Jahangir (d. 1627), aristocratic court portraiture came into fashion in India. The new genre reflects the influence of European art and suggests, at once, a relaxation of the Muslim prohibition against the representation of the human figure. Relatively small in comparison with the aristocratic portraits executed by Rigaud or van Dyck (figures 23.1 and 23.18), the painted likeness of Jahangir (the name means "world seizer") reflects nevertheless, the will to glorify the ruler (figure 23.24). The artist Bichitr (fl. 1625), whose self-portrait appears in the lower left corner, shows the Shah enthroned atop an elaborate hourglass. Jahangir welcomes a *mullah* (a Muslim scholar) in the company of such Western dignitaries as King James I of England, also shown at the lower left. Four western-style angels frame the scene: the upper two seem to lament that Jahangir has chosen

heavenly over worldly power, while the bottom two inscribe the base of the hourglass with a prayer: "O Shah, may the span of your life be a thousand years." Just as Louis XIV assumed the guise of the Sun King, so Jahangir—as notorious for his overconsumption of wine and opium as Louis was for fine food and sex—is apotheosized by a huge halo consisting of the sun and the moon.

Well before the seventeenth century, Mogul rulers had initiated the tradition of building huge ceremonial complexes from which they might administer the state. Such complexes symbolized Muslim wealth and authority in India. Comparable with Versailles, Akbar's palace complex near Agra consisted of an elaborate residence surrounded by courtyards and mosques, as well as by formal gardens embellished with artificial pools and fountains. The garden, a this-worldly counterpart of the Garden of Paradise described in the Koran (chapter 10) and a welcome refuge from India's intense heat, was a chracteristic feature of the Mogul palace complex. Inspired by the elaborate ceremonial centers built by his father and his grandfather, Shah Jahan (d. 1658) commissioned the most sumptuous of all Mogul palaces, the Shahjahanabad (present-day Old Delhi). The red sandstone walls of the Shahjahanabad (nicknamed the "Red Fort") enclosed a palatial residence of white marble, flanked by magnificent gardens, public and private audience halls, courtyards, pavilions, baths, and the largest mosque in India (figure 23.25). The 3:4 rectangle of the complex was bisected by an axis that led through successive courts to the public audience hall, a pattern that anticipated the rigid symmetry of Versailles (figure 23.3).

The hot Indian climate inclined Mogul architects to open up interior space by means of foliated arcades (compare figure 10.7) and latticed screens through which breezes might blow uninterrupted. These graceful architectural features are apparent in the Shah's palace at the Red Fort (figure 23.26). The most ornate of all of Mogul interiors, Shah Jahan's audience hall consists of white marble arcades and ceilings decorated with geometric and floral patterns of precious and semiprecious stones inlaid in a technique called *pietra dura* ("hard stone"), which the Moguls borrowed from Italy (figure 23.27). At the center of the hall, the Shah once sat on the prized (but no longer existing) Peacock Throne, fashioned in solid gold and studded with emeralds, rubies, diamonds, and pearls. Above the throne was a canopy on which stood two gold peacocks, and above the canopy, around the ceiling of the hall, were inscribed the words, "If there is a paradise on the face of the earth, It is this, oh! it is this, oh! it is this."

FIGURE 23.25 Drawing of the Red Fort, Delhi. Shah Jahan, after 1638. Painting by a Delhi artist, ca. 1820. Courtesy of the British Library.

FIGURE 23.26 Diwan-i-Khas, the Private Audience Hall of the Red Fort, Delhi. Shah Jahan, after 1638. Nineteenth century watercolor of the interior. From M. Wheeler *Splendors of the East: Temples, Tombs, Palaces and Fortresses of Asia* G. P. Putnam's Sons, © 1965.

FIGURE 23.27 *Pietra dura* inlay in the Mussamman Burj. Red Fort, Agra Mogul, Shah Jahan period, ca. 1637. © The Bettmann Archive.

FIGURE 23.28   Agra, Taj Mahal. Mogul, Shah Jahan period, completed in 1653. © Jim W. Grace/Photo Researchers, Inc.

Surpassing the palace at Delhi (which was badly damaged by the British army during the nineteenth century) is Shah Jahan's most magnificent gift to the world: the Taj Mahal (figure 23.28). Shah Jahan built this mausoleum to honor the memory of his favorite wife, Mumtaz Mahal. When Mumtaz died giving birth to their fourteenth child, her husband, legend has it, was inconsolable. He directed his architects to construct alongside the Jumma River a glorious tomb, a twin to one he planned for himself on the adjoining riverbank. Fabricated of cream-colored marble, the Taj rises majestically above a tree-lined pool that mirrors its elegant silhouette. Although the individual elements of the building—minarets, bulbous domes, and octagonal base—recall Byzantine and Persian prototypes (figures 9.10 and 23.22), the total effect is unique: shadowy voids and bright solids play against one another on the surface of the exterior, while similar patterns of light and dark are repeated in the latticed marble screens and exquisitely carved walls of the interior. Gardens partitioned into geometric shapes and broad walkways flank the oblong reflecting pool and its fountains—the whole, an image of the Muslim garden of paradise. The Taj Mahal is the product of some twenty thousand West Asian builders and craftsmen working under the direction of a Persian architect. It is a brilliant fusion of the best aspects of Byzantine, Muslim, and Hindu traditions and, hence, an emblem of Islamic cohesion. But, it is also an extravagant expression of conjugal devotion and, to generations of Western visitors, an eloquent symbol of romantic love.

FIGURE 23.29 Peking, Forbidden City, throne room of the T'ai-ho tien. Ch'ing dynasty. Ostasiatiska Museet, Stockholm. Photo: O'Siren.

Imperial China under the Ming and Manchu Rulers

From the earliest days of Chinese history, Chinese emperors—the "Sons of Heaven"—ruled on earth by divine authority, or, as the Chinese called it, "the Mandate of Heaven" (chapter 3). In theory, all of China's emperors were absolute rulers. Nevertheless, over the centuries, their power frequently had been contested by feudal lords, military generals, and government officials. In 1368, native Chinese rebels drove out the last of the Mongol rulers (chapter 14) and established the Ming dynasty, which ruled China until 1644. The Ming dynasty governed the largest and most sophisticated empire on earth, an empire of some 120 million people. In the highly centralized Chinese state, Ming emperors oversaw a bureaucracy that in-

cluded offices of finance, laws, military affairs, and public works. They rebuilt the Great Wall (figure 7.26) and revived such old Chinese traditions as the examination system, which had been suspended by the Mongols. By the seventeenth century, however, the Ming had become autocrats who, like the foreigners they had displaced, took all power into their own hands. They transformed the civil service into a non-hereditary bureaucracy that did not dare to threaten the emperor's authority. The rigid court protocol that developed around the imperial rulers of the late Ming dynasty symbolized this shift toward autocracy. Officials, for instance, knelt in the presence of the emperor, who, as the Son of Heaven, sat on an elevated throne in the center of the imperial precinct (figure 23.29).

Beset by court corruption and popular revolts, the Ming fell prey to the invading hordes of Tartars (descendants of Mongols, Turks, and other tribes) known as the Manchu. But under the Manchu, who established the Ch'ing dynasty (1644–1911), the conditions of imperial autocracy intensified. As a symbol of submission, every Chinese male was required to adopt the Manchu hairstyle, by which one shaved the front of his head and wore a pigtail at the back. Ch'ing rulers retained the administrative traditions of their predecessors, but government posts often were sold rather than earned by merit. When the Ch'ing dynasty reached its zenith—during the very years that Louis XIV ruled France—it governed the largest, most populous, and one of the most unified states in the world (Map 23.1). Despite internal peace, however, uprisings were common. They reflected the discontent of peasant masses beset by high taxes and rents and periodic famines. Like the lower classes of France and India, Chinese villagers and urban workers supported the luxuries of royal princes, government officials, and large landholders, who (as in France and India) were themselves exempt from taxation. The early Manchu rulers imitated their predecessors as royal sponsors of art and architecture. Like Louis XIV or Shah Jahan, the Chinese emperor and his huge retinue resided in a ceremonial city. This metropolis, the symbol of entrenched absolutism and the majesty of the ruler, was known as the Forbidden City—so-called because of its inaccessibility to ordinary Chinese citizens.

FIGURE 23.30 Grand audience hall of the imperial palace, Forbidden City, Peking, anonymous drawing, eighteenth century. National Palace Museum, Peking.

The Forbidden City

Comparable in size and conception to Versailles in the West and to the Mogul palaces of India, the Forbidden City—a walled complex of palaces, tombs, and gardens located in Peking—was the most elaborate imperial monument of the Ming and Ch'ing eras. Construction on the Imperial Palace began under sixteenth-century Ming emperors and was continued by the Manchus. For almost five hundred years, this vast ceremonial complex—which, like Versailles, is now a park and museum—was the adminstrative center of China and the home of Chinese emperors, their families, and the members of their courts.

Inside the walls of the Forbidden City are grand avenues, broad courtyards, government offices, mansions of princes and dignitaries, artificial lakes, lush gardens, spacious temples, theaters, a library and a printing house (figure 23.30). Entering from the south, one passes under the majestic, five-towered entranceway through a succession of courtyards and gates reminiscent of the intriguing boxes within boxes at which Chinese artisans excel. At the heart of the rectangular complex, one proceeds up the three-tiered stone terrace (figure 23.31), into the Hall of Supreme Harmony (approximately 200 by 100 feet), where the Sons of Heaven once sat enthroned (figure 23.29), and beyond, to the imperial living quarters at the rear of the complex. Fragrant gardens, watered by fountains and artificial pools, once graced the private quarters of the royal officials here. During the seventeenth century, courtyard gardening itself developed into a fine art. Often flanked by a covered walkway from which it could be viewed, the garden was an arrangement of seemingly random (but actually carefully placed) rocks, plants, and trees—a miniature version of the natural world. Like the Chinese landscape scroll, the Chinese garden was designed to be enjoyed progressively, as an object of gentle contemplation. Such gardens, with their winding, narrow paths, delicate ferns, and quivering bamboos, have become a hallmark of Far Eastern culture.

The Forbidden City was the nucleus of imperial power and the symbol of Chinese absolutism. Laid out with a gridiron regularity that rivaled Mogul and French palatial complexes, the arrangement of buildings, courtyards, gates, and terraces was nevertheless uniquely Chinese. This ceremonial arrangement reflects an adherence to ancient Confucian principles of correctness and to the Chinese taste for self-enclosure. Buildings are lined up along the traditional north/south axis (chapter 14), and their relative sizes and functions determined by the rigors of Chinese court procedure, a strict protocol based on rank, age, and sex. During the Ming Era, for instance, imperial legislation prescribed nine rooms for the emperor, seven for a prince, five for a court official, and three for an ordinary citizen. Most of the buildings of the Forbidden City are no more than a single story high, their walls serving only as screens that divide interior space. What the Chinese sacrificed in monumentality, however, they recovered in elegance,

FIGURE 23.31 Peking, Forbidden city, T'ai-ho tien. Ming dynasty. Len Sirman Press, Geneva.

and in the creation of an architecture that harmonized with (rather than dominated over) nature. The richly ornamented buildings of the Forbidden City—the work of thousands of artisans—recall those of Mogul and French palace complexes. Chinese architects, however, deliberately preserved such traditional features as the rectangular hall with fully exposed wooden rafters and the pitched roof with projecting eaves and gleaming yellow tiles—the latter symbolic of the mantle of heaven. In the Forbidden City, as in all of Chinese culture prior to the twentieth century, tradition prevailed over innovation. And, in seventeenth-century China, as in neoclassical France, tradition and ritual enhanced the majesty of the ruler.

Ming and Manchu Patronage of the Arts

The Ming and Manchu emperors were great patrons of the arts. They encouraged the traditional schools of landscape painting and oversaw the production of such luxury items as inlaid bronzes, carved ivories and jades, lacquer ware, embroidered silk, and painted ceramics. Chinese porcelains of the seventeenth century were world famous, so much so that in the West the word "Ming" became synonymous with porcelain, and the word "china" came into use in the English language to describe fine ceramics and tableware.

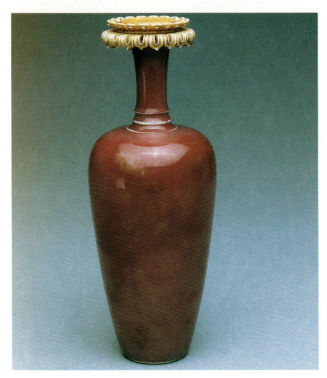

FIGURE 23.32 Flower vase. Chinese Pottery. Ch'ing dynasty. "Peach-bloom" glaze, 7 3/4 in. high. Courtesy of the Freer Gallery of Art, Smithsonian Institution, Washington, D.C. (42.20).

Ming artists used bright colors more freely than in earlier times. Vessels with solid color glazes of ox-blood red and peach-blossom pink (figure 23.32) alternated with colorful landscapes filled with songbirds, flowering trees, human figures, and mythical animals. One Ch'ing bowl ornamented with a rich five-color palette shows a group of elegantly attired men, women, and servants in a luxurious interior (figure 23.33). As this delightful scene suggests, neither in the porcelains nor in the paintings of this period did the Chinese develop any interest in the kinds of heroic and moralizing themes that dominated baroque art in the West. This difference notwithstanding, imperial tastes dictated the style of aristocratic art in China every bit as much as the royal academies of France influenced seventeenth-century French style. By 1680, there were over thirty official palace workshops serving the imperial court. Out of these workshops poured increasingly flamboyant works of art: exotic jewelry, painted enamels, *cloisonné* vessels (figure 23.34), intricate jade carvings, and lavishly embroidered silk and gold tapestries (figure 23.35). Many of these objects found their way into Europe, where they inspired *chinoiserie,* a style reflecting the influence of Chinese art. East-West influence, however, was mutual: Delegations of Jesuits, who arrived in China in 1601, introduced the rules of linear perspective to Chinese art, even as they transmitted to Europe (often by means of prints and engravings) a knowledge of

FIGURE 23.33 *Famille verte,* foliated porcelain bowl, Ch'ing dynasty, early eighteenth century. Diameter 6 1/2 in. Ashmolean Museum, Oxford, Dept. of Eastern Art.

Chinese techniques and materials. And French prints in turn prompted early Manchu rulers to build a Chinese version of Versailles, complete with fountains, at the imperial summer palace northwest of Peking.

Chinese Literature and the Theater Arts

Ming and Manchu rulers worked hard to preserve the rich literary heritage of China. Under Ming patronage, a group of 2,000 scholars began the enormous task of collecting and copying the most famous of China's literary and historical works. The Manchu contemporary of Louis XIV, Emperor K'ang-hsi (d. 1722), hired 15,000 calligraphers and 360 editors to compile a vast assortment of dictionaries, encyclopedias, and anthologies of the Chinese classics. Increasing numbers of literate middle-class men and women in China's growing cities demanded printed

FIGURE 23.34 Incense burner, Ming dynasty, sixteenth century. Cloisonné enamel. Freer Gallery of Art, Smithsonian Institution, Washington, D.C.

FIGURE 23.35 Silk and gold tapestry, Ming dynasty. Ke si, Length, 78 in. Cleveland Museum of Art. Gift of Mr. & Mrs. J. H. Wade. CMA 16.1334.

books for everyday use. These included almanacs, guides to letter writing, short stories, collections of proverbs and maxims, chronicles, ballads, and romances. Novels, a literary genre that had emerged as early as the twelfth century in China, remained extremely popular during the Ming and Ch'ing eras. The typical novel recounted Chinese historical events and often made fun of religious and secular authorities. In the mid-eighteenth century, Ts'ao Hsüeh-ch'in produced China's greatest novel, *The Dream of the Red Chamber* (also known as *The Story of the Stone*), a four-thousand page work that offers a detailed picture of upper-class Ch'ing society. Plots drawn from popular novels often provided the themes for dramatic performances, and drama itself was the most widely appreciated kind of public entertainment.

Chinese theatrical performances almost always included vocal and intrumental music. Performers were exclusively male, and, since troupes of players moved from city to city, elaborate costumes and stage scenery were rare. In place of costumes and scenery, a system of conventions arose in the performance of Chinese plays to indicate setting or circumstance: a chair might represent a mountain, a whip might signify that the actor was on horseback, and a black cloth might be used to indicate that a character was invisible. Colors symbolized stock characters and types: red represented loyalty and dignity, white symbolized villainy or treachery, and so on. During the Ming Era, when sumptuous costumes and masklike makeup became popular, such earlier stage symbols and conventions were still preserved. Indeed, to this day, Chinese drama retains traditional, highly stylized features that set it apart from early modern Western theater.

During the seventeenth century, at the same time that Europeans were producing some of their first operas, the Chinese were staging elaborate regional performances that combined drama, dance, song, and instrumental music. By the late eighteenth century, the first permanent Chinese opera company appeared in the capital city of Peking. Chinese opera[21] was, however, distinctly different from Western opera. Like Chinese music in general, Chinese opera was rich in melodic and rhythmic nuances, but lacked the dramatic contrasts in texture and timbre that characterized Western music since the Renaissance. Other differences are notable: though elaborately staged, Chinese opera was less aristocratic than European opera. While European operas usually employed themes from Greco-Roman mythology and biblical history—themes often employed to glorify a royal patron—Chinese operas mainly drew on a conven-

---

[21]See Music Listening Selection I–12, an excerpt from a Chinese opera described in chapter 14.

tional repertory of love stories, social events, and the adventures of popular heroes. Such operas often featured stock characters resembling those of Molière's plays, and, like Molière's plays, they had wide and lasting appeal.

Summary

The aristocratic style in the arts of the seventeenth century reflects the influence of absolutism in the political history of the West, as well as in Asia and the Far East. In the West, the most notable figure of the Age of Absolutism was Louis XIV. Under Louis' leadership, the arts worked to serve the majesty of the ruler. At Versailles, the classical baroque style—an amalgam of Greco-Roman subject matter, classical principles of design (often derived from Renaissance models), and baroque theatricality—became the vehicle of French royal authority. Luxury, grandeur, and technical refinement became the hallmarks of elitism.

Louis XIV was instrumental in founding most of the royal academies of France, whose members established neoclassical guidelines for painting, sculpture, music, literature, and dance. Poussin's canvases, Giraudon's sculptures, La Rochfoucauld's maxims, Lully's operas, Racine's tragedies, and Molière's comedies all assert the neoclassical view that the mind must prevail over the passions. Under Louis' leadership, the ballet emerged as an independent art form and one that epitomized neoclassical order and grace. Outside of France, Velásquez and van Dyck painted elegant portraits that flattered aristocratic patrons, while Rubens produced dramatic allegories of royal authority.

In the Near East, the Ottoman emperor, Suleiman the Magnificent, established a pattern of princely patronage that was imitated by Muslim rulers for at least two centuries. The Persian Shah Abbas and the Mogul rulers of India, Akbar, Jahangir, and Shah Jahan, were great patrons of the arts and commissioned some of the most magnificent monuments in architectural history. Like Versailles in France, the Imperial Mosque at Isfahan, the Red Fort at Old Delhi, and the Taj Mahal—though serving different functions—epitomize the wealth, authority, and artistic vision of a privileged minority. So too, the imperial complex at the Forbidden City in Peking stands as a symbol of the absolute authority of China's rulers.

Though the aristocratic style has a rich history whose origins may be traced back to the pharoahs of Egypt, that style held a particularly important place in the seventeenth century, when it served to legitimatize and glorify the power of the ruling elite throughout Europe and Asia. Flamboyant and lavish, the aristocratic style touched all forms of intellectual and artistic expression, including drama, opera, architecture, and dance. And although the artists of Asia tapped a heritage that was essentially different from that of Europeans, the East produced works of art that in every way rivaled those of the West.

GLOSSARY

chinoiserie   a style (also the objects made in that style) that reflects the influence of Chinese art and Chinese decorative motifs

choreography   the art of symbolically representing dance movements

comédie-ballet   (French), a dramatic performance that features interludes of song and dance

marquetry   a decorative technique in which patterns are created on a wooden surface by means of inlaid wood, shell, or ivory

maxim   a short, concise, and often witty saying

objets d'art   (French), art objects

pietra dura   (Italian, "hard stone") an ornamental technique involving inlaid precious and semiprecious stones

salon   (French, "drawing room") an elegant apartment or drawing room

SUGGESTIONS FOR READING

Davies, Philip. *The Splendors of the Raj.* New York: Viking Penguin, 1985.

Desai, Vishakha N. *Life at Court: Art for India's Rulers 16th–19th Centuries.* Boston: Boston Museum of Fine Arts, 1985.

Gascoigne, Bamber. *The Great Moghuls.* New York: Harper and Row, 1971.

Hatton, Ragnhild M., ed. *Louis XIV and Absolutism.* Columbus: Ohio University Press, 1976.

Howarth, W. D. *Molière: A Playwright and his Audience.* Cambridge: Cambridge University Press, 1982.

Mitford, Nancy. *The Sun King: Louis XIV at Versailles.* New York: Harper and Row, 1966.

Volwahsen, Andreas. *Living Architecture: Islamic Indian.* New York: Grosset and Dunlap, 1970.

Walker, Hallam, *Molière.* Boston: Twayne, 1990.

Wright, Christopher. *The French Painters of the Seventeenth Century.* New York: New York Graphic Society, 1986.

Yu Zhuoyun, ed. *Palaces of the Forbidden City.* Translated by Ng Mau-Sang and others. New York: Viking Press, 1984.

3287 Versailles - Buste de Voltaire
(Houdon)

II
THE EUROPEAN ENLIGHTENMENT

The Age of the Enlightenment, as the eighteenth century is often called, was a time of buoyant optimism. Educated Europeans envisioned themselves as the most civilized people in history: having survived a millennium of darkness, they now ushered in a new era of light—the light of reason. Reason, they optimistically predicted, would dispel the mists of human ignorance, superstition, and prejudice. Eighteenth-century intellectuals were the heirs to Newtonian science. They viewed the universe as a great machine that operated according to "natural" laws. Just as Newton had systematized the laws of the physical universe, so these rationalists tried to regulate the laws of human behavior. Such practical powers, they argued, were not only attainable, but they were essential to the progress and betterment of human kind. The ideals of rationalism, humanitarianism, and social progress fueled the Enightenment—the major cultural and intellectual movement of the eighteenth century. And although this movement did not directly touch the lives of millions of peasants and villagers, it profoundly influenced the course of modern history.

During the eighteenth century, learning freed itself from the Church, and literacy became widespread. Among middle-class Europeans, ninety to one hundred percent of the males and almost seventy-five percent of the females could read and write. This new, more literate middle class competed with a waning aristocracy for social and political prestige. The public interest in literature and the arts spurred the rise of the newspaper, the novel, and the symphony. Satire became a popular vehicle for dramatizing the contradictions between the polite society of the upper classes and the poverty and illiteracy of the lower classes. In educated circles, debate raged over the powers of rulers versus those of the ruled. And in France and North America, visionary treatises defended the unalienable rights of citizens and fanned the flames of revolt.

The chapters that follow examine the Enlightenment as the central theme of the eighteenth century and as a shaping force in the evolution of the humanistic tradition. Chapter 24, "The Promise of Reason," deals with the Enlightenment concepts of natural law and the social contract as manifested

Continued

in the writings of Thomas Hobbes, John Locke, Thomas Jefferson, and Adam Smith. The crusade for human progress is illustrated in the birth of the encyclopedia and the writings of Condorcet, while the middle-class interest in the particulars of everyday life is seen in the rise of the novel. In chapter 25, entitled "The Limits of Reason," we hear the voices of intellectuals whose faith in reason was tempered by cynicism, pessismism, and skepticism. Voltaire's brilliant satire, *Candide,* the controversial treatises of Rousseau, and the caustic prints of William Hogarth are featured in this chapter. Chapter 26, "Eighteenth-Century Art, Music, and Society," examines the rococo and neoclassical styles in art and architecture and the rise of classical music. The paintings of Fragonard and David and the music of Haydn and Mozart are discussed here, along with other glorious artworks that mirror the tastes and values of eighteenth-century society.

24

THE PROMISE OF REASON

In the year 1680, a comet blazed across the skies over Western Europe. The English astronomer Edmund Halley (d. 1742) observed the celestial body, calculated its orbit, and predicted its future appearances. Stripped of its former role as a portent of catastrophe or a harbinger of natural calamity, Halley's comet now became merely another natural phenomenon, the behavior of which invited scientific investigation. This new, objective attitude toward nature and the accompanying confidence in the liberating role of reason were hallmarks of the Enlightenment, as the period between 1687 (the date of Newton's *Principia*) and 1789 (the beginning of the French Revolution) is often called. Indeed, the eighteenth century marks the divide between the essentially medieval view of the world as controlled by an omnipotent God and governed by the principles of faith, and the modern, secular view of the world as controlled by humankind and governed by the principles of reason. It also marks the beginning and an optimistic faith in the human ability to create a kind of happiness on earth that in former ages had been thought to exist only in heaven.

One of the principal occupations of Enlightenment thinkers was the effort to understand human nature in scientific terms—that is, without reference to divine authority. "Theology," wrote one Enlightenment skeptic, "is only ignorance of natural causes." Just as Halley explained the operations of the celestial bodies as a logical part of nature's mechanics, so eighteenth-century intellectuals explained human nature in terms of *natural law*. The unwritten and divinely sanctioned law of nature, or natural law, included certain "natural rights": the right to life, liberty, property, and just treatment by the ruling order. Moreover, Enlightenment thinkers argued that a true understanding of the human condition was the first step toward progress, that is, towards the gradual betterment of human life. It is no wonder, then, that the eighteenth century saw the formation of the social sciences: anthropology, sociology, economics, and political science. As the social scientists hoped to prove, the promise of reason lay in the achievement of an enlightened social order.

FIGURE 24.1 *Portrait of John Locke,* John Greenhill, ca. 1672. National Portrait Gallery, London.

The Political Theories of Hobbes and Locke

An enlightened social order required a redefinition of the role of government and the rights of citizens. Not since the Golden Age of Athens had the relationship between the ruler and the ruled received so much intellectual attention as in the early modern era, the age of the rising European nation-state. During the sixteenth century, the political theorist Machiavelli (d. 1527) had argued that the survival of the state was more important than the well-being of its citizens. Later in that century, the French Lawyer Jean Bodin (d. 1576) had used biblical precepts and long-standing tradition to defend theories of divine right monarchy. In the seventeenth century, the Dutch statesman Hugo Grotius (d. 1645) proposed a more all-embracing system of international law based on reason, which he identified with nature. Grotius' idea of a political contract based in natural law profoundly influenced the thinking of two English philosophers, Thomas Hobbes (d. 1679) and John Locke (figure 24.1), the latter of whom we met in chapter 22 as a champion of the empirical method.

Hobbes and Locke took up the urgent question of human rights versus the sovereignty of the ruler. Fully aware of the conflict between royalist and anti-royalist factions that had fueled the English Civil War (see chapter 21), both thinkers rejected the principle of divine right monarchy. Instead, in treatises published some forty years apart, they advanced the idea that government must be based in a **social contract**. For Hobbes, the social contract was a covenant among individuals who willingly surrendered a portion of their freedom to a governing authority. Locke agreed with Hobbes that government must be formed by a contract that laid the basis for social order and individual happiness. But while Hobbes held that ultimate authority should rest in the hands of the ruler, Locke believed that power must remain with the ruled.

The divergent positions of Hobbes and Locke proceeded from their contrasting perceptions of human nature. Whereas Locke perceived human beings as naturally equal, free, and capable (through reason) of defining the common good, Hobbes viewed human beings as selfish, greedy, and warlike. Without the state, he argued, human life was "solitary, poor, nasty, brutish, and short." Bound by an irrevocable and irreversible social contract, government under one individual or a ruling assembly was, according to Hobbes, society's only hope for peace and security. The collective safety of society lay in its willingness to submit to a higher authority, which Hobbes dubbed the "Leviathan," after the mythological marine monster described in the Bible. Hobbes aired these views in the treatise called the *Leviathan,* which he published in 1651—only two years after England's anti-royalist forces had beheaded the English monarch Charles I.

READING 84 From Hobbes' *Leviathan*

Part I. Chapter 13: Of the Natural Condition of Mankind as Concerning their Felicity and Misery.

Nature has made men so equal in the faculties of the   1
body and mind as that, though there be found one man
sometimes manifestly stronger in body or of quicker
mind than another, yet, when all is reckoned together,
the difference between man and man is not so
considerable as that one man can thereupon claim to
himself any benefit to which another may not pretend as
well as he. For as to the strength of body, the weakest
has strength to kill the strongest, either by secret
machination or by confederacy with others that are in   10
the same danger with himself. . . .

From this equality of ability arises equality of hope in
the attaining of our ends. And therefore if any two men
desire the same thing, which nevertheless they cannot
both enjoy, they become enemies; and in the way to
their end, which is principally their own conservation,

and sometimes their delectation only, endeavor to destroy or subdue one another. And from hence it comes to pass that where an invader has no more to fear than another man's single power, if one plant, sow, build, or possess a convenient seat, others may probably be expected to come prepared with forces united to dispossess and deprive him, not only of the fruit of his labor, but also of his life or liberty. And the invader again is in the like danger of another. . . .

So that in the nature of man we find three principal causes of quarrel: first, competition; secondly, diffidence;[1] thirdly, glory.

The first makes men invade for gain, the second for safety, and the third for reputation. The first use violence to make themselves masters of other men's persons, wives, children, and cattle; the second, to defend them; the third, for trifles, as a word, a smile, a different opinion, and any other sign of undervalue, either direct in their persons or by reflection in their kindred, their friends, their nation, their profession, or their name.

Hereby it is manifest that, during the time men live without a common power to keep them all in awe, they are in that condition which is called war, and such a war as is of every man against every man. For WAR consists not in battle only, or the act of fighting, but in a tract of time wherein the will to contend by battle is sufficiently known; and therefore the notion of *time* is to be considered in the nature of war as it is in the nature of weather. For as the nature of foul weather lies not in a shower or two of rain but in an inclination thereto of many days together, so the nature of war consists not in actual fighting but in the known disposition thereto, during all the time there is no assurance to the contrary. All other time is PEACE.

Whatsoever, therefore, is consequent to a time of war where every man is enemy to every man, the same is consequent to the time wherein men live without other security than what their own strength and their own invention shall furnish them withal. In such condition there is no place for industry, because the fruit thereof is uncertain; and consequently no culture of the earth; no navigation nor use of the commodities that may be imported by sea; no commodious building; no instruments of moving and removing such things as require much force; no knowledge of the face of the earth; no account of time; no arts; no letters; no society; and, which is worst of all, continual fear and danger of violent death; and the life of man solitary, poor, nasty, brutish, and short. . . .

Part II. Chapter 17: Of the Causes, Generation, and Definition of a Commonwealth

The final cause, end, or design of men, who naturally love liberty and dominion over others, in the introduction of that restraint upon themselves in which we see them live in commonwealths, is the foresight of their own preservation, and of a more contented life thereby—that is to say, of getting themselves out from that miserable condition of war which is necessarily consequent . . . to the natural passions of man when there is no visible power to keep them in awe and tie them by fear of punishment to the performance of their covenants and observations of [the] laws of nature. . . .

For the laws of nature—as *justice, equity, modesty, mercy,* and, in sum, *doing to others as we would be done to*—of themselves, without the terror of some power to cause them to be observed, are contrary to our natural passions, that carry us to partiality, pride, revenge, and the like. And covenants without the sword are but words, and of no strength to secure a man at all. Therefore, notwithstanding the laws of nature. . . , if there be no power erected, or not great enough for our security, every man will—and may lawfully—rely on his own strength and art for caution against all other men. . . .

The only way to erect such a common power as may be able to defend them from the invasion of foreigners and the injuries of one another, and thereby to secure them in such sort as that by their own industry and by the fruits of the earth they may nourish themselves and live contentedly, is to confer all their power and strength upon one man, or upon one assembly of men that may reduce all their wills, by plurality of voices, unto one will; which is as much as to say, to appoint one man or assembly of men to bear their person, and everyone to own and acknowledge to himself to be author of whatsoever he that so bears their person shall act or cause to be acted in those things which concern the common peace and safety, and therein to submit their wills every one to his will, and their judgments to his judgment. This is more than consent or concord; it is a real unity of them all in one and the same person, made by covenant of every man with every man, in which manner as if every man should say to every man, *I authorize and give up my right of governing myself to this man, or to this assembly of men, on this condition, that you give up your right to him and authorize all his actions in like manner.* This done, the multitude so united in one person is called a COMMONWEALTH, in Latin CIVITAS. This is the generation of that great LEVIATHAN (or rather, to speak more reverently, of that *mortal god*) to which we owe, under the *immortal God,* our peace and defense. For by this authority, given him by every particular man in the commonwealth, he has the use of so much power and strengh conferred on him that, by terror thereof, he is enabled to form the wills of them all to peace at home and mutual aid against their enemies abroad. And in him consists the essence of the commonwealth, which, to define it, is *one person, of whose acts a great multitude, by mutual covenants one with another, have made themselves every one the author, to the end he may use the strength and means of them all as he shall think expedient for their peace and common defense.* And he that carries this person is called SOVEREIGN and said to have *sovereign power:* and everyone besides, his SUBJECT.

[1]Mistrust.

The attaining to this sovereign power is by two ways. One, by natural force. . . . The other is when men agree among themselves to submit to some man or assembly of men voluntarily, on confidence to be protected by him against all others. This latter may be called a political commonwealth, or commonwealth by *institution,* and the former a commonwealth by *acquisition.* . . .

Part II. Chapter 30: Of the Office of the Sovereign Representative

The office of the sovereign, be it a monarch or an assembly, consists in the end for which he was trusted with the sovereign power, namely, the procuration of *the safety of the people;* to which he is obliged by the law of nature, and to render an account thereof to God, the author of that law, and to none but him. But by safety here is not meant a bare preservation but also all other contentments of life which every man by lawful industry, without danger or hurt to the commonwealth, shall acquire to himself.

And this is intended should be done, not by care applied to individuals further than their protection from injuries when they shall complain, but by a general providence contained in public instruction, both of doctrine and example, and in the making and executing of good laws, to which individual persons may apply their own cases.

And because, if the essential rights of sovereignty. . . . be taken away, the commonwealth is thereby dissolved and every man returns into the condition and calamity of a war with every other man, which is the greatest evil that can happen in this life, it is the office of the sovereign to maintain those rights entire, and consequently against his duty, first, to transfer to another or to lay from himself any of them. For he that deserts the means deserts the ends. . . .

◆

Locke's Government of the People

Locke disagreed with Hobbes' view of humankind as self-serving and aggressive. He held that since human beings were born without any preexisting qualities (chapter 21), their natural state was one of perfect freedom. Whether people became brutish or otherwise depended solely upon their experiences and their environment. People have, by their very nature as human beings, said Locke, the right to life, liberty, and estate (or "property"). Government must arbitrate between the exercise of one person's liberty and that of the next. The social contract thus preserves the natural rights of the governed. And, although individuals may willingly consent to give up some of their liberty in return for the ruler's protection, they never relinquish their ultimate authority. If a ruler is tyrannical or oppressive, the people have not only the right but the obligation to rebel and seek a new ruler. Locke's defense of political rebellion in the face of tyranny served as justification for the "Glorious Revolution" of 1688, as well as for the revolutions that took place in America and in France toward the end of the eighteenth century.

If for Hobbes the state was sovereign, for Locke sovereignty rested with the people, and government existed only to protect the natural rights of its citizens. In his *First Treatise on Government,* Locke argued that individuals might attain their maximum development only in a society free from the unnatural restrictions imposed by absolute rulers. In his second treatise, called *Of Civil Government* (an excerpt from which follows), Locke expounded on the idea that government must rest upon the consent of the governed. While Locke's views were basic to the development of modern liberal thought, Hobbes' views provided the justification for all forms of tyranny, including the enlightened despotism of such eighteenth-century rulers as Frederick of Prussia and Catherine II of Russia, who claimed that their authority was founded in the general consent of the people. Nevertheless, the notion of government as the product of a social contract between the ruler and the ruled has become one of the dominating ideas of modern Western—and more recently of Eastern European and Asian—political life.

READING 85 From Locke's *Of Civil Government*

Book II, Chapter II: Of the State of Nature.

To understand political power right and derive it from its original, we must consider what state all men are naturally in, and that is a state of perfect freedom to order their actions and dispose of their possessions and persons as they think fit, within the bounds of the law of nature without asking leave or depending upon the will of any other man.

A state also of equality, wherein all the power and jurisdiction is reciprocal, no one having more than another; there being nothing more evident than that creatures of the same species and rank, promiscuously born to all the same advantages of nature and the use of the same faculties, should also be equal one amongst another without subordination or subjection; unless the Lord and Master of them all should, by any manifest declaration of his will, set one above another and confer on him, by an evident and clear appointment, an undoubted right to dominion and sovereignty. . . .

Chapter V: Of Property

God, who hath given the world to men in common, hath also given them reason to make use of it to the best advantage of life and convenience. The earth and all that is therein is given to men for the support and comfort of their being. And though all the fruits it naturally produces and beasts it feeds belong to mankind in common . . . , there must of necessity be a means to appropriate them some way or other before they can be of any use, or at all beneficial to any particular man. . . .

Though the earth and all inferior creatures be common to all men, yet every man has a property in his own person: this nobody has any right to but himself. The labor of his body, and the work of his hands we may say, are properly his. Whatsoever then he removes out of the state that nature has provided and left it in, he has mixed his labor with and joined to it something that is his own, and thereby makes it his property. . . . 30

Chapter VIII: The Beginning of Political Societies

Men being, as has been said, by nature all free, equal, and independent, no one can be put out of this estate and subjected to the political power of another without his own consent. The only way whereby any one divests 40 himself of his natural liberty and puts on the bonds of civil society is by agreeing with other men to join and unite into a community for their comfortable, safe, and peaceable living one amongst another, in a secure enjoyment of their properties, and a greater security against any that are not of it. This any number of men may do, because it injures not the freedom of the rest; they are left as they were in the liberty of the state of nature. When any number of men have so consented to make one community or government, they are thereby 50 presently incorporated and make one body politic, wherein the majority have a right to act and conclude the rest.

For when any number of men have, by the consent of every individual, made a community, they have thereby made that community one body, with a power to act as one body, which is only by the will and determination of the majority: . . . And therefore we see that in assemblies empowered to act by positive laws, where no number is set by that positive law which 60 empowers them, the act of the majority passes for the act of the whole and of course determines; as having, by the law of nature and reason, the power of the whole.

And thus every man, by consenting with others to make one body politic under one government, puts himself under an obligation to every one of that society to submit to the determination of the majority and to be concluded by it; or else this original compact whereby he with others incorporate into one society, would signify nothing and be no compact if he be left free and 70 under no other ties than he was in before in the state of nature. . . .

Chapter IX: Of the Ends of Political Society and Government

If man in the state of nature be so free as has been said; if he be absolute lord of his own person and possessions, equal to the greatest, and subject to nobody, why will he part with his freedom, why will he give up this empire and subject himself to the dominion and control of any other power? To which it is obvious to answer that though in the state of nature he has such

a right, yet the enjoyment of it is very uncertain and 80 constantly exposed to the invasion of others; for all being kings as much as he, every man his equal and the greater part no strict observers of equity and justice, the enjoyment of the property he has in this state is very unsafe, very unsecure. This makes him willing to quit a condition, which, however free, is full of fears and continual dangers: and it is not without reason that he seeks out and is willing to join in society with others who are already united or have a mind to unite for the mutual preservation of their lives, liberties, and estates, 90 which I call by the general name property.

The great and chief end, therefore, of men's uniting into commonwealths, and putting themselves under government, is the preservation of their property. . . .

Chapter XVIII: Of Tyranny

As usurpation is the exercise of power, which another hath a right to, so tyranny is the exercise of power beyond right, which nobody can have a right to. And this is making use of the power any one has in his hands, not for the good of those who are under it, but for his own private, separate advantage—when the 100 governor, however entitled, makes not the law, but his will, the rule; and his commands and actions are not directed to the preservation of the properties of his people, but [to] the satisfaction of his own ambition, revenge, covetousness, or any other irregular passion. . . .

Wherever law ends, tyranny begins, if the law be transgressed to another's harm; and whosoever in authority exceeds the power given him by the law, and makes use of the force he has under his command, . . . 110 ceases in that to be a [magistrate]; and, acting without authority, may be opposed as any other man who by force invades the right of another. . . .

"May the commands then of a prince be opposed? may he be resisted as often as any one shall find himself aggrieved, and but imagine he has not right done him? This will unhinge and overturn all politics, and, instead of government and order, leave nothing but anarchy and confusion."

To this I answer that force is to be opposed to 120 nothing but to unjust and unlawful force; whoever makes any opposition in any other case, draws on himself a just condemnation both from God and man.

———————◆———————

The Influence of Locke on Montesquieu and Jefferson

Locke's political treatises were read widely. So too, his defense of religious toleration (issued even as Louis XIV forced all Calvinists to leave France), his plea for equality of education among men and women, and his arguments for the use of modern languages in place of Latin won the attention of many intellectuals. Published during the last decades of the seventeenth century, Locke's writings became the wellspring of the Enlightenment in both Europe and America.

In France, the keen-minded aristocrat Charles Louis de Secondat Montesquieu (d. 1755) championed Locke's views on political freedom and expanded on his theories. Intrigued by the ways in which nature seemed to govern social behavior, the Baron de Montesquieu investigated the effects of climate and custom on human conduct, thus pioneering the field of sociology. In his elegantly written, thousand-page treatise *The Spirit of the Laws,* (1748), Montesquieu defended liberty as the free exercise of the will and condemned slavery as fundamentally "unnatural and evil." A proponent of constitutional monarchy, he advanced the idea of a separation of powers among the executive, legislative, and judicial agencies of government, advising that each monitor the activities of the others in order to ensure a balanced system of government. He warned that when legislative and executive powers were united in the same person (or body of magistrates), or when judicial power was inseparable from legislative and executive powers, human liberty was gravely theatened. Montesquieu's system of checks and balances was later enshrined in the Constitution of the United States of America (1787).

Across the Atlantic, the most eloquent expression of Locke's ideas appeared in the preamble to the statement declaring the independence of the North American colonies from the rule of the British king George III. Written by the leading American apostle of the Enlightenment, Thomas Jefferson (d. 1823, figure 26.23), and adopted by the Continental Congress on July 4, 1776, the American Declaration of Independence echoes Locke's ideology of revolt as well as his view that governments derive their just powers from the consent of the governed. Following Locke and Montesquieu, Jefferson justified the establishment of a social contract between ruler and ruled as the principal means of fulfilling natural law—the "unalienable right" to life, liberty, and the pursuit of happiness.

READING 86 From Jefferson's *Declaration of Independence*

When in the course of human events, it becomes necessary for one people to dissolve the political bands which have connected them with another, and to assume among the powers of the earth, the separate and equal station to which the laws of nature and of nature's God entitle them, a decent respect to the opinions of mankind requires that they should declare the causes which impel them to separation.

We hold these truths to be self-evident: That all men are created equal; that they are endowed by their Creator with certain unalienable rights; that among these are life, liberty and the pursuit of happiness; that to secure these rights governments are instituted among men, deriving their just powers from the consent of the governed; that whenever any form of government becomes destructive of these ends, it is the right of the people to alter or to abolish it, and to institute new government, laying its foundation on such principles and organizing its powers in such form, as to them shall seem most likely to effect their safety and happiness.

◆

The Declaration of Independence made clear the belief of America's "founding fathers" in equality among *men.* Equality between the sexes was, however, another matter: although both Locke and Jefferson acknowledged that women held the same natural rights as men, they did not consider women—or slaves, or children, for that matter—capable of exercising such rights. Recognizing this bias, Abigail Adams (d. 1818) wrote to her husband, John, who was serving as a delegate to the Second Continental Congress (1777), as follows:

I . . . hear that you have declared an independency, and, by the way, in the new code of laws which I suppose it will be necessary for you to make, I desire you would remember the ladies and be more generous and favorable to them than were your ancestors. Do not put such unlimited power into the hands of husbands. Remember all men would be tyrants if they could. If particular care and attention are not paid to the ladies we are determined to foment a rebellion, and will not hold ourselves bound to obey any laws in which we have no voice or representation.[2]

Despite the future First Lady's spirited admonitions, however, American women did not secure the legal right to vote or to hold political office until well into the twentieth century.

---

[2]Letter of March 31, 1776, in *Familiar Letters of John Adams and His Wife Abigail Adams During the Revolution,* ed. Charles Francis Adams (New York: Hurd and Houghton, 1876. Reprint: Freeport, N.Y.: Books for Library Press, 1970), p. 148.

Adam Smith and the Birth of Economic Theory

While Enlightenment thinkers were primarily concerned with matters of political equality, they also addressed questions related to the economy of the modern European state. The Scottish philosopher Adam Smith (d. 1790) applied the idea of natural law to the domains of human labor, productivity, and the exchange of goods. In his epoch-making, nine-hundred page synthesis of ethics and economics, *An Inquiry into the Nature and Causes of the Wealth of Nations,* published in 1776, Smith set forth the "laws" of labor, production, and trade with an exhaustiveness reminiscent of Newton's *Principia Mathematica* (chapter 22). Smith contended that labor, a condition natural to humankind (as Locke had observed), was the foundation for prosperity. A nation's wealth is not its land or its money, said Smith, but its labor force. In the "natural" economic order, individual self-interest guides the progress of economic life, and certain natural forces, such as the "law of supply and demand," motivate a market economy. Since government interference would infringe on this order, reasoned Smith, such interference is undesirable. He thus opposed all artificial restraints on the economy associated with government regulation and control. The modern concepts of free enterprise and *laissez-faire* (literally, "leave alone") economics spring from Smith's incisive formulations. In the following excerpt, Smith examines the origin of the division of labor among human beings and defends the natural and unimpeded operation of trade and competition among nations.

READING 87 From Smith's *Inquiry into the Nature and Causes of the Wealth of Nations*

Book I, Chapter II: The Principle which Occasions the Division of Labor

[The] division of labor, from which so many advantages 1
are derived, is not originally the effect of any human
wisdom, which foresees and intends that general
opulence to which it gives occasion. It is the necessary,
though very slow and gradual, consequence of a certain
propensity in human nature which has in view no such
extensive utility; the propensity to truck, barter, and
exchange one thing for another.

. . . [This propensity] is common to all men, and to
be found in no other race of animals, which seem to 10
know neither this nor any other species of contracts.
Two greyhounds, in running down the same hare, have
sometimes the appearance of acting in some sort of
concert. Each turns her towards his companion, or
endeavors to intercept her when his companion turns

her towards himself. This, however, is not the effect of
any contract, but of the accidental concurrence of their
passions in the same object at that particular time.
Nobody ever saw a dog make a fair and deliberate
exchange of one bone for another with another 20
dog. . . . In almost every other race of animals each
individual, when it is grown up to maturity, is entirely
independent, and in its natural state has occasion for
the assistance of no other living creature. But man has
almost constant occasion for the help of his brethren,
and it is in vain for him to expect it from their
benevolence only. He will be more likely to prevail if he
can interest their self-love in his favor, and show them
that it is for their own advantage to do for him what he
requires of them. Whoever offers to another a bargain of 30
any kind, proposes to do this. Give me that which I
want, and you shall have this which you want, is the
meaning of every such offer; and it is in this manner that
we obtain from one another the far greater part of those
good offices which we stand in need of. It is not from
the benevolence of the butcher, the brewer, or the
baker, that we expect our dinner, but from their regard
to their own interest. We address ourselves, not to their
humanity, but to their self-love; and never talk to them of
our own necessities, but of their advantages. . . . 40

As it is by treaty, by barter, and by purchase, that
we obtain from one another the greater part of those
mutual good offices which we stand in need of, so it is
this same trucking disposition which originally gives
occasion to the division of labor. In a tribe of hunters or
shepherds a particular person makes bows and arrows,
for example, with more readiness and dexterity than any
other. He frequently exchanges them for cattle or for
venison with his companions; and he finds at last that
he can in this manner get more cattle and venison, than 50
if he himself went to the field to catch them. From a
regard to his own interest, therefore, the making of
bows and arrows grows to be his chief business. . . .

Book IV, Chapter III, Part II: Of the Unreasonableness of Restraints [on Trade]

Nations have been taught that their interest consisted in
beggaring all their neighbors. Each nation has been
made to look with an invidious eye upon the prosperity
of all the nations with which it trades, and to consider
their gain as its own loss. Commerce, which ought
naturally to be, among nations as among individuals, a
bond of union and friendship, has become the most 60
fertile source of discord and animosity. The capricious
ambition of kings and ministers has not, during the
present and the preceding century, been more fatal to
the repose of Europe, than the impertinent jealousy of
merchants and manufacturers. The violence and
injustice of the rulers of mankind is an ancient evil, for
which, I am afraid, the nature of human affairs can
scarce admit of a remedy. But the mean rapacity, the
monopolizing spirit of merchants and manufacturers,
who neither are, nor ought to be, the rulers of mankind, 70
though it cannot perhaps be corrected, may very easily
be prevented from disturbing the tranquility of anybody
but themselves.

FIGURE 24.2 *Assembly in a Salon,* François Dequevauviller after N. Lavréince, 1745–1807. Engraving 15 13/16 × 19 5/8 in. The Metropolitan Museum of Art, Harris Brisbane Dick Fund, 1935 (35.100.17).

That it was the spirit of monopoly which originally both invented and propagated this doctrine, cannot be doubted; and they who first taught it were by no means such fools as they who believed it. In every country it always is and must be the interest of the great body of the people to buy whatever they want of those who sell it cheapest. The proposition is so very manifest, that it seems ridiculous to take any pains to prove it; not could it ever have been called in question had not the interested sophistry of merchants and manufacturers confounded the common sense of mankind. Their interest is, in this respect, directly opposed to that of the great body of the people. . . . 80

The wealth of a neighboring nation, though dangerous in war and politics, is certainly advantageous in trade. In a state of hostility it may enable our enemies to maintain fleets and armies superior to our own; but in a state of peace and commerce it must likewise enable them to exchange with us to a greater value and to afford a better market, either for the immediate produce of our own industry or for whatever is purchased with that produce. As a rich man is likely to be a better customer to the industrious people in his neighborhood, than a poor, so is likewise a rich nation. . . . 90

The *Philosophes*

The individuals who dominated the intellectual activity of the Age of the Enlightenment were known as *philosophes* (the French word for "philosophers"). These upper- and middle-class thinkers met in the London coffeehouses and in the fashionable *salons* of Paris townhouses, where they exchanged views on morality, politics, and religion and voiced opinions on everything ranging from diet to the latest fashions in theater and dress (figure 24.2). Such meetings were usually organized and directed by intellectually and socially ambitious women, who championed a freer and more public role for their sex. The men and women who graced the *salons* were the humanists of their time. Intellectuals rather than philosophers in the strict sense of the word, the *philosophes* constituted a small—less than five percent of the population—circle of well-educated individuals. Like the humanists of fifteenth-century Florence, their interests were mainly secular and social. Unlike their Renaissance counterparts, however, the *philosophes* scorned all forms of authority—they believed that they had surpassed the ancients, and they looked beyond the present state of knowledge to the establishment of a superior moral and social order.

Most *philosophes* held to the deist view of God (chapter 22) as Creator rather than as personal Redeemer, and as the providential force behind nature and natural law. They believed in the immortality of the soul, not out of commitment to any religious doctrine, but because they saw human beings as fundamentally different from other living creatures. They viewed the Bible as mythology rather than as revealed truth, and scorned Church hierarchy and ritual. Their antipathy to irrationality, superstition, and religious dogma (as reflected, for instance, in the Catholic doctrine of original sin) alienated them from the Church

the *Sciences, Arts and Crafts*—was the largest compendium of contemporary social, philosophic, artistic, scientific, and technological knowledge ever produced in the West. A collection of "all the knowledge scattered over the face of the earth," as Diderot explained, it manifested the zealous desire of the *philosophes* to dispel human ignorance and transform society. It was also, in part, a response to rising literacy and to the widespread public interest in the facts of everyday life. Not all members of society welcomed the enterprise, however: King Louis XV, who claimed that the *Encyclopédie* was doing "irreparable damage to morality and religion," twice banned the printing of its volumes, some of which were published and distributed secretly.

Diderot's *Encyclopédie* was the most ambitious and influential literary undertaking of the eighteenth century. Some two hundred individuals contributed seventy-two thousand entries on subjects ranging from political theory and cultural history to the technology of theater machinery, the making of silk stockings, and the varieties of wigs (figure 24.4). Articles on Islam, India, and China indicate a more than idle curiosity about civilizations that remained to most Westerners

FIGURE 24.3 *Diderot,* Jean Antoine Houdon, 1773. Marble, height 20 7/16 in. The Metropolitan Museum of Art, New York City. Gift of Mr. and Mrs. Charles Wrightsman, 1974. (1974.291)

and set them at odds with the established authorities—a position memorably expressed in Diderot's acerbic pronouncement that "men will not be free until the last king is strangled with the entrails of the last priest." The quest for a nonauthoritarian, secular morality led the *philosophes* to challenge all existing forms of intolerance, inequality, and injustice. The banner cry of the *philosophes,* "*Ecrasez l'infame*" ("Wipe out all evils"), sparked a commitment to social reforms that fueled—at least in France—the flames of bitter revolt (chapter 25).

Diderot and the Encyclopédie

The basic ideals of the Enlightenment were summed up in a monumental literary endeavor to which many of the *philosophes* contributed: the thirty-five-volume *Encyclopédie* (including eleven volumes of engraved plates), published between 1752 and 1784 under the leadership of Denis Diderot (d. 1789, figure 24.3). Modeled on the two-volume Chamber's Encyclopedia printed in England in 1751, Diderot's *Encyclopédie*—also known as *The Analytical Dictionary of*

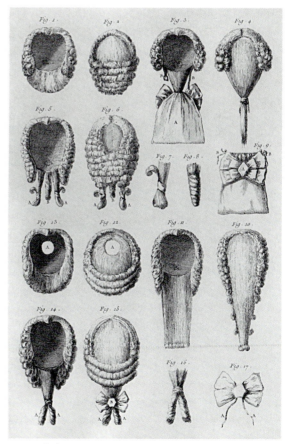

FIGURE 24.4 *Wigs,* a plate from the *Encyclopédie* illustrating the varieties of men's wigs that were fashionable in Europe in the 1750s. Thomas J. Watson Library, The Metropolitan Museum of Art, New York City.

FIGURE 24.5 *Gabrielle-Emilie le Tonnelier de Breteuil, Marquise du Chatelet*, Nicolas de Largillière, ca. 1740. Oil on canvas, 51 1/2 × 40 1/4 in. Columbus Museum of Art, Columbus, Ohio. Bequest of Frederick W. Schumacher.

remote and exotic. The list of contributors to the *Encyclopédie* reads like a who's who of the Enlightenment: François Marie Arouet (d. 1778), known as Voltaire (chapter 25—a historian of comparative cultures and the most brilliant thinker of the age—wrote on "matters of nature and of art"; the French philosopher and educator Jean Jacques Rousseau (d. 1778, chapter 25) provided articles on music; François Quesnay wrote on political economy; Montesquieu (whose articles were published posthumously) examined the different types of governments; Jean Le Rond d'Alembert (d. 1783) treated the matter of higher education; and Diderot himself prepared numerous entries on art and politics.

Although women contributed moral and financial support to the *Encyclopédie,* none was invited to participate in its production. Moreover, not one of the thirty-one entries on women makes reference to the contributions of exceptional eighteenth-century women such as Gabrielle Emilie Le Tonnelier de Breteuil (d. 1749), the Marquise du Châtelet (figure 24.5). Madame du Châtelet translated the Latin works of Virgil, Horace, and Ovid into eloquent French; she wrote original poetry and conducted experiments in

physics, chemistry, and mathematics. She was also a reckless gambler, a champion of the fashionably low-cut neckline, and the mistress of Voltaire. In their assessment of the abilities and the rights of women, the *philosophes* were ambivalent at best, their personal sentiments characterized by Rousseau's self-scorning complaint that one of his great misfortunes was "always to be connected with some literary woman." Nevertheless, the *Encyclopédie* remains a monument to secular knowledge and to the Enlightenment faith in the promise of reason—a spirit summed up in Voltaire's proclamation, "Let the facts prevail." The following excerpts come from the entry on natural law written by the French lawyer Antoine-Gaspart Boucher d'Argis and from the long article on Black Africans by Le Romain (whose first name and dates are unkown).

READING 88 From the *Encyclopédie*

Law of Nature or Natural Law

In its broadest sense the term is taken to designate   1
certain principles which nature alone inspires and which
all animals as well as all men have in common. On this
law are based the union of male and female, the
begetting of children as well as their education, love of
liberty, self-preservation, concern for self-defense.

It is improper to call the behavior of animals natural
law, for, not being endowed with reason, they can know
neither law nor justice.

More commonly we understand by natural law certain   10
laws of justice and equity which only natural reason has
established among men, or better, which God has
engraved in our hearts.

The fundamental principles of law and all justice are:
to live honestly, not to give offense to anyone, and to
render unto each whatever is his. From these general
principles derive a great many particular rules which
nature alone, that is, reason and equity, suggest to
mankind.

Since this natural law is based on such fundamental   20
principles, it is perpetual and unchangeable: no
agreement can debase it, no law can alter it or exempt
anyone from the obligation it imposes. . . .

The principles of natural law, therefore, form part of
the law of nations, particularly the primitive law of
nations; they also form part of public and of private law:
for the principles of natural law, which we have stated,
are the purest source of the foundation of most of
private and public law. . . .

The authority of natural laws stems from the fact that   30
they owe their existence to God. Men submit to them
because to observe them leads to the happiness of men
and society. This is a truth demonstrated by reason. It is
equally true that virtue by itself is a principle of inner
satisfaction whereas vice is a principle of unrest and
trouble. It is equally certain that virtue produces great
external advantage, while vice produces great ills. . . .

Negroes

For the last few centuries the Europeans have carried on a trade in Negroes whom they obtain from Guinea and other coasts of Africa and whom they use to maintain the colonies established in various parts of America and in the West Indies. To justify this loathsome commerce, which is contrary to natural law, it is argued that ordinarily these slaves find the salvation of their souls in the loss of their liberty, and that the Christian teaching they receive, together with their indispensable role in the cultivation of sugar cane, tobacco, indigo, etc., softens the apparent inhumanity of a commerce where men buy and sell their fellow men as they would animals used in the cultivation of the land.

Trade in Negroes is carried on by all the nations which have settlements in the West Indies, and especially by the French, the English, the Portuguese, the Dutch, the Swedes, and the Danes. The Spaniards, in spite of the fact that they possess the greatest part of the Americas, have no direct way of acquiring slaves but have concluded treaties with other nations to furnish them with Negroes. . . .

As soon as the trade is completed no time must be lost in setting sail. Experience has shown that as long as these unfortunates are still within sight of their homeland, they are overcome by sorrow and gripped by despair. The former is the cause of many illnesses from which a large number perish during the crossing; the latter inclines them to suicide, which they effect either by refusing nourishment or by shutting off their breathing. This they do in a way they know of turning and twisting their tongues which unfailingly suffocates them. Others again shatter their head against the sides of the ship or throw themselves into the sea if the occasion presents itself. . . .

Punishment of the Negroes, policing, and regulations concerning these matters:

If the Negro commits a slight offense the overseer may on his own responsibility punish him with a few strokes of the whip. If, however, it is a serious matter, the master has the culprit clapped in irons and then decides the number of strokes with which he will be punished. If all men were equally just, these necesary punishments would be kept within limits, but it often happens that certain masters abuse the authority which they claim over their slaves and chastise these unfortunates too harshly. Yet the masters themselves may be responsible for the situation which led to the offense. To put an end to the cruelties of these barbarous men who would be capable of leaving their slaves without the basic necessities of life while driving them to forced labor, the officers of His Majesty, who are resident in the colonies, have the responsibility of enforcing the edict of the king, which is called the Black Code. In the French islands of America this code regulates the governing and the administration of justice and of the police, as well as the discipline of the slaves and the slave-trade. . . .

———————— ◆ ————————

The Encyclopedic Cast of Mind

The *Encyclopédie* had an enormous impact on eighteenth-century culture. Although few individuals actually read or understood all of it, it fostered an encyclopedic cast of mind. Indeed, the emphasis on the accumulation, codification, and systematic preservation of knowledge linked the eighteenth century to the Scientific Revolution and to that other Enlightenment "bible," Newton's *Principia*.

Eighteenth-century scientists made notable advances in the fields of chemistry, electricity, biology, and the medical sciences. They produced the mercury thermometer and the stethoscope and introduced the science of immunology to the West—some seven centuries after the Chinese had invented the first inoculations against smallpox. Antoine Lavoisier's *Elementary Treatise of Chemistry*, published in 1789, launched chemistry as an exact science. The Swede Carolus Linnaeus (d. 1778) produced taxonomic treatises in botany, and the French naturalist George Louis Leclerc, Comte de Buffon (d. 1788) made similar advances in zoology.

Valuable efforts to accumulate and classify knowledge took place in the arts as well: the English critic and poet Samuel Johnson (d. 1784) published the first dictionary of the English language. Voltaire wrote a lengthy historical account of the age of Louis XIV. And Edward Gibbon (d. 1788) undertook to analyze the sociological forces at work within ancient cultures—an enterprise that led him to blame Christianity for the collapse and fall of the Roman Empire.

Eighteenth-century China lay beyond the immediate influence of the European Enlightenment; nevertheless, an encyclopedic impulse similar to that prevailing in the West occurred at this time (and even earlier) in the East. Ch'ing rulers followed their Ming predecessors in directing groups of scholars to assemble exhaustive collections of information, some filling as many as 36,000 manuscript volumes. These "encyclopedias" were actually anthologies of the writings of former Chinese artists and scholars, rather than comprehensive collections of contemporary knowledge. Nevertheless, as in France, some of China's rulers deemed the indiscriminate accumulation of information itself dangerous, and at least one eighteenth-century Ch'ing emperor authorized the official burning of thousands of books.

The Enlightenment Crusade for Progress

Among European intellectuals, the belief in the reforming powers of reason became the basis for a progressive view of human history. The German mathematician and philosopher Gottfried Wilhelm

Leibniz (d. 1716) systematically defended the idea that human beings live in perfect harmony with God and nature. Leibniz linked optimism to the logic of probability: his *principle of sufficient reason* held, simply, that there must be a reason or purpose for everything in nature. In response to the question, Why does evil exist in a world created by a good God? Leibniz answered that all events conformed to the preestablished harmony of the universe. Even evil, according to Leibniz, was necesary in a world that was "better than any other possible world"—a position that came to be called "philosophic optimism."

For the *philosophes,* the key to social reform lay in a true understanding of human nature, which, they argued, might best be acquired by examining human history. They interpreted the transition from hunting and gathering to the birth of civilization as clear evidence of the steady march toward social improvement. Faith in that steady march motivated the Enlightenment crusade for progress. The Italian lawyer and social reformer Cesare de Beccaria (d. 1794) enlisted in this crusade when he wrote his treatise *On Crimes and Punishments,* in which he suggested that torturing criminals did not work to deter crime. Rather, argued Beccaria, society should seek methods by which to rehabilitate those who commit crimes. Though Beccaria's book generated no immediate changes, it went through six editions in eighteen months and ultimately contributed to movements for prison reform in Europe and the United States. The questions that Beccaria raised concerning the value of punishment are still being debated today.

The most passionate warrior in the Enlightenment crusade for progress was the French aristocrat Antoine Nicolas de Condorcet (d. 1794). Condorcet was a mathematician, a social theorist, and a political moderate amidst revolutionary extremists. His *Sketch for a Historical Picture of the Progress of the Human Mind,* written during the early days of the French Revolution, was the preface to a longer work he never completed, for he committed suicide shortly after being imprisoned as an "enemy" of the Revolution. Condorcet believed that human nature could be perfected through reason and the sciences. All errors in politics and morals, he argued, were based in philosophical and scientific errors. "There is not a religious system nor a supernatural extravagance," wrote Condorcet, "that is not founded on ignorance of the laws of nature." Fiercely optimistic about the future of humankind, Condorcet was one of the first modern champions of sexual equality. He called for the "complete annihilation of the prejudices that have brought about an inequality of rights between the sexes, an inequality fatal even to the party in whose favor it works." Such inequality, he protested "has its origin solely in an abuse of strength, and all the later sophistical attempts that have been made to excuse it are vain."

In his visionary *Sketch,* Condorcet traced the "progress" of humankind through ten stages: from ignorance and tyranny to the threshold of enlightenment and equality. The utopian tenth stage, subtitled "The Future Progress of the Human Mind" (an excerpt of which follows), sets forth ideas that were well ahead of their time, such as a guaranteed livelihood for the aged, a universal system of education, fewer work hours, and the refinement of a technology for the accumulation of knowledge. (How computers would have delighted this prophet of the Information Age!) The educational goals that Condorcet outlines toward the end of the excerpt still carry the force of sound judgment.

READING 89 From Condorcet's *Sketch for a Historical Picture of the Progress of the Human Mind*

If man can, with almost complete assurance, predict   1
phenomena when he knows their laws, and if, even
when he does not, he can still, with great expectation of
success, forecast the future on the basis of his
experience of the past, why, then, should it be regarded
as a fantastic undertaking to sketch, with some
pretense to truth, the future destiny of man on the basis
of his history? The sole foundation for belief in the
natural sciences is this idea that the general laws
directing the phenomena of the universe, known or   10
unknown, are necessary and constant. Why should this
principle be any less true for the development of the
intellectual and moral faculties of man than for the other
operations of nature? Since beliefs founded on past
experience of like conditions provide the only rule of
conduct for the wisest of men, why should the
philosopher be forbidden to base his conjectures on
these same foundations, so long as he does not
attribute to them a certainty superior to that warranted
by the number, the constancy, and the accuracy of his   20
observations? . . .

The time will therefore come when the sun will shine
only on free men who know no other master but their
reason; when tyrants and slaves, priests and their
stupid or hypocritical instruments will exist only in works
of history and on the stage; and when we shall think of
them only to pity their victims and their dupes; to
maintain ourselves in a state of vigilance by thinking on
their excesses; and to learn how to recognize and so to
destroy, by force of reason, the first seeds of tyranny   30
and superstition, should they ever dare to reappear
among us.

In looking at the history of societies we shall have
had occasion to observe that there is often a great
difference between the rights that the law allows its
citizens and the rights that they actually enjoy, and,

again, between the equality established by political codes and that which in fact exists among individuals. . . .

These differences have three main causes: inequality in wealth, inequality in status between the man whose means of subsistence are hereditary and the man whose means are dependent on the length of his life, or, rather, on that part of his life in which he is capable of work; and, finally, inequality in education. 40

We therefore need to show that these three sorts of real inequality must constantly diminish without however disappearing altogether: for they are the result of natural and necessary causes which it would be foolish and dangerous to wish to eradicate. . . . 50

[As to education] we can teach the citizen everything that he needs to know in order to be able to manage his household, administer his affairs, and employ his labor and his faculties in freedom; to know his rights and to be able to exercise them; to be acquainted with his duties and fulfill them satisfactorily; to judge his own and other men's actions according to his own lights and to be a stranger to none of the high and delicate feelings which honor human nature; not to be in a state of blind dependence upon those to whom he must 60 entrust his affairs or the exercise of his rights; to be in a proper condition to choose and supervise them; to be no longer the dupe of those popular errors which torment man with superstitious fears and chimerical hopes; to defend himself against prejudice by the strength of his reason alone; and, finally, to escape the deceits of charlatans who would lay snares for his fortune, his health, his freedom of thought, and his conscience under the pretext of granting him health, wealth, and salvation. . . . 70

The real advantages that should result from this progress, of which we can entertain a hope that is almost a certainty, can have no other term than that of the absolute perfection of the human race; since, as the various kinds of equality come to work in its favor by producing ampler sources of supply, more extensive education, more complete liberty, so equality will be more real and will embrace everything which is really of importance for the happiness of human beings. . . .

———————◆———————

The Journalistic Essay and the Birth of the Modern Novel

As Condorcet's treatise attests, social criticism assumed an important place in Enlightenment literature. Such criticism now also manifested itself in a new literary genre known as the journalistic essay. Designed to address the middle-class reading public, prose essays and editorials were the stuff of magazines and daily newspapers. The first daily emerged in London during the eighteenth century, although a weekly had been published since 1642. With the rise of newspapers and periodicals, the "poetic" prose of

the seventeenth century—characterized by long sentences and magisterial phrases (see Bacon's *Of Studies,* Reading 79)—gave way to a more informal prose style, one that reflected the conversational chatter of the *salons* and the *cafés.* Journalistic essays brought "philosophy out of the closets and libraries, schools and colleges, to dwell in clubs and assemblies, at tea-tables and in coffee houses," explained Richard Addison (d. 1719), the leading British prose stylist of his day. In collaboration with his lifelong friend, Richard Steele (d. 1729), Addison published two London periodicals, the *Tatler* and the *Spectator,* which featured penetrating commentaries on current events and social behavior. The *Spectator* had a circulation of some twenty-five-thousand readers. Anticipating modern newsmagazines, eighteenth-century broadsheets and periodicals offered the literate public timely reports and diverse opinions on all aspects of popular culture. They provided entertainment even as they helped to shape popular opinion.

The most important new form of eighteenth-century literary entertainment, however, was the novel. The novel first appeared in world literature in China and Japan. The most famous of the early Japanese novels, *The Tale of Genji,* was written by an unknown eleventh-century author known as Lady Shikibu Murasaki. In China, where the history of the novel reached back to the twelfth century, prose tales of travel, love, and adventure were popular sources for operas and plays (chapters 14 and 23). Neither Japanese nor Chinese prose fiction had any direct influence on Western writers. Nevertheless, the vernacular novel became a major form of social entertainment in both Asia and the West during the eighteenth century. In both East and West, the rise of the novel reflected the demands of a larger reading public, although in China, literacy was still confined to the educated elite—only ten percent of Chinese women, for instance, could read and write.

The modern novel made its appearance in England at the beginning of the eighteenth century with the publication of Daniel Defoe's popular adventure story, *Robinson Crusoe* (1719). Defoe's stories, based in actual experience, were sharply realistic and thus quite different from the fantasy-laden novels of his sixteenth-century predecessors, Cervantes and Rabelais (chapter 18). The novels of Defoe and his somewhat later contemporaries Samuel Richardson (d. 1761) and Henry Fielding (d. 1771) featured graphic accounts of the personalities and daily lives of the lower and middle classes. With an exuberance reminiscent of Chaucer, these prose narratives—peppered with alehouse brawls and scenes of lusty seduction—brought to life tales of criminals, pirates, and prostitutes. Not surprisingly, such novels appealed to the tastes of the same individuals who enjoyed the spicy realism and journalistic prose of contemporary broadsheets.

Alexander Pope: Poet of the Age of Reason

Alexander Pope (d. 1744), the greatest English poet of the eighteenth century, typified the spirit of the Enlightenment. Pope was a great admirer of Newton and a champion of the scientific method. He was also a staunch neoclassicist who devotedly revived the wit and polish of the Golden Age Roman poets Virgil and Horace. Pope defended the value of education in Greek and Latin, and his own love of the classics inspired him to produce new translations of Homer's *Iliad* and *Odyssey*. "A *little learning* is a dangerous thing," warned Pope in pleading for a broader and more thorough survey of the past. Pope's poems are as controlled and refined as a Poussin painting or a Bach fugue. His epigrammatic verses, written in **heroic couplets**, ring with concentrated brilliance. Pope's choice of the heroic couplet reflects his commitment to the qualities of balance and order; and his mastery of that verse form bears out his claim that "True ease in writing comes from art, not chance,/As those move easiest who have learned to dance."

Pope's most famous poem was his *Essay on Man.* Like Milton's *Paradise Lost,* but on a smaller scale, Pope's *Essay* tried to explain humankind's place in the universal scheme. But whereas Milton had explained evil in terms of human will, Pope—a Catholic turned deist—believed that evil was simply part of God's design for a universe that Pope described as "A mighty maze! but not without a plan." According to Pope (and to Leibniz, whom Pope admired), whatever occurs in nature has been "programmed" by God and is part of God's benign and rational order. Pope lacked the reforming zeal of the *philosophes,* but he caught the optimism of the Enlightenment in a single statement: "Whatever is, is right." In the *Essay on Man,* Pope warns that we must not presume to understand the whole of nature. Nor should we aspire to a higher place in the great "chain of being." Rather, he counsels the reader, "Know then thyself, presume not God to scan;/The proper study of Mankind is Man."

READING 90   From Pope's *Essay on Man*

Epistle I

. . . .

IX. What if the foot, ordain'd the dust to tread,   1
Or hand, to toil, aspir'd to be the head?
What if the head, the eye, or ear repin'd[3]
To serve mere engines to the ruling Mind?
Just as absurd for any part to claim
To be another, in his gen'ral frame:
Just as absurd, to mourn the tasks or pains.
The great directing Mind of All ordains.

All are but parts of one stupendous whole,
Whose body Nature is, and God the soul;   10
That, chang'd thro' all, and yet in all the same;
Great in the earth, as in th' ethereal frame;
Warms in the sun, refreshes in the breeze,
Glows in the stars, and blossoms in the trees,
Lives thro' all life, extends thro' all extent,
Spreads undivided, operates unspent;
Breathes in our soul, informs our mortal part,
As full, as perfect, in a hair as heart:
As full, as perfect, in vile Man that mourns,
As the rapt Seraph[4] that adores and burns: 20
To him no high, no low, no great, no small;
He fills, he bounds, connects, and equals all.

X. Cease then, nor Order Imperfection name:
Our proper bliss depends on what we blame.
Know thy own point: This kind, this due degree
Of blindness, weakness, Heav'n bestows on thee.
Submit—In this, or any other sphere,
Secure to be as blest as thou canst bear:
Safe in the hand of one disposing Pow'r,
Or in the natal, or the mortal hour.   30
All Nature is but Art,[5] unknown to thee;
All Chance, Direction, which thou canst not see;
All Discord, Harmony not understood;
All partial Evil, universal Good:
And, spite of Pride, in erring Reason's spite,
One truth is clear, WHATEVER IS, IS RIGHT.

Epistle II

I. Know then thyself, presume not God to scan;[6]
The proper study of Mankind is Man.
Plac'd on this isthmus of a middle state,[7]
A Being darkly wise, and rudely great: 40
With too much knowledge for the Sceptic side,
With too much weakness for the Stoic's pride,
He hangs between; in doubt to act, or rest;
In doubt to deem himself a God, or Beast;
In doubt his Mind or Body to prefer,
Born but to die, and reas'ning but to err;
Alike in ignorance, his reason such.

---

[3]Complained.
[4]A member of the highest order of angels.
[5]Compare Hobbes: "Nature is the art whereby God governs the world."
[6]Investigate.
[7]Between the angels (above) and the animal kingdom (below). Compare Pico della Mirandola's view of human beings as creatures who partake of both earthly and celestial qualities and can therefore ascend or descend the great "chain of being" (chapter 16).

Whether he thinks too little, or too much:
Chaos of Thought and Passion, all confus'd;
Still by himself abus'd, or disabus'd;   50
Created half to rise, and half to fall;[8]
Great lord of all things, yet a prey to all;
Sole judge of Truth, in endless Error hurl'd:[9]
The glory, jest, and riddle of the world!

---

[8]See note 7.
[9]Cast back and forth.

Summary

The Age of the European Enlightenment marks the beginnning of the Western notion of social progress and human perfectibility. In political thought, Thomas Hobbes and John Locke advanced the idea of government based on a social contract between ruler and ruled. While Hobbes envisioned this contract as a bond between individuals who surrendered some portion of their freedom to a sovereign authority, Locke saw government as an agent of the people—bound to exercise the will of the majority. According to Locke, government must operate according to the consent of the governed.

Locke's writings provided the intellectual foundation for the Enlightenment faith in reason as the sure guide to social progress. Jefferson, Montesquieu, and Adam Smith adapted Locke's views on natural law to political and economic life. The idea that human beings, free from the bonds of ignorance and superstition and operating according to the principles of reason, might achieve the good life here on earth inspired the philosophic optimism of Leibniz in Germany and the progressive theories of Beccaria in Italy and Condorcet in France.

The symbol of the Enlightenment zeal for knowledge was the *Encyclopédie,* produced by Diderot with the assistance of the *philosophes.* A similar zeal for the ordering of socially useful information inspired the writing of dictionaries, biographies, and histories. The journalistic essay and the early modern novel entertained the new reading public, even as they offered an intimate examination of everyday, secular life. And in poetry, the elegant verbal tapestries of Alexander Pope optimistically pictured human beings as the enlightened inhabitants of an orderly and harmonious universe.

The promise of reason and the gospel of progress—two fundamental ideas of the Enlightenment—have shaped the course of modern Western culture. Imported to America during the eighteenth century, they became the informing ideals of a new order of society. They served a "cult of utility," which promoted the idea that rational thought and its application in science and technology would advance and improve the quality of life for all members of society. More recently, the promise of reason and the gospel of progress have worked to challenge tyranny and injustice in many other parts of the world, including Africa and Asia—a sign of the durability of Enlightenment thought within the humanistic tradition.

GLOSSARY

heroic couplet   a pair of rhymed iambic pentameter lines that reach completion in structure and in sense at the end of the second line

laissez-faire   (French, "leave alone") a general policy of noninterference in the economy, defended by such classical economists as Adam Smith

philosophes   (French, "philosophers") the intellectuals of the European Enlightenment

social contract   an agreement made between citizens leading to the establishment of the state

SUGGESTIONS FOR READING

Becker, Carl L. *The Heavenly City of the Eighteenth-Century Philosophers.* New Haven: Yale University Press, 1932.

Gay, Peter. *The Enlightenment: An Interpretation.* 2 Vols. New York: Norton, 1977.

Hampson, Norman. *A Cultural History of the Enlightenment.* New York: Pantheon Books, 1968.

Havens, George R. *The Age of Ideas.* New York: Henry Holt, 1955.

Krieger, Leonard. *Kings and Philosophies 1689–1789.* Vol. 3 of *The Norton History of Modern Europe.* New York: Norton, 1970.

Vyverberg, Henry. *Human Nature, Cultural Diversity, and the French Enlightenment.* New York: Oxford University Press, 1989.

Watt, Ian. *The Rise of the Novel: Studies in Defoe, Richardson, and Fielding.* Berkeley: University of California Press, 1957.

25

THE LIMITS OF REASON

Even that most enthusiastic optimist, Alexander Pope, acknowledged in his *Essay on Man* that human beings were "Born to die and reas'ning but to err"—that is, that people were finite and fallible. Pope and other eighteenth-century champions of reason were, in fact, ambivalent: while generally committed to the belief in human perfectibility and the rational potential of humankind, they observed that people often acted in ways that were wholly irrational. Reason—that infallible guide to Enlightenment wisdom—was all too frequently ignored or abandoned altogether. Moreover, the critical exercise of reason, when taken to an extreme, often deteriorated into bitter skepticism and cynicism.

Perhaps the greatest obstacle to the belief in the promise of reason, however, lay in the hard realities of everyday life. In eighteenth-century Europe, where Enlightenment intellectuals were exalting the ideals of human progress, there was clear evidence of human ignorance, depravity, and despair. Upon visiting the much-acclaimed city of Paris, Jean Jacques Rousseau discovered "dirty, stinking streets, filthy black houses, an air of slovenliness" and alleys filled with beggars. Beyond the elegant drawing rooms of Paris and London lay clear signs of poverty, violence, and degradation. In some areas of England only half of the newborn children reached the age of ten. The triumph of science and technology spawned a new barbarism in the form of machines that were as potentially destructive as they were beneficial. In England, the invention of the "flying shuttle" (1733), the "spinning jenny" (1765), and the power loom (1785)—machines for the manufacture of textile goods—encouraged the rise of the factory system and sparked the Industrial Revolution. James Watts' steam engine (1775) provided a new power source for textiles and other industries. But such technological achievements, allied with unregulated capitalism, gave rise to dangerous working conditions and the exploitation of labor. In many of London's factories, children tended the new machines for twelve- to fourteen-hour shifts and were boarded in shabby barracks. And in the mines of Cornwall and Durham, women and children were paid a pittance to labor like animals, pulling carts laden with coal. Some miners worked such long hours that they never saw the light of day. The discrepancies between squalid reality and perfumed ideals provoked indignant protests, and none so potent as those coached in literary satire.

Satire: Weapon of the Enlightenment

The eighteenth century was history's greatest age of satire. The favorite weapon of many Enlightenment intellectuals, satire fused wit and irony to underscore human folly and error. The genre that had served Juvenal in imperial Rome (chapter 7) and Erasmus in the Age of the Reformation (chapter 18) now became the favorite tool of social reformers, who drew attention to the vast contradictions between morals and manners, intentions and actions, and, more generally, between Enlightenment aspirations and realities.

The satire of the eighteenth century reflected a new interest in cultural differences, especially those that prevailed between Europe and Asia. Europe's commercial expansion into China and India, the activities of the Jesuits in the Far East, and the circulation of illustrated travel books encouraged the study of "exotic" civilizations. While the *philosophes* did not embrace all non-European cultures—Diderot, for instance, pronounced the Arabs "bellicose and thievish"—they found much to admire in the exotic East—Voltaire, for example, esteemed Confucius as the quintessential philosopher-sage. From this position of cultural relativism, the *philosophes* took a hard look at Western values and habits as they might have been perceived by incredulous foreigners. The Baron de Montesquieu led the way in 1721 with his publication of the *Persian Letters,* a series of satiric descriptions of Parisian society viewed through the eyes of a Persian tourist. Equally incisive was *The Citizen of the World,* a set of letters allegedly written by a Chinese philosopher visiting London, but actually fabricated by the Irish playwright Oliver Goldsmith (d. 1774). *The Citizen of the World* (an excerpt from which follows) describes the strange habits and fashions of European society, including the eighteenth-century practice of wearing powdered wigs (figure 24.4) and "beauty" patches as signs of social and political status (figure 25.1).

READING 91 From Goldsmith's *Citizen of the World*

To make a fine gentleman, several trades are   1
required, but chiefly a barber: you have undoubtedly
heard of the Jewish champion, whose strength lay in his
hair:[1] one would think that the English were for placing
all wisdom there: To appear wise, nothing more is
requisite here than for a man to borrow hair from the
heads of all his neighbors, and clap it like a bush on his

own: the distributors of law . . . stick on such
quantities, that it is almost impossible, even in idea to
distinguish between the head and the hair.   10

Those whom I have been now describing, affect the
gravity of the lion: those I am going to describe more
resemble the pert vivacity of smaller animals. The
barber, who is still master of the ceremonies, cuts their
hair close to the crown; and then with a composition of
meal and dog's lard, plasters the whole in such a
manner, as to make it impossible to distinguish whether
the patient wears a cap or a plaster;[2] but to make the
picture more perfectly striking, conceive the tail of some
beast, a grey-hound's tail, or a pig's tail for instance,   20
appended to the back of the head, and reaching down
to that place where tails in other animals are generally
seen to begin; thus betailed and bepowdered, the man
of taste fancies he improves in beauty, dresses up his
hard-featured face in smiles, and attempts to look
hideously tender. Thus equipped, he is qualified to make
love, and hopes for success more from the powder on
the outside of his head, than the sentiments within.

Yet when I consider what sort of a creature the fine
lady is, to whom he is supposed to pay his addresses, it   30
is not strange to find him thus equipped in order to
please. She is herself every whit as fond of powder, and
tails, and hog's lard as he: to speak my secret
sentiments, most reverend Fum,[3] the ladies here are
horridly ugly; . . .

They like to have the face of various colors . . .
frequently sticking on, with spittle, little black patches[4]
on every part of it, except on the tip of the nose, which I
have never seen with a patch. You'll have a better idea
of their manner of placing these spots, when I have   40
finished a map of an English face patched up to the
fashion, which shall shortly be sent to increase your
curious collection of paintings, medals, and monsters.[5]

But what surprises more than all the rest, is, what I
have just now been credibly informed by one of this
country; 'Most ladies here, says he, have two faces; one
face to sleep in, and another to show in company: the
first is generally reserved for the husband and family at
home, the other put on to please strangers abroad; the
family face is often indifferent enough, but the out-door   50
one looks something better; this is always made at the
toilet, where the looking-glass and toad-eater[6] sit in
council, and settle the complexion of the day.'

I can't ascertain the truth of this remark; however, it
is actually certain, that they wear more clothes within
doors than without; and I have seen a lady who seemed
to shudder at a breeze in her own apartment, appear
half naked in the streets. Farewell.

---

[1]The biblical Samson.

[2]The combination of lime, water, and hair that constituted the wig.
[3]The fictional Chinese friend to whom the author of the letter writes.
[4]Artificial "beauty" marks.
[5]Popular among eighteenth-century European aristocrats was the *schatzkammer,* or "cabinet of marvels," which included curiosities, drawings, prints, coins, porcelains, and other intimate items.
[6]A toady, that is, one who flatters in the hope of winning favor.

FIGURE 25.1 *Marriage à la Mode: The Marriage Transaction,* William Hogarth, 1742–46. Engraving. Reproduced by courtesy of the Trustees of the British Museum, London.

Satire in Chinese Literature

The satirical travel tale also came into vogue in other parts of the world. Toward the end of the great age of prose fiction—the seventeenth and eighteenth centuries—the Chinese philologist Li Ju-chen (d. 1830) wrote *Flowers in the Mirror,* a series of loosely woven stories that recount the adventures of a hero who journeys to many strange lands, such as the Country of Two-Faced People, the Country of Long-Armed People, and the Country of Women. In the last of these fictional lands, the traditional roles of the sexes are reversed, and the ruling women of the country set upon the hero to prepare him as "royal concubine": they plait his hair, apply lipstick and powder to his face, pierce his ears, and, to his ultimate dismay, bind his feet in the traditional Chinese manner. Chinese writers produced other satires, such as *The Scholars* by Wu Ching-tse (d. 1754), a collection of stories that poked fun at China's privileged class of scholars. But the blunt kind of social criticism represented by *Flowers in the Mirror* did not appear in China until the late eighteenth century. And, despite the fact that Manchu rulers censured from Chinese custom by forbidding Manchu women to bind their feet, Li Ju-chen's bold assertion of equal rights for women fell on deaf ears in China at large.

The Satires of Jonathan Swift

The premier British satirist of the eighteenth century was Jonathan Swift (d. 1745). Unlike the *philosophes,* this Dublin-born Anglican priest took a pessimistic view of human nature. He once confided (in a letter to Alexander Pope) that he hated the human race, whose misuse of reason produced, in his view, a corrupt society. Such negativism accompanied Swift's self-acclaimed "savage indignation." Yet, Swift was not a man of despair, for no despairing personality could have produced such a profoundly moralizing body of literature. Swift wrote many political pamphlets and letters publicizing the wretched condition of the Irish peasants, who were exploited unmercifully by the English government. In *A Modest Proposal,* a satirical treatise subtitled "for Preventing the Children of the Poor People in Ireland from Being a Burden to their Parents or Country, and for Making them Beneficial to the Public," Swift observed that many Irish peasants were too poor to feed their families; he proposed with deadpan frankness that Irish children should be bred and butchered for the English dining table, thus providing income for the poor and alleviating the misery of all.

In 1726, Swift published his most famous work, *Gulliver's Travels.* At one level, *Gulliver's Travels* is an adventure story that describes the fortunes of a hero in imaginary lands peopled with midgets, giants, and other fabulous creatures. At a second, symbolic level, however, it is a social statement on the vagaries of human behavior. In one chapter, Gulliver visits the Lilliputians, "little people" whose moral pettiness and inhumanity seem to characterize humankind at its worst; in another, he meets noble horses whose rational behavior contrasts with the bestiality of their human-looking slaves, the Yahoos. While *A Modest Proposal* mocked particular contemporary ills, *Gulliver's Travels* attacked conditions that are universal and, unfortunately, timeless. An immediate popular sensation, *Gulliver's Travels* has become a landmark in fantasy literature and social satire.

Voltaire and Candide

Swift's satires were an inspiration to that most scintillating of French *philosophes,* François Marie Arouet (d. 1778), who used the pen name Voltaire (figure 25.2). Born into a rising Parisian middle-class family and educated by Jesuits, Voltaire became a poet, playwright, and critic, as well as the central figure of the French *salons.* His historical and expository works attacked bigotry as man-made evil and injustice as institutional evil, and on two separate occasions, his controversial verse-satires led to his imprisonment in the Bastille (the French state prison).

Like other *philosophes,* Voltaire condemned organized religion and all forms of superstition and fanaticism. A declared deist, he compared human beings to mice, who, living in the recesses of an immense ship, had no cognizance of its captain or its destination. Any confidence Voltaire might have had in beneficent Providence was dashed by the terrible Lisbon earthquake and tidal wave of 1755, which took the lives of some fifteen thousand people. For Voltaire, the realities of natural disaster and human cruelty were not easily reconciled with the belief that a good God created the universe or the idea that humans were by nature good—views basic to Enlightenment optimism. In the satirical tale *Candide* (subtitled *Optimism*), Voltaire addressed the age-old question of how evil could exist in a universe created and governed by the forces of good. More important, he leveled a major blow at the optimistic credo that this world was "the best of all possible worlds."

A parody of the adventure romances in vogue in Voltaire's time, *Candide* describes the exploits of a naive and unsophisticated young man whose blissful optimism is daunted by a series of terrible (and hilarious) experiences. Initially, the youthful Candide (literally, "candid" or "frank") approaches life with the glib optimism taught to him by Dr. Pangloss ("all tongue"), Voltaire's embodiment of the philosopher Leibniz (see chapter 24). But Candide soon discovers

FIGURE 25.2 *Voltaire in Old Age,* Jean Antoine Houdon, 1781. Marble, height 20 in. Château de Versailles. © The Bettmann Archive.

the folly of believing that "all is for the best in this best of all possible worlds." He experiences the horrors of war (the consequence of two equally self-righteous opposing armies), the evils of religious fanaticism (as manifested by the Spanish Inquisition), the disasters of nature (the Lisbon earthquake), and the dire effects of human greed (an affliction especially prevalent among the aristocracy and derived, according to Voltaire, from boredom). Experience becomes the antidote to the comfortable fatalism of Pope's "Whatever is, is right." After a lifetime of sobering misadventures, Candide ends his days settled on a farm in the company of his long-lost friends. "We must cultivate our garden," he concludes. This metaphor for achieving personal satisfaction in a hostile world relieves the otherwise devastating skepticism that underlies *Candide.* It is Voltaire's answer to blind optimism and the foolish hope that human reason can allay evil.

Voltaire's genius, and the quality that separates his style from that of Goldsmith or Swift, is his penetrating wit. Like a sword, Voltaire's satire is sharply pointed, precise in its aim, and devastating in its effect.

With a sure hand, Voltaire manipulates the principal satirical devices: irony, understatement, and overstatement. Using irony—the contradiction between literal and intended meanings—he mocks serious matters and deflates lofty pretensions; he calls war, for instance, "heroic butchery" and refers to Paquette's venereal disease as a "present" she received from "a very learned Franciscan." He exploits understatement when he notes, for example, that Pangloss "only lost one eye and one ear" (as the result of syphilis). And, he uses overstatement for moral effect: the 350-pound baroness of Westphalia is "greatly respected;" thus corpulence—actually an indication of self-indulgence—becomes a specious sign of dignity and importance.

Voltaire's mock optimism, dispatched by Candide's persistent view that this is "the best of all possible worlds" even as he encounters repeated horrors, underscores the contradiction between the ideal and the real that lies at the heart of all satire. Although *Candide* was censored in many parts of Europe, the book was so popular that forty editions were published in Voltaire's lifetime. A classic of Western satire, *Candide* has survived numerous adaptations, including a superb twentieth-century version as a comic-operetta with lyrics by the American poet Richard Wilber and music by the American composer Leonard Bernstein.[7] Approximately one-third of Voltaire's masterpiece is included in the following excerpt.

READING 92 From Voltaire's *Candide*

Chapter 1

How Candide Was Brought Up in a Fine Castle, and How He Was Expelled From Thence

There lived in Westphalia,[8] in the castle of my Lord the Baron of Thunder-ten-tronckh, a young man, on whom nature had bestowed the most agreeable manners. His face was the index to his mind. He had an upright heart, with an easy frankness; which, I believe, was the reason he got the name of *Candide*. He was suspected, by the old servants of the family, to be the son of my Lord the Baron's sister, by a very honest gentleman of the neighborhood, whom the young lady declined to marry, because he could only produce seventy-one armorial quarterings;[9] the rest of his genealogical tree having been destroyed through the injuries of time.

The Baron was one of the most powerful lords in Westphalia; his castle had both a gate and windows; and his great hall was even adorned with tapestry. The dogs of his outer yard composed his hunting pack upon occasion, his grooms were his huntsmen, and the vicar of the parish was his chief almoner. He was called My Lord by everybody, and everyone laughed when he told his stories.

My Lady the Baroness, who weighed about three hundred and fifty pounds, attracted, by that means, very great attention, and did the honors of the house with a dignity that rendered her still more respectable. Her daughter Cunegonde, aged about seventeen years, was of a ruddy complexion, fresh, plump, and well calculated to excite the passions. The Baron's son appeared to be in every respect worthy of his father. The preceptor, Pangloss,[10] was the oracle of the house, and little Candide listened to his lectures with all the simplicity that was suitable to his age and character.

Pangloss taught metaphysico-theologo-cosmoloonigology.[11] He proved most admirably, that there could not be an effect without a cause; that, in this best of possible worlds,[12] my Lord the Baron's castle was the most magnificent of castles, and my Lady the best of Baronesses that possibly could be.

"It is demonstrable," said he, "that things cannot be otherwise than they are: for all things having been made for some end, they must necessarily be for the best end. Observe well, that the nose has been made for carrying spectacles; therefore, we have spectacles. The legs are visibly designed for stockings, and therefore we have stockings. Stones have been formed to be hewn, and make castles; therefore my Lord has a very fine castle; the greatest baron of the province ought to be the best accommodated. Swine were made to be eaten; therefore we eat pork all the year round: consequently, those who have merely asserted that all is good, have said a very foolish thing; they should have said all is the best possible."

Candide listened attentively, and believed implicitly; for he thought Miss Cunegonde extremely handsome, though he never had the courage to tell her so. He concluded, that next to the good fortune of being Baron of Thunder-ten-tronckh, the second degree of happiness was that of being Miss Cunegonde, the third to see her every day, and the fourth to listen to the teachings of Master Pangloss, the greatest philosopher of the province, and consequently of the whole world.

One day Cunegonde having taken a walk in the environs of the castle, in a little wood, which they called a park, espied Doctor Pangloss giving a lesson in experimental philosophy to her mother's chambermaid; a little brown wrench, very handsome, and very docile. As Miss Cunegonde had a strong inclination for the sciences, she observed, without making any noise, the reiterated experiments that were going on before her eyes; she saw very clearly the sufficient reason of the

---

[7]The 1985 New York City Opera House version is available on record, cassette, and CD, New World label: NW–340/41.

[8]A province in western Germany.

[9]Genealogical degrees of noble ancestry; since each quartering represents one generation, the family "tree" is over two thousand years old—an obvious impossibility.

[10]The tutor's name is (literally) "all-tongue."

[11]Note the French *nigaud* ("booby") included in the elaborate title of this pompous-sounding discipline.

[12]One of many allusions in *Candide* to the philosophic optimism systematized by Leibniz and popularized by Pope (see chapter 24, pp. 107–8, 110–11).

Doctor, the effects and the causes; and she returned 70
greatly flurried, quite pensive, and full of desire to be
learned; imagining that she might be a sufficient reason
for young Candide, who also, might be the same to her.

On her return to the castle, she met Candide, and
blushed; Candide also blushed; she wished him good
morrow with a faltering voice, and Candide answered
her, hardly knowing what he said. The next day, after
dinner, as they arose from table, Cunegonde and
Candide happened to get behind the screen.
Cunegonde dropped her handkerchief, and Candide 80
picked it up; she, not thinking any harm, took hold of his
hand; and the young man, not thinking any harm
neither, kissed the hand of the young lady, with an
eagerness, a sensibility, and grace, very particular; their
lips met, their eyes sparkled, their knees trembled, their
hands strayed.——— The Baron of Thunder-ten-tronckh
happening to pass close by the screen, and observing
this cause and effect, thrust Candide out of the castle,
with lusty kicks. Cunegonde fell into a swoon and as
soon as she came to herself, was heartily cuffed on the 90
ears by my Lady the Baroness. Thus all was thrown into
confusion in the finest and most agreeable castle
possible.

Chapter 2

What Became of Candide Among the Bulgarians[13]

Candide being expelled the terrestrial paradise, rambled
a long while without knowing where, weeping, and lifting
up his eyes to heaven, and sometimes turning them
towards the finest of castles, which contained the
handsomest of baronesses. He laid himself down,
without his supper, in the open fields, between two
furrows, while the snow fell in great flakes. Candide, 100
almost frozen to death, crawled next morning to the
neighboring village, which was called Waldber-ghoff-
trarbk-dikdorff. Having no money, and almost dying with
hunger and fatigue, he stopped in a dejected posture
before the gate of an inn. Two men, dressed in blue,[14]
observing him in such a situation, ''Brother,'' says one
of them to the other, ''there is a young fellow well built,
and of a proper height.'' They accosted Candide, and
invited him very civilly to dinner.

''Gentlemen,'' replied Candide, with an agreeable 110
modesty, ''you do me much honor, but I have no money
to pay my share.''

''O sir,'' said one of the blues, ''persons of your
appearance and merit never pay anything; are you not
five feet five inches high?''

''Yes, gentlemen, that is my height,'' returned he,
making a bow.

''Come, sir, sit down at table; we will not only treat
you, but we will never let such a man as you want
money; men are made to assist one another.'' 120

''You are in the right,'' said Candide; ''that is what
Pangloss always told me, and I see plainly that
everything is for the best.''

They entreated him to take a few crowns, which he
accepted, and would have given them his note; but they
refused it, and sat down to table.

''Do not you tenderly love———''

''O yes,'' replied he, ''I tenderly love Miss
Cunegonde.''

''No,'' said one of the gentlemen; ''we ask you if you 130
do tenderly love the King of the Bulgarians?''

''Not at all,'' said he, ''for I never saw him.''

''How! he is the most charming of kings, and you
must drink his health.''

''O, with all my heart, gentlemen,'' and drinks.

''That is enough,'' said they to him; ''you are now the
bulwark, the support, the defender, the hero of the
Bulgarians; your fortune is made, and you are certain of
glory.'' Instantly they put him in irons, and carried him to
the regiment. They made him turn to the right, to the 140
left, draw the ramrod, return the ramrod, present, fire,
step double; and they gave him thirty blows with a
cudgel. The next day, he performed his exercises not
quite so badly, and received but twenty blows; the third
day the blows were restricted to ten, and he was looked
upon by his fellow-soldiers, as a kind of prodigy.

Candide, quite stupefied, could not well conceive
how he had become a hero. One fine Spring day he
took it into his head to walk out, going straight forward,
imagining that the human, as well as the animal species, 150
were entitled to make whatever use they pleased of
their limbs. He had not travelled two leagues, when four
other heroes, six feet high, came up to him, bound him,
and put him into a dungeon. He is asked by a Court-
martial, whether he chooses to be whipped six and
thirty times through the whole regiment, or receive at
once twelve bullets through the forehead? He in vain
argued that the will is free, and that he chose neither
the one nor the other; he was obliged to make a choice;
he therefore resolved, in virtue of God's gift called *free-* 160
will, to run the gauntlet six and thirty times. He
underwent this discipline twice. The regiment being
composed of two thousand men, he received four
thousand lashes, which laid open all his muscles and
nerves, from the nape of the neck to the back. As they
were proceeding to a third course, Candide, being quite
spent, begged as a favor that they would be so kind as
to shoot him; he obtained his request; they hoodwinked
him, and made him kneel; the King of the Bulgarians
passing by, inquired into the crime of the delinquent; 170
and as this prince was a person of great penetration, he
discovered from what he heard of Candide, that he was
a young metaphysician, entirely ignorant of the things of
this world; and he granted him his pardon, with a
clemency which will be extolled in all histories, and
throughout all ages. An experienced surgeon cured
Candide in three weeks, with emollients prescribed by
no less a master than Dioscorides.[15] His skin had
already began to grow again, and he was able to walk,
when the King of the Bulgarians gave battle to the King 180
of the Abares.

---

[13]Voltaire's name for the troops of Frederick the Great, King of Prussia, who, like their king, were widely regarded as Sodomites; the association between the name and the French *bougre* (''to bugger'') is patent.

[14]The color of the uniforms worn by the soldiers of Frederick the Great.

---

[15]A famous Greek physician of the first century A.D. whose book on medicine was for centuries a standard text.

Chapter 3

How Candide Made His Escape From the Bulgarians, and What Afterwards Befel Him.

Nothing could be so fine, so neat, so brilliant, so well ordered, as the two armies.[16] The trumpets, fifes, hautboys, drums, and cannon, formed an harmony superior to what hell itself could invent. The cannon swept off at first about six thousand men on each side; afterwards, the musketry carried away from the best of worlds, about nine or ten thousand rascals that infected its surface. The bayonet was likewise the sufficient reason of the death of some thousands of men. The whole number might amount to about thirty thousand souls. Candide, who trembled like a philosopher, hid himself as well as he could, during this heroic butchery.

At last, while each of the two kings were causing *Te Deum*—glory to God—to be sung in their respective camps, he resolved to go somewhere else, to reason upon the effects and causes. He walked over heaps of the dead and dying; he came at first to a neighboring village belonging to the Abares, but found it in ashes; for it had been burnt by the Bulgarians, according to the law of nations. Here were to be seen old men full of wounds, casting their eyes on their murdered wives, who were holding their infants to their bloody breasts. You might see in another place, virgins outraged after they had satisfied the natural desires of some of those heroes, whilst breathing out their last sighs. Others, half-burnt, praying earnestly for instant death. The whole field was covered with brains, and with legs and arms lopped off.

Candide betook himself with all speed to another village. It belonged to the Bulgarians, and had met with the same treatment from the Abarian heroes. Candide, walking still forward over quivering limbs, or through rubbish of houses, got at last out of the theatre of war, having some small quantity of provisions in his knapsack, and never forgetting Miss Cunegonde. His provisions failed him when he arrived in Holland;[17] but having heard that every one was rich in that country, and that they were Christians, he did not doubt but he should be as well treated there as he had been in my Lord the Baron's castle, before he had been expelled thence on account of Miss Cunegonde's sparkling eyes.

He asked alms from several grave looking persons, who all replied, that if he continued that trade, they would confine him in a house of correction, where he should learn to earn his bread.

He applied afterwards to a man, who for a whole hour had been discoursing on the subject of charity, before a large assembly. This orator, looking at him askance, said to him:

"What are you doing here? are you for the good cause?"

"There is no effect without a cause," replied Candide, modestly; "all is necessarily linked, and ordered for the best. A necessity banished me from Miss Cunegonde; a necessity forced me to run the gauntlet; another necessity makes me beg my bread, till I can get into some business by which to earn it. All this could not be otherwise."

"My friend," said the orator to him, "do you believe that the Anti-Christ is alive?"

"I never heard whether he is or not," replied Candide; "but whether he is, or is not, I want bread!"

"You do not deserve to eat any," said the other; "get you gone, you rogue; get you gone, you wretch; never in thy life come near me again!"

The orator's wife, having popped her head out of the chamber window, and seeing a man who doubted whether Anti-Christ was alive, poured on his head a full vessel of. . . . Oh heavens! to what excess does religious zeal transport the fair sex!

A man who had not been baptized, a good Anabaptist,[18] named *James,* saw the barbarous and ignominious manner with which they treated one of his brethren, a being with two feet, without feathers, and endowed with a rational soul.[19] He took him home with him, cleaned him, gave him bread and beer, made him a present of two florins,[20] and offered to teach him the method of working in his manufactories of Persian stuffs, which are fabricated in Holland. Candide, prostrating himself almost to the ground, cried out, "Master Pangloss argued well when he said, that everything is for the best in this world; for I am infinitely more affected with your very great generosity, than by the hard-heartedness of that gentleman with the cloak, and the lady his wife."

Next day, as he was taking a walk, he met a beggar, all covered over with sores, his eyes half dead, the tip of his nose eaten off, his mouth turned to one side of his face, his teeth black, speaking through his throat, tormented with a violent cough, with gums so rotten, that his teeth came near falling out every time he spit.

Chapter 4

How Candide Met His Old Master of Philosophy, Dr. Pangloss, and What Happened to Them.

Candide moved still more with compassion than with horror, gave this frightful mendicant the two florins which he had received of his honest Anabaptist James. The spectre fixed his eyes attentively upon him, dropt some tears, and was going to fall upon his neck. Candide, affrighted, drew back.

"Alas!" said the one wretch to the other, "don't you know your dear Pangloss?"

"What do I hear! Is it you, my dear master! you in this dreadful condition! What misfortune has befallen you? Why are you no longer in the most magnificent of

---

[16]A mocking reference to the Seven Years' War (1756–63) fought between the Prussians (Bulgars) and the French-Austrian coalition, to whom Voltaire gives the name Abares—a tribe of semicivilized Scythians.

[17]Holland, a mecca of religious freedom for over two centuries, had given asylum to the Anabaptists and other radical religious sects.

[18]See *The Humanistic Tradition*, Book 4, p. 29.

[19]The minimalist definition of man ascribed to the philosopher Plato and used here to suggest James' sympathy with all humankind.

[20]Gold coins.

castles? What has become of Miss Cunegonde, the nonpareil of the fair sex, the master-piece of nature?''

''I have no more strength,'' said Pangloss.

Candide immediately carried him to the Anabaptist's stable, where he gave him a little bread to eat. When Pangloss was refreshed a little, ''Well,'' said Candide, ''what has become of Cunegonde?'' 290

''She is dead,'' replied the other.

Candide fainted away at this word; but his friend recovered his senses, with a little bad vinegar which he found by chance in the stable.

Candide opening his eyes, cried out, ''Cunegonde is dead! Ah, best of worlds, where art thou now? But of what distemper did she die? Was not the cause, her seeing me driven out of the castle by my Lord, her father, with such hard kicks on the breech?''

''No,'' said Pangloss, ''she was gutted by some 300 Bulgarian soldiers, after having been barbarously ravished.[21] They knocked my Lord the Baron on the head, for attempting to protect her; my Lady the Baroness was cut in pieces; my poor pupil was treated like his sister; and as for the castle, there is not one stone left upon another, nor a barn, nor a sheep, nor a duck, nor a tree. But we have been sufficiently revenged; for the Abarians have done the very same thing to a neighboring barony, which belonged to a Bulgarian Lord.'' 310

At this discourse, Candide fainted away a second time; but coming to himself, and having said all that he ought to say, he enquired into the cause and the effect, and into the sufficient reason that had reduced Pangloss to so deplorable a condition. ''Alas,'' said the other, ''it was love; love, the comforter of the human race, the preserver of the universe, the soul of all sensible beings, tender love.'' ''Alas!'' said Candide, ''I know this love, the sovereign of hearts, the soul of our soul; yet it never cost me more than a kiss, and twenty kicks. But how 320 could this charming cause produce in you so abominable an effect?''

Pangloss made answer as follows: ''Oh my dear Candide, you knew Paquetta, the pretty attendant on our noble Baroness; I tasted in her arms the delights of Paradise, which produced those torments of hell with which you see me devoured. She was infected,[22] and perhaps she is dead. Paquetta received this present from a very learned Franciscan, who had it from an old countess, who received it from a captain of horse, who 330 was indebted for it to a marchioness, who got it from one of the companions of Christopher Columbus. For my part, I shall give it to nobody, for I am dying.''

''Oh Pangloss!'' cried Candide, ''what a strange genealogy! Was not the devil at the head of it?'' ''Not at all,'' replied the great man; ''it was a thing indispensable; a necessary ingredient in the best of worlds; for if Columbus had not caught, in an island of

America, this disease, we should have had neither chocolate nor cochineal. It may also be observed, that 340 to this day, upon our continent, this malady is as peculiar to us, as is religious controversy. The Turks, the Indians, the Persians, the Chinese, the Siamese, and the Japanese, know nothing of it yet. But there is sufficient reason why they, in their turn, should become acquainted with it, a few centuries hence. In the mean time, it has made marvellous progress among us, and especially in those great armies composed of honest hirelings, well disciplined, who decide the fate of states; for we may rest assured, that when thirty thousand men 350 in a pitched battle fight against troops equal to them in number, there are about twenty thousand of them on each side who have the pox.''

''This is admirable,'' said Candide; ''but you must be cured.'' ''Ah! how can I?'' said Pangloss; ''I have not a penny, my friend; and throughout the whole extent of this globe, we cannot get any one to bleed us, or give us a glister, without paying for it, or getting some other person to pay for us.''

This last speech determined Candide. He went and 360 threw himself at the feet of his charitable Anabaptist James, and gave him so touching a description of the state his friend was reduced to, that the good man did not hesitate to entertain Dr. Pangloss, and he had him cured at his own expense. During the cure, Pangloss lost only an eye and an ear. As he wrote well, and understood arithmetic perfectly, the Anabaptist made him his bookkeeper. At the end of two months, being obliged to go to Lisbon on account of his business, he took the two philosophers along with him, in his ship. 370 Pangloss explained to him how every thing was such as it could not be better; but James was not of this opinion. ''Mankind,'' said he, ''must have somewhat corrupted their nature; for they were not born wolves, and yet they have become wolves; God has given them neither cannon of twenty-four pounds, nor bayonets; and yet they have made cannon and bayonets to destroy one another, I might throw into the account bankrupts; and the law which seizes on the effects of bankrupts only to bilk the creditors.'' ''All this was 380 indispensable,'' replied the one-eyed doctor, '' and private misfortunes constitute the general good; so that the more private misfortunes there are, the whole is the better.'' While he was thus reasoning, the air grew dark, the winds blew from the four quarters of the world, and the ship was attacked by a dreadful storm, within sight of the harbor of Lisbon.

Chapter 5

Tempest, Shipwreck, Earthquake and What Became of Dr. Pangloss, Candide and James the Anabaptist.

One half of the passengers being weakened, and ready to breathe their last, with the inconceivable anguish which the rolling of the ship conveyed through the 390 nerves and all the humors of the body, which were quite disordered, were not capable of being alarmed at the

---

[21]Raped.

[22]With venereal disease; syphilis, which entered Europe in the late fifteenth century, was one of the most virulent legacies of the Euro-American exchange.

danger they were in. The other half uttered cries and made prayers; the sails were rent, the masts broken, and the ship became leaky. Every one worked that was able, nobody cared for any thing, and no order was kept. The Anabaptist contributed his assistance to work the ship. As he was upon deck, a furious sailor rudely struck him, and laid him sprawling on the planks; but with the blow he gave him, he himself was so violently jolted, that he tumbled overboard with his head foremost, and remained suspended by a piece of a broken mast. Honest James ran to his assistance, and helped him on deck again; but in the attempt, he fell into the sea, in the sight of the sailor, who suffered him to perish, without deigning to look upon him. Candide drew near and saw his benefactor, one moment emerging, and the next swallowed up for ever. He was just going to throw himself into the sea after him, when the philosopher Pangloss hindered him, by demonstrating to him, that the road to Lisbon had been made on purpose for this Anabaptist to be drowned in. While he was proving this, *a priori*, the vessel foundered, and all perished except Pangloss, Candide, and the brutal sailor, who drowned the virtuous Anabaptist. The villain luckily swam ashore, whither Pangloss and Candide were carried on a plank.

When they had recovered themselves a little, they walked towards Lisbon. They had some money left, with which they hoped to save themselves from hunger, after having escaped from the storm.

Scarce had they set foot in the city, bewailing the death of their benefactor, when they perceived the earth to tremble under their feet,[23] and saw the sea swell in the harbor, and dash to pieces the ships that were at anchor. The whirling flames and ashes covered the streets and public places, the houses tottered, and their roofs fell to the foundations, and the foundations were scattered; thirty thousand inhabitants of all ages and sexes were crushed to death in the ruins. The sailor, whistling and swearing, said "There is some booty to be got here." "What can be the sufficient reason of this phenomenon?" said Pangloss. "This is certainly the last day of the world," cried Candide. The sailor ran quickly into the midst of the ruins, encountered death to find money, found it, laid hold of it, got drunk, and having slept himself sober, purchased the favors of the first willing girl he met with, among the ruins of the demolished houses, and in the midst of the dying and the dead. While he was thus engaged, Pangloss pulled him by the sleeve; "My friend," said he, "this is not right; you trespass against universal reason, you choose your time badly." "Brains and blood!" answered the other; "I am a sailor, and was born at Batavia; . . . you have found the right man, this time, with your universal reason."

Some pieces of stone having wounded Candide, he lay sprawling in the street, and covered with rubbish. "Alas!" said he to Pangloss, "get me a little wine and oil; I am dying." "This trembling of the earth is no new thing," answered Pangloss. "The City of Lima, in America, experienced the same concussions last year;

the same cause has the same effects; there is certainly a train of sulphur under the earth, from Lima to Lisbon." "Nothing is more probable," said Candide; "but, for God's sake, a little oil and wine." "How probable?" replied the philosopher; "I maintain that the thing is demonstrable." Candide lost all sense, and Pangloss brought him a little water from a neighbouring fountain.

The day following, having found some provisions, in rumaging through the rubbish, they recruited their strength a little. Afterwards, they employed themselves like others, in administering relief to the inhabitants that had escaped from death. Some citizens that had been relieved by them, gave them as good a dinner as could be expected amidst such a disaster. It is true that the repast was mournful, and the guests watered their bread with their tears. But Pangloss consoled them by the assurance that things could not be otherwise; "For," said he, "all this must necessarily be for the best. As this volcano is at Lisbon, it could not be elsewhere; as it is impossible that things should not be what they are, as all is good."

A little man clad in black, who belonged to the Inquisition,[24] and sat at his side, took him up very politely, and said: "It seems, sir, you do not believe in original sin; for if all is for the best, then there has been neither fall nor punishment."

"I most humbly ask your excellency's pardon," answered Pangloss, still more politely; "for the fall of man and the curse necessarily entered into the best of worlds possible." "Then, sir, you do not believe there is liberty," said the inquisitor. "Your Excellency will excuse me," said Pangloss; "liberty can consist with absolute necessity; for it was necessary we should be free; because, in short, the determinate will————"

Pangloss was in the middle of his proposition, when the inquisitor made a signal with his head to the tall armed footman in a cloak, who waited upon him, to bring him a glass of port wine.

Chapter 6

How a Fine *Auto-da-Fé*[25] Was Celebrated to Prevent Earthquakes, and How Candide Was Whipped.

After the earthquake, which had destroyed three-fourths of Lisbon, the sages of the country could not find any means more effectual to prevent a total destruction, than to give the people a splendid *auto-da-fé*. It had been decided by the university of Coimbra, that the spectacle of some persons burnt to death by a slow fire, with great ceremony, was an infallible antidote for earthquakes.

---

[23]The first Lisbon earthquake and fire took place on November 1, 1755. It destroyed much of the city and took almost 40,000 lives.

[24]An officer of the Inquisition, a special church court designed to try heretics; the officer was empowered to arrest anyone he suspected of heresy.

[25]The public ceremony (literally, "act of faith") by which those found guilty of heresy were punished.

In consequence of this resolution, they had seized a Biscayan, convicted of having married his god-mother,[26] and two Portuguese, who, in eating a pullet, had stripped off the bacon.[27] After dinner, they came and secured Dr. Pangloss, and his disciple Candide; the one for having spoke too freely, and the other for having heard with an air of approbation. They were both conducted to separate apartments, extremely damp, and never incommoded with the sun.[28] Eight days after, they were both clothed with a gown and had their heads—adorned with paper crowns.[29] Candide's crown and gown were painted with inverted flames, and with devils that had neither tails nor claws; but Pangloss' devils had claws and tails, and the flames were pointed upwards. Being thus dressed, they marched in procession, and heard a very pathetic speech followed by fine music on a squeaking organ. Candide was whipped on the back in cadence, while they were winging; the Biscayan, and the two men who would not eat lard, were burnt; and Pangloss, though it was contrary to custom, was hanged. The same day, the earth shook anew,[30] with a most dreadful noise.

Candide, affrighted, interdicted, astonished, all bloody, all panting, said to himself: "If this is the best of possible worlds, what then are the rest? Supposing I had not been whipped now, I have been so, among the Bulgarians; but, Oh, my dear Pangloss; thou greatest of philosophers, that it should be my fate to see thee hanged without knowing for what! Oh! my dear Anabaptist! thou best of men, that it should be thy fate to be drowned in the harbor! Oh! Miss Cunegonde! the jewel of ladies, that it should be thy fate to have been outraged and slain!"

He returned, with difficulty, supporting himself, after being lectured, whipped, absolved, and blessed, when an old woman accosted him, and said: "Child, take courage, and follow me."

Chapter 7

How an Old Woman Took Care of Candide, and How He Found the Object He Loved.

Candide did not take courage, but he followed the old woman to a ruinated house. She gave him a pot of pomatum[31] to annoint himself, left him something to eat and drink, and showed him a very neat little bed, near which was a complete suit of clothes. "Eat, drink, and sleep," said she to him, "and may God take care of you. I will be back to-morrow." Candide, astonished at all he

had seen, at all he had suffered, and still more at the charity of the old woman, offered to kiss her hand. "You must not kiss my hand," said the old woman, "I will be back to-morrow. Rub yourself with the pomatum, eat and take rest."

Candide, notwithstanding so many misfortunes, ate, and went to sleep. Next morning, the old woman brought him his breakfast, looked at his back, and rubbed it herself with another ointment; she afterwards brought him his dinner; and she returned at night, and brought him his supper. The day following she performed the same ceremonies. "Who are you," would Candide always say to her; "Who has inspired you with so much goodness? What thanks can I render you?" The good woman made no answer; she returned in the evening, but brought him no supper. "Come along with me," said she, "and say not a word." She took him by the arm, and walked with him into the country about a quarter of a mile; they arrived at a house that stood by itself, surrounded with gardens and canals. The old woman knocked at a little door, which being opened, she conducted Candide by a private stair-case into a gilded closet, and leaving him on a brocade couch, shut the door and went her way. Candide thought he was in a revery, and looked upon all his life as an unlucky dream, but at the present moment, a very agreeable vision.

The old woman returned very soon, supporting with difficulty a woman trembling, of a majestic port, glittering with jewels, and covered with a veil. "Take off that veil," said the old woman to Candide. The young man approached and took off the veil with a trembling hand. What joy! what surprise! he thought he saw Miss Cunegonde; he saw her indeed! it was she herself. His strength failed him, he could not utter a word, but fell down at her feet. Cunegonde fell upon the carpet. The old woman applied aromatic waters; they recovered their senses, and spoke to one another. At first, their words were broken, their questions and answers crossed each other, amidst sighs, tears and cries. The old woman recommended them to make less noise, and then left them to themselves. "How! is it you?" said Candide; "are you still alive? do I find you again in Portugal? You were not ravished then, as the philosopher Pangloss assured me?" "Yes, all this was so," said the lovely Cunegonde; "but death does not always follow from these two accidents." "But your father and mother! were they not killed?" "It is but too true," answered Cunegonde, weeping. "And your brother?" "My brother was killed too." "And why are you in Portugal? and how did you know that I was here? and by what strange adventure did you contrive to bring me to this house?" "I will tell you all that, presently," replied the lady; "but first you must inform me of all that has happened to you, since the harmless kiss you gave me, and the rude kicking which you received for it."

Candide obeyed her with the most profound respect; and though he was forbidden to speak, though his voice was weak and faltering, and though his back still pained

---

[26]A swipe at papal efforts to condemn as incestuous marriages in which the parties might be bound by family relation.

[27]Unwittingly revealing that they were secretly Jews—Jewish dietary laws prohibit the eating of pork. Under the pressure of the Spanish and Portuguese Inquisitions, many Iberian Jews had converted to Christianity.

[28]Prison cells.

[29]Yellow penitential garments worn by the confessed heretic.

[30]A second earthquake occurred in Lisbon on December 21, 1755.

[31]Ointment.

him, yet he related to her, in the most artless manner, every thing that had befallen him since the moment of their separation. Cunegonde lifted up her eyes to heaven; she shed tears at the death of the good Anabaptist, and of Pangloss; after which she thus related her adventures to Candide, who lost not a word, but looked on her, as if he would devour her with his eyes.

Chapter 8

The History of Cunegonde

"I was in my bed and fast asleep, when it pleased heaven to send the Bulgarians to our fine castle of Thunder-ten-tronckh; they murdered my father and my brother, and cut my mother to pieces. A huge Bulgarian, six feet high, perceiving the horrible sight had deprived me of my senses, set himself to ravish me. This abuse made me come to myself; I recovered my senses, I cried, I struggled, I bit, I scratched, I wanted to tear out the huge Bulgarian's eyes, not considering that what had happened in my father's castle, was a common thing in war. The brute gave me a cut with his knife, the mark of which I still bear about me." "Ah! I anxiously wish to see it," said the simple Candide. "You shall," answered Cunegonde; "but let me finish my story." "Do so," replied Candide.

She then resumed the thread of her story, as follows: "A Bulgarian captain came in, and saw me bleeding; but the soldier was not at all disconcerted. The Captain flew into a passion at the little respect the brute showed him, and killed him upon my body. He then caused me to be dressed, and carried me as a prisoner of war to his own quarters. I washed the scanty linen he had, and cooked his meals. He found me very pretty, I must say it; and I cannot deny but he was well shaped, and that he had a white, soft skin; but for the rest, he had little sense or philosophy; one could plainly see that he was not bred under Dr. Pangloss. At the end of three months, having lost all his money, and being grown out of conceit with me, he sold me to a Jew, named *Don Issachar,* who traded to Holland and Portugal, and had a most violent passion for women. This Jew laid close siege to my person, but could not triumph over me; I have resisted him better that I did the Bulgarian soldier. A woman of honor may be ravished once, but her virtue gathers strength from such rudeness. The Jew, in order to render me more tractable, brought me to this country-house that you see. I always imagined hitherto, that no place on earth was so fine as the castle of Thunder-ten-tronckh; but I am now undeceived.

"The grand inquisitor observing me one day ogled me very strongly, and sent me a note, saying he wanted to speak with me upon private business. Being conducted to his palace, I informed him of my birth; upon which he represented to me, how much it was below my family to belong to an Israelite. A proposal was then made by him to Don Issachar, to yield me up to my Lord. But Don Issachar, who is the court-banker, and a man of credit, would not come into his measures. The inquisitor threatened him. At last, my Jew, being affrighted, concluded a bargain, by which the house and myself should belong to them both in common; the Jew to have possession Monday, Friday, and Saturday, and the inquisitor, the other days of the week. This agreement has now continued six months. It has not, however, been without quarrels; for it has been often disputed whether Saturday night or Sunday belonged to the old, or to the new law. For my part, I have hitherto disagreed with them both; and I believe that this is the reason I am still beloved by them.

"At length, to avert the scourge of earthquakes and to intimidate Don Issachar, it pleased his Lordship the inquisitor to celebrate. He did me the honor to invite me to it. I got a very fine seat, and the ladies were served with refreshments between the ceremonies. I was seized with horror at seeing them burn the two Jews, and the honest Biscayan who married his godmother; but how great was my surprise, my consternation, my anguish, when I saw in a sanbenito and mitre, a person that somewhat resembled Pangloss! I rubbed my eyes, I looked upon him very attentively, and I saw him hanged. I fell into a swoon, and scarce had I recovered my senses, when I saw you stripped stark naked; this was the height of horror, consternation, grief, and despair. I will frankly own to you, that your skin is still whiter, and of a better complexion than that of my Bulgarian captain. This sight increased all the sensations that oppressed and distracted my soul. I cried out, I was going to say stop, barbarians; but my voice failed me, and all my cries would have been to no purpose. When you had been severely whipped: How is it possible, said I, that the amiable Candide, and the sage Pangloss, should both be at Lisbon;—the one to receive a hundred lashes and the other to be hanged by order of my Lord the Inquisitor, by whom I am so greatly beloved? Pangloss certainly deceived me most cruelly, when he said that everything was for the best in this world.

"Agitated, astonished, sometimes beside myself, and sometimes ready to die with weakness; my head filled with the massacre of my father, my mother, and my brother, the insolence of the vile Bulgarian soldier, the stab he gave me with his hanger, my abject servitude, and my acting as a cook to the Bulgarian captain; the rascal Don Issachar, my abominable inquisitor; the execution of Dr. Pangloss, the grand music on the organ while you were whipped, and especially the kiss I gave you behind the screen, the last day I saw you. I praised the Lord for having restored you to me after so many trials. I charged my old woman to take care of you, and to bring you hither as soon as she could. She has executed her commission very well; I have tasted the inexpressible pleasure of seeing you, hearing you, and speaking to you. You must have a ravenous appetite, by this time; I am hungry myself, too; let us therefore, sit down to supper."

On this, they both sat down to table; and after supper, they seated themselves on the fine couch before mentioned. They were there, when Signor Don Issachar, one of the masters of the house, came in. It was his Sabbath day, and he came to enjoy his right, and to express his tender love.

[*Candide, Cunegonde and the old woman travel to Cadiz. The old woman recounts her past misfortunes. They sail to America, where Candide finds a South American paradise, El Dorado, filled with kind and reasonable people; however, he loses Cunegonde to a Spanish colonial nobleman. On his way back to Europe, Candide meets the disillusioned pessimist, Martin, who opens Candide's eyes to the evil in the world. Following various adventures in Europe, Candide travels to Turkey and encounters Pangloss, whom he had thought dead.*]

Chapter 29

How Candide Found Cunegonde and the Old Woman Again

While Candide, the Baron, Pangloss, Martin, and Cacambo, were relating their adventures to each other, and disputing about the contigent and non-contigent events of this world, and while they were arguing upon effects and causes, on moral and physical evil, on liberty and necessity, and on the consolations a person may experience in the galleys in Turkey, they arrive on the banks of the Propontis, at the house of the Prince of Transylvania. The first objects which presented themselves were Cunegonde and the old woman, hanging out some table-linen on the line to dry.

The Baron grew pale at this sight. Even Candide, the affectionate lover, on seeing his fair Cunegonde awfully tanned, with her eye-lids reversed, her neck withered, her cheeks wrinkled, her arms red and rough, was seized with horror, jumped near three yards backwards, but afterwards advanced to her, but with more politeness than passion. She embraced Candide and her brother, who, each of them, embraced the old woman, and Candide ransomed them both.

There was a little farm in the neighborhood, which the old woman advised Candide to hire, till they could meet with better accommodations for their whole company. As Cunegonde did not know that she had grown ugly, nobody having told her of it, she put Candide in mind of his promise to marry her, in so peremptory a manner, that he durst not refuse her. But when this thing was intimated to the Baron, "I will never suffer," said he, "such meanness on her part, nor such insolence on yours. With this infamy I will never be reproached. The children of my sister shall never be enrolled in the chapters[32] of Germany. No; my sister shall never marry any but a Baron of the empire. Cunegonde threw herself at her brother's feet, and bathed them with her tears, but he remained inflexible. "You ungrateful puppy, you," said Candide to him, "I have delivered you from the galleys; I have paid your

ransom; I have also paid that of your sister, who was a scullion here, and is very homely; I have the goodness, however, to make her my wife, and you are fool enough to oppose it; I have a good mind to kill you again, you make me so angry." "You may indeed kill me again," said the Baron; "but you shall never marry my sister, while I have breath."

Chapter 30

Conclusion

Candide had no great desire, at the bottom of his heart, to marry Cunegonde. But the extreme impertinence of the Baron determined him to conclude the match, and Cunegonde pressed it so earnestly, that he could not retract. He advised with Pangloss, Martin, and the trusty Cacambo. Pangloss drew up an excellent memoir, in which he proved, that the Baron had no right over his sister, and that she might, according to all the laws of the empire, espouse Candide with her left hand.[33] Martin was for throwing the Baron into the sea: Cacambo was of opinion that it would be best to send him back again to the Levant captain, and make him work at the galleys. This advice was thought good; the old woman approved it, and nothing was said to his sister about it. The scheme was put in execution for a little money, and so they had the pleasure of punishing the pride of a German Baron.

It is natural to imagine that Candide, after so many disasters, married to his sweetheart, living with the philosopher Pangloss, the philosopher Martin, the discreet Cacambo, and the old woman, and especially as he had brought so many diamonds from the country of the ancient Incas, must live the most agreeable life of any man in the whole world. But he had been so cheated by the Jews,[34] that he had nothing left but the small farm; and his wife, growing still more ugly, turned peevish and insupportable. The old woman was very infirm, and worse humored than Cunegonde herself. Cacambo, who worked in the garden, and went to Constantinople to sell its productions, was worn out with labor, and cursed his fate. Pangloss was ready to despair, because he did not shine at the head of some university in Germany. As for Martin, as he was firmly persuaded that all was equally bad throughout, he bore things with patience. Candide, Martin, and Pangloss, disputed sometimes about metaphysics and ethics. They often saw passing under the windows of the farmhouse boats full of effendis, bashaws, and cadis,[35] who were going into banishment to Lemnos, Mitylene, and Erzerum. They observed that other cadis, other bashaws, and other effendis, succeeded in the posts of those who were exiled, only to be banished themselves

---

[32]Noble assemblies.

[33]A marriage that denies noble status to the party of the lower rank.
[34]Voltaire's anti-semitism seems to have been the result of financial losses he suffered from the bankruptcies of Jewish moneylenders.
[35]Highranking members of the Turkish nobility.

in turn. They saw heads nicely impaled, to be presented to the Sublime Porte. These spectacles increased the number of their disputations; and when they were not disputing, their *ennui* was so tiresome that the old woman would often say to them, "I want to know which is the worst;—to be ravished an hundred times by negro pirates, to run the gauntlet among the Bulgarians, to be whipped and hanged, to be dissected, to row in the galleys; in a word, to have suffered all the miseries we have undergone, or to stay here, without doing anything?" "That is a great question," said Candide. 820

This discourse gave rise to new reflections, and Martin concluded upon the whole, that mankind were born to live either in the distractions of inquietude, or in the lethargy of disgust. Candide did not agree with that opinion, but remained in a state of suspense. Pangloss confessed, that he had always suffered dreadfully; but having once maintained that all things went wonderfully well, he still kept firm to his hypothesis, though it was quite opposed to his real feelings. 830

What contributed to confirm Martin in his shocking principles, to make Candide stagger more than ever, and to embarrass Pangloss, was, that one day they saw Paquetta and Girofflee, who were in the greatest distress, at their farm. They had quickly squandered away their three thousand piastres,[36] had parted, were reconciled, quarrelled again, had been confined in prison, had made their escape, and Girofflee had at length turned Turk. Paquetta continued her trade wherever she went, but made nothing by it. "I could easily foresee," said Martin to Candide, "that your presents would soon be squandered away, and would render them more miserable. You and Cacambo have spent millions of piastres, and are not a bit happier than Girofflee and Paquetta." "Ha! ha!" said Pangloss to Paquetta, "has Providence then brought you amongst us again, my poor child? Know, then, that you have cost me the tip of my nose, one eye, and one of my ears, as you see. What a world this is!" This new adventure set them a philosophizing more than ever. 840

850

There lived in the neighborhood a very famous dervish, who passed for the greatest philosopher in Turkey. They went to consult him. Pangloss was chosen speaker, and said to him, "Master, we are come to desire you would tell us, why so strange an animal as man was created." 860

"What's that to you?" said the dervish; "is it any business of yours?" "But, my reverend father," said Candide, "there is a horrible amount of evil in the world." "What does it matter," said the dervish, "whether there be good or evil? When his Sublime Highness send a vessel to Egypt, does it trouble him, whether the mice on board are at their ease or not?" "What would you have one do then?" said Pangloss. "Hold your tongue," said the dervish. "I promised myself the pleasure," said Pangloss, "of reasoning with 870

you upon effects and causes, the best of possible worlds, the origin of evil, the nature of the soul, and the pre-established harmony."—The dervish, at these words, shut the door in their faces.

During this conference, news was brought that two viziers and a mufti were strangled at Constantinople, and a great many of their friends impaled. This catastrophe made a great noise for several hours. Pangloss, Candide, and Martin, on their way back to the little farm, met a good-looking old man, taking the air at his door, under an arbor of orange trees. Pangloss, who had as much curiosity as philosophy, asked him the name of the mufti who was lately strangled. "I know nothing at all about it," said the good man; "and what's more, I never knew the name of a single mufti, or a single vizier, in my life. I am an entire stranger to the story you mention; and presume that, generally speaking, they who trouble their heads with state affairs, sometimes die shocking deaths, not without deserving it. But I never trouble my head about what is doing at Constantinople; I content myself with sending my fruits thither, the produce of my garden, which I cultivate with my own hands!" Having said these words, he introduced the strangers into his house. His two daughters and two sons served them with several kinds of sherbet, which they made themselves, besides caymac, enriched with the peels of candied citrons, oranges, lemons, ananas, pistachio nuts, and Mocha coffee, unadulterated with the bad coffee of Batavia and the isles. After which, the two daughters of this good Muslim perfumed the beards of Candide, Pangloss, and Martin. 880

890

900

"You must certainly," said Candide to the Turk, "have a very large and very opulent estate!" "I have only twenty acres," said the Turk; "which I, with my children, cultivate. Labor keeps us free from three of the greatest evils; boredom, vice, and need."

As Candide returned to his farm, he made deep reflections on the discourse of the Turk. Said he to Pangloss and Martin, "The condition of this good old man seems to me preferable to that of the six kings with whom we had the honor to dine." "The grandeurs of royalty," said Pangloss, "are very precarious, in the opinion of all philosophers. For, in short, Eglon, king of the Moabites, was assassinated by Ehud; Absalom was hung by the hair of his head, and pierced through with three darts; King Nadab, the son of Jeroboam, was killed by Baasha; King Elah by Zimri; Ahaziah by Jehu; Athaliah by Jehoiadah; the kings Joachim, Jechonias, and Zedekias, were carried into captivity. You know the fates of Croesus, Astyages, Darius, Dionysius of Syracuse, Pyrrhus, Perseus, Hannibal, Jugurtha, Ariovistus, Caesar, Pompey, Nero, Otho, Vitellius, Domitian, Richard II, Edward II, Henry VI, Richard III, Mary Stuart, Charles I of England, the three Henrys of France, and the Emperor Henry IV.[37] You know———" 910

920

---

[36]Spanish dollars; pieces of eight.

[37]All rulers who came to a bad end.

"I know very well," said Candide, "that we ought to look after our garden." "You are in the right," said Pangloss, "for when man was placed in the garden of Eden, he was placed there, *ut operatur cum*, to cultivate it; which 930 proves that mankind are not created to be idle." "Let us work," said Martin, "without disputing; it is the only way to render life supportable."

All their little society entered into this laudable design, according to their different abilities. Their little piece of ground produced a plentiful crop. Cunegonde was indeed very homely, but she became an excellent pastry cook. Paquetta worked at embroidery, and the old woman took care of the linen. There was no idle person in the company, not excepting even Girofflee; he 940 made a very good carpenter, and became a very honest man.

As to Pangloss, he evidently had a lurking consciousness that his theory required unceasing exertions, and all his ingenuity, to sustain it. Yet he stuck to it to the last; his thinking and talking faculties could hardly be diverted from it for a moment. He seized every occasion to say to Candide, "All the events in this best of possible worlds are admirably connected. If a single link in the great chain were omitted, the harmony 950 of the entire universe would be destroyed. If you had not been expelled from that beautiful castle, with those cruel kicks, for your love to Miss Cunegonde; if you had not been imprisoned by the inquisition; if you had not travelled over a great portion of America on foot; if you had not plunged your sword through the baron; if you had not lost all the sheep you brought from that fine country, Eldorado, together with the riches with which they were laden, you would not be here to-day, eating preserved citrons, and pistachio nuts." 960

"That's very well said, and may all be true," said Candide; "but let's cultivate our garden."

◆

The Visual Satires of William Hogarth

Like Voltaire and Swift, the English artist William Hogarth (d. 1764) was a master of that most potent weapon of ridicule: satire. Hogarth's paintings and prints are a living record of the ills of eighteenth-century British society. He illustrated the novels of Defoe and Swift, including *Gulliver's Travels,* and executed a series of paintings based on John Gay's *The Beggar's Opera*—a mock-heroic comedy that equated low-class crime with high-class corruption. Popular novels and plays provided inspiration for what Hogarth called his "modern moral subjects"; while the theater itself prompted many of the devices he used for pictorial representation: the boxlike staging, the lighting from below, and a wealth of "props." "I have

endeavored," he wrote, "to treat my subjects as a dramatic writer: my picture is my stage, and men and women my actors."

Hogarth made engraved versions of his own paintings and sold them, just as Diderot sold the volumes of the *Encyclopédie,* by subscription. So popular were these prints that they were pirated and sold without his authorization (a practice that continued even after Parliament passed the first copyright law in 1735). Especially successful were two series of prints based on his paintings. The first series illustrated the misfortunes of a young woman who becomes a London prostitute (*The Harlot's Progress*); the second reported the comic misadventures of an antihero and ne'er-do-well named Tom Rakewell (*The Rake's Progress*). Following these, Hogarth published a series of six engravings entitled *Marriage à la Mode* (1742–64), which depicted the tragic consequences of a marriage of convenience between the son of a poverty-stricken nobleman and the daughter of a wealthy and ambitious merchant. The first print in the series, *The Marriage Transaction,* shows the two families transacting the terms of the matrimonial union (figure 25.1). The scene unfolds as if upon a stage: the corpulent Lord Squanderfield, victim of the gout (an ailment traditionally linked with rich food and drink) sits pompously in his ruffed velvet waistcoat, pointing to his family tree, which springs from the loins of William the Conqueror. Across the table, the wealthy merchant and father of the bride carefully peruses the financial terms of the marriage settlement. On a settee in the corner of the room, the pawns of this socially expedient match turn away from each other in attitudes of mutual dislike. The earl's son, young Squanderfield, sporting a beauty patch, opens his snuffbox and vainly gazes at himself in a mirror, while his bride-to-be idly dangles her betrothal ring on a kerchief. She leans forward to hear the honeyed words of her future seducer, a lawyer named Lord Silvertongue. A combination of **caricature** (exaggeration of peculiarities or defects), comic irony, and symbolic detail, Hogarth's "stylish marriage" is drawn with a stylus as sharp as Voltaire's pen.

Like Voltaire's Paris, Hogarth's London was not yet an industrial city, but it was plagued by some of the worst urban conditions of the day. It lacked sewers, streetlights, and adequate law enforcement. A city of vast contrasts between rich and poor, it was crowded with thieves, drunks, and prostitutes, all of whom threatened the jealously guarded privileges of the rich. Hogarth represented mid-eighteenth-century London at its worst in the famous engraving *Gin Lane* (figure 25.3). This devastating attack on the combined evils of urban poverty and alcoholism portrays poor, ragged,

FIGURE 25.3 *Gin Lane,* William Hogarth, 1751. Engraving. Reproduced by courtesy of the Trustees of the British Museum, London.

and drunk men and women in various stages of depravity. Some pawn their possessions to support their expensive addictions (*lower left*); others commit suicide (*upper right corner*) and one pours gin down the throat of a babe-in-arms, following the common practice of using liquor and other drugs to quiet noisy infants (*far right*). In the center of the print is the figure of a besotted mother—her leg covered with syphilitic sores—who carelessly allows her child to fall over the edge of the stair rail. Hogarth's visual satirization of gin addiction was a heroic attack on the social conditions of his time and on drug abuse in general. But even Parliament's passage of the Gin Law in 1751, which more than doubled the gin tax, did little to reduce the widespread use of gin in eighteenth-century England. While Hogarth's prints failed to reduce the ills and inequities of his society, they remain an enduring condemnation of human hypocrisy, cruelty, vanity, and greed.

Rousseau's Revolt Against Reason

Jean Jacques Rousseau, introduced in chapter 24 as a contributor to Diderot's *Encyclopédie,* was a novelist, playwright, composer, and educator. He was also one of the Enlightenment's most outspoken critics. Rousseau took issue with some of the basic precepts of Enlightenment thought, including the idea that the progress of the arts and sciences might improve human conduct. Human beings may be good by nature, argued Rousseau, but they are ultimately corrupted by society and its institutions. "God makes all things good," wrote Rousseau; "man meddles with them and they become evil." Rousseau flatly rejected the artificiality of civilized life, and although he did not advocate that humankind should return to a "state of nature," he exalted the "noble savage" as the model of the uncorrupted individual. Rousseau's philosophy of the heart elevated the role of instinct over reason and encouraged a new appreciation of nature and the natural—principles that underlay the romantic movement of the early nineteenth century (chapters 27–29). In the following excerpt from *Discourse on the Origin of Inequality among Men* (1755), Rousseau gives an eloquent account of how human beings came to lose their freedom and innocence.

READING 93 From Rousseau's *Discourse on the Origin of Inequality among Men*

The first man who, having enclosed a piece of land, thought of saying "This is mine" and found people simple enough to believe him, was the true founder of civil society. How many crimes, wars, murders; how much misery and horror the human race would have been spared if someone had pulled up the stakes and filled in the ditch and cried out to his fellow men: "Beware of listening to this impostor. You are lost if you forget that the fruits of the earth belong to everyone and that the earth itself belongs to no one!" But it is highly probable that by this time things had reached a point beyond which they could not go on as they were; for the idea of property, depending on many prior ideas which could only have arisen in successive stages, was not formed all at once in the human mind. It was necessary for men to make much progress, to acquire much industry and knowledge, to transmit and increase it from age to age, before arriving at this final stage of the state of nature. Let us therefore look farther back, and try to review from a single perspective the slow succession of events and discoveries in their most natural order.

Man's first feeling was that of his existence, his first concern was that of his preservation. The products of the earth furnished all the necessary aids; instinct prompted him to make use of them. While hunger and other appetites made him experience in turn different modes of existence, there was one appetite which urged him to perpetuate his own species; and this blind impulse, devoid of any sentiment of the heart, produced only a purely animal act. The need satisfied, the two sexes recognized each other no longer, and even the child meant nothing to the mother, as soon as he could do without her.

Such was the condition of nascent[38] man; such was the life of an animal limited at first to mere sensation; and scarcely profiting from the gifts bestowed on him by nature, let alone was he dreaming of wresting anything from her. But difficulties soon presented themselves and man had to learn to overcome them. The height of trees, which prevented him from reaching their fruits; the competition of animals seeking to nourish themselves on the same fruits; the ferocity of animals who threatened his life—all this obliged man to apply himself to bodily exercises; he had to make himself agile, fleet of foot, and vigorous in combat. Natural weapons—branches of trees and stones—were soon found to be at hand. He

learned to overcome the obstacles of nature, to fight when necessary against other animals, to struggle for his subsistence even against other men, or to indemnify[39] himself for what he was forced to yield to the stronger.

[Rousseau then describes how people devised a technology for hunting and fishing, invented fire, and developed superiority over other creatures.]

Instructed by experience that love of one's own wellbeing is the sole motive of human action, he found himself in a position to distinguish the rare occasions when common interest justified his relying on the aid of his fellows, and those even rarer occasions when competition should make him distrust them. In the first case, he united with them in a herd, or at most in a sort of free association that committed no one and which lasted only as long as the passing need which had brought it into being. In the second case, each sought to grasp his own advantage, either by sheer force, if he believed he had the strength, or by cunning and subtlety if he felt himself to be the weaker. . . .

. . . the habit of living together generated the sweetest sentiments known to man, conjugal love and paternal love. Each family became a little society, all the better united because mutual affection and liberty were its only bonds; at this stage also the first differences were established in the ways of life of the two sexes which had hitherto been identical. Women became more sedentary and accustomed themselves to looking after the hut and the children while men went out to seek their common subsistence. The two sexes began, in living a rather softer life, to lose something of their ferocity and their strength; but if each individual became separately less able to fight wild beasts, all, on the other hand, found it easier to group together to resist them jointly. . . .

To the extent that ideas and feelings succeeded one another, and the heart and mind were exercised, the human race became more sociable, relationships became more extensive and bonds tightened. People grew used to gathering together in front of their huts or around a large tree; singing and dancing, true progeny[40] of love and leisure, became the amusement, or rather the occupation, of idle men and women thus assembled. Each began to look at the others and to want to be looked at himself; and public esteem came to be prized. He who sang or danced the best; he who was the most handsome, the strongest, the most adroit[41] or the most eloquent became the most highly regarded, and this was the first step toward inequality and at the same time toward vice. From those first preferences there arose, on the one side, vanity and scorn, on the other, shame and envy, and the fermentation produced by these new leavens[42] finally produced compounds fatal to happiness and innocence.

---

[38]Early, developing.

[39]Compensate.
[40]Offspring.
[41]Skillful.
[42]Significant changes.

As soon as men learned to value one another and the idea of consideration was formed in their minds, everyone claimed a right to it, and it was no longer possible for anyone to be refused consideration without affront. This gave rise to the first duties of civility, even among savages: and henceforth every intentional wrong became an outrage, because together with the hurt which might result from the injury, the offended party saw an insult to his person which was often more unbearable than the hurt itself. Thus, as everyone punished the contempt shown him by another in a manner proportionate to the esteem he accorded himself, revenge became terrible, and men grew bloodthirsty and cruel. This is precisely the stage reached by most of the savage peoples known to us; and it is for lack of having sufficiently distinguished between different ideas and seen how far those peoples already are from the first state of nature that so many authors have hastened to conclude that man is naturally cruel and needs civil institutions to make him peaceable, whereas in truth nothing is more peaceable than man in his primitive state. Placed by nature at an equal distance from the stupidity of brutes[43] and the fatal enlightenment of civilized man, limited equally by reason and instinct to defending himself against evils which threaten him, he is restrained by natural pity from doing harm to anyone, even after receiving harm himself: for according to the wise Locke: "Where there is no property, there is no injury."

But it must be noted that society's having come into existence and relations among individuals having been already established meant that men were required to have qualities different from those they possessed from their primitive constitution. . . .

As long as men were content with their rustic huts, as long as they confined themselves to sewing their garments of skin with thorns or fishbones, and adorning themselves with feathers or shells, to painting their bodies with various colors, to improving or decorating their bows and arrows; and to using sharp stones to make a few fishing canoes or crude musical instruments; in a word, so long as they applied themselves only to work that one person could accomplish alone and to arts that did not require the collaboration of several hands, they lived as free, healthy, good and happy men. . . .

. . . but from the instant one man needed the help of another, and it was found to be useful for one man to have provisions enough for two, equality disappeared, property was introduced, work became necessary, and vast forests were transformed into pleasant fields which had to be watered with the sweat of men, and where slavery and misery were soon seen to germinate and flourish with the crops.

---

[43]Beasts.

◆

Rousseau was haunted by contradictions within the social order and within his own mind (he fought insanity during the last fifteen years of his life). The opening words of his treatise, *The Social Contract* (1762), "Man is born free, and everywhere he is in chains," reflect his apprehension concerning the inhibiting role of institutional authority. In order to safeguard individual liberty, said Rousseau, people should form a contract among themselves. Unlike Hobbes, whose social contract involved transferring absolute authority from the citizens to a sovereign ruler, or Locke, whose social contract gave limited power to the ruler, Rousseau defined the state as nothing more than "the general will" of its citizens. "The general will alone," he explained, "can direct the State according to the object for which it was instituted, that is, the common good." Rousseau insisted, moreover, that whoever refused to obey the general will should be constrained to do so by the whole society; that is, all humans should "be forced to be free." "As nature gives each man absolute power over all his members," wrote Rousseau, "the social compact gives the body politic absolute power over all its members also." Such views might have contributed to nascent theories of democracy, but they were equally effective in justifying totalitarian constraints leveled in the name of the people.

Rousseau's wish to preserve the natural also led him to propose revolutionary changes in education. If society is indeed hopelessly corrupt, then let children grow up in accord with nature, argued Rousseau. In *Émile* (1762), his treatise on education, Rousseau advanced the hypothesis—unheard of in his time—that the education of a child begins at birth. He divided childhood development into five stages over a twenty-five-year span and outlined the type of rearing desirable for each stage. "Hands-on" experience was essential to education, according to Rousseau, especially in the period just prior to the development of reason and intellect, which he placed between the ages of twelve and fifteen. "Nature provides for the child's growth in her own fashion, and this should never be thwarted. Do not make him sit still when he wants to run about, nor run when he wants to be quiet." Rousseau also made a clear distinction between the education of men and that of women. Arguing that a woman's place was in the home and beside the cradle, he proposed for her a domestic education that cultivated modesty, obedience, and other virtues agreeable to her mate. Thus, Rousseau's views on women's education were not radically different from those advanced by Castiglione some two hundred years earlier in *The Book of the Courtier* (chapter 16). Nevertheless, *Émile* became a land-mark in educational theory, and Rousseau's new approach to education—particularly his emphasis on the cultivation of natural inquisitiveness over and above rote learning—influenced modern teaching methods ories such as those developed by the Italian educator Maria Montessori (d. 1952). Ironically, however, Rousseau saw fit to put all five of his own children in a foundling hospital rather than raise them himself.

Kant's Revolt Against Reason

The German philosopher Immanuel Kant (d. 1804) was the last and greatest philosopher of the Enlightenment. "Awakened from his slumber," as he put it, by reading the writings of Rousseau and the treatises of the Scottish philosopher David Hume (d. 1776), Kant shifted the focus of philosophic debate from a concern with the empirical method and the nature of objective reality to the question of cognition itself—the process by which the mind comprehends experience. Hume had proposed that human knowledge depended on habits of the mind that connected the individual units of sense experience. Such habits, said Hume, led to mistaken notions of cause and effect. In attacking the principle of causality, Hume undermined all knowledge. "The gentle skeptic," as Hume was called, doubted that individuals could know anything other than the contents of their own consciousness. One could neither prove the existence of God nor rely on reason to account for moral action, since human values, argued Hume, were based on sentiment, not rational thought.

Kant rejected Hume's skepticism by asserting that human beings have knowledge of what is physical through certain innate capabilities of the mind. The "categories" of causality, space, and time, for instance, which exist in the mind from birth, transform and order the experience that comes to us through our senses, said Kant. In the *Critique of Pure Reason* (1781), Kant described the mechanics of human cognition—an effort that required some nine hundred pages of dense German prose. His view of the mind as an active agent that constructs our idea of the world laid the basis for philosophic **idealism**, the theory that reality consists of the mind and its ideas.

Like most eighteenth-century intellectuals, Kant was a moralist who tried to define general rules for human behavior. Recognizing that notions of good and evil varied widely among different groups of people, Kant sought an absolute ethical system that would transcend individual circumstances. In the *Critique of Practical Reason* (1788), he proposed a general moral law called the "categorical imperative": We should act as we wish everyone else would act, that is, act as if we could will our actions to

become laws for all humankind. The basis of this moral law is "good will," which, said Kant, operates from within human beings and can not be imposed from without. It is not enough that our acts have good effects; what is necessary is that we *will* the good. Such goodwill is not, however, identical with love. Kant's "categorical imperative" differs from Jesus' commandment to "Do to others as you would wish them to do to you," because for Kant, ethical conduct is based not in love for humankind but in respect for the imperative to do what is good, a respect essential to human dignity.

The Revolutions of the Late Eighteenth Century

The American and French Revolutions drew inspiration from the Enlightenment faith in the reforming power of reason. Both, however, demonstrated the limits of reason in achieving social change. As early as 1776, America's thirteen colonies had rebelled against the long-standing political control of the British government. In the Declaration of Independence (Reading 86), Jefferson restated Locke's assertion that government must protect the rights of citizens in their life, liberty, and property. The British government, however, in making unreasonable demands for revenues, threatened colonial liberty. In 1783, following some seven years of armed conflict, several thousand battle deaths, and a war expense estimated at over $100 million, the thirteen North American colonies achieved their independence. And, in 1789, they began to function under the Constitution of the United States of America. The American hero Thomas Paine (d. 1809) asserted that the Revolution had done more to enlighten the world and diffuse a spirit of freedom among humankind than any event that had preceded it.

The American Revolution did not go unnoticed in France. French intellectuals followed its every turn; the French government secretly aided the American cause and eventually joined in the war against Great Britain. However, the revolution that began on French soil in 1789 involved circumstances that were quite different from those in America. The British colonies had not sought to overturn long-standing social and political institutions or to end upper-class privilege, for, in North America, there was neither a manorial system nor a feudal aristocracy. The French Revolution, on the other hand, was the product of two major sets of problems: class inequality and a serious financial crisis—brought about by some five hundred years of costly wars and royal extravagances (chapter 23). With his nation on the verge of bankruptcy, King Louis XVI sought new measures for raising revenue.

FIGURE 25.4 **The Siege of the Bastille, July 14, 1789. Engraving. Pierpont Morgan Library, New York City, bequest of Gordon N. Ray, GNR 78 (plate #16).**

Throughout French history, taxes had fallen exclusively on the shoulders of the lower and middle classes, the so-called Third Estate. Almost four-fifths of the average peasant's income went to pay taxes, which supported the privileged upper classes. In a population of some 25 million people, the First Estate (the clergy) and the Second Estate (the nobility)—a total of only 200,000 citizens—controlled nearly half the land in France; yet they were exempt from paying taxes. When, in 1789, in an effort to obtain public support for new taxes, King Louis XVI called a meeting of the Estates General—its first meeting in 175 years—the Third Estate withdrew and, declaring itself representative of the general will of the people, formed a separate body claiming the right to approve or veto all taxation. This daring act set the Revolution in motion. No sooner had the Third Estate declared itself a national assembly than great masses of peasants and laborers began to riot throughout France. Peasant grievances were not confined to matters of taxation: population growth and rising prices led to severe

shortages of bread, the principal food of the lower classes. In Paris, a working-class mob attacked a symbol of royal power, the state prison known as the Bastille (figure 25.4). The spirit of revolt animates the following excerpt from the eyewitness account of J. B. Humbert, a French clockmaker who participated in the storming of the Bastille on July 14, 1789.

READING 94 From Humbert's *Account of July 14, 1789*

I immediately made my way to the Bastille, passing   1
through the courtyard of the Arsenal; it was about half-
past three; the first bridge had been lowered, and the
chains cut; but the portcullis[44] barred the way; people
were trying to bring in some cannon which had
previously been dismantled; I crossed over by the small
bridge and from the further side helped to bring in the
two guns.

---

[44]The iron gateway at the entrance to the Bastille.

When they had been set up on their gun-carriages again, everybody with one accord drew up in rows of five or six, and I found myself in the front rank. 10

In this array we marched to the drawbridge of the fortress; on either side of this I saw two dead soldiers lying; the one on my left was wearing the uniform of the Vintimille regiment;[45] I could not make out that of the soldier lying on my right.

The cannon were then levelled: the bronze gun at the large drawbridge and a small iron one, inlaid with silver, at the small bridge. . . .

We each fired half-a-dozen shots. Then a paper was 20 thrust through an oval gap a few inches across; we ceased fire; one of our number stepped forward and went to the kitchen to fetch a plank so as to collect the paper; this plank was laid on the parapet; many people stood on it to weigh it down: one man started out along it, but just as he was about to take the paper, he was killed by a shot and fell into the moat.

Another man, carrying a flag, immediately dropped his flag and went to fetch the paper, which was then read out loud and clearly, so that everyone could hear. 30

The contents of this message, which offered capitulation, proving unsatisfactory, we decided to fire the gun; everyone stood aside to let the cannon-ball pass.

Just as we were about to fire, the small drawbridge was lowered; it was promptly filled by a crowd of people, of whom I was about tenth. We found the gate behind the drawbridge closed: after a couple of minutes a Pensioner[46] came to open it, and asked what we wanted: 'Give up the Bastille,' I replied, as did everyone 40 else: then he let us in. My first concern was to call for the bridge to be lowered; this was done.

Then I entered the main courtyard (I was about eighth or tenth). The Pensioners were lined up on the right, the Swiss guards on the left; we shouted; 'lay down your arms,' which they did, except for one Swiss officer. I went up to him and threatened him with my bayonet, repeating: 'lay down your arms.' He appealed to all present: 'Gentlemen, please believe me, I never fired.' 50

I immediately said to him: 'How dare you say you never fired, when your lips are still black from biting your cartridge?' As I said this, I pounced on his sword; another fellow did the same; as the two of us were arguing as to which should have the sword, I happened to glance at a staircase on my left, and I saw three citizens who had gone up five or six steps and were hurrying down again; I immediately left the sword and, armed with my rifle, which I had never abandoned, I rushed over to the staircase to help the citizens, whom I 60 assumed to have been driven back; I rapidly climbed up to the keep. . . . In the keep I found a Swiss soldier squatting down with his back to me: I aimed my rifle at him, shouting: 'lay down your arms;' he turned round in surprise, and laid down his weapons saying: 'Comrade,

don't kill me, I'm for the Tiers État[47] and I will defend you to the last drop of my blood; you know I'm obliged to do my job; but I haven't fired.'

While he was speaking thus I picked up his rifle, then, poking him in the stomach with my bayonet, I 70 ordered him to hand over his cartridge-case and sling it round my neck, which he did.

Immediately afterwards I went to the cannon that stood just above the drawbridge of the Bastille, in order to push it off its gun-carriage and render it unusable. But as I stood for this purpose with my shoulder under the mouth of the cannon, someone in the vicinity fired at me, and the bullet pierced my coat and waistcoat and wounded me in the neck; I fell down senseless; the Swiss soldier whose life I had spared dragged me on to 80 the staircase, still clutching my gun, so he told me. . . .

When I recovered from my swoon I found myself sitting on the stairs; the Swiss guard had been shaking me to restore me to consciousness, and he had tried to staunch the blood that was pouring out of my wound with a piece of linen he had cut off my shirt.

[His wound is tended and he attempts to rejoin his comrades at the Bastille but is persuaded to return home to rest.]

I rested until about midnight, when I was woken by repeated cries of 'to arms! to arms!' Then I could not resist my longing to be of some further use; I got up, armed myself and went to the guardroom, where I found M. Poirier, the Commanding Officer, under whose orders 90 I remained until the following morning.

---

[47]Third Estate.

<hr />
◆
<hr />

The crowds that stormed the Bastille destroyed the visible symbol of the old French regime. Less than one month later, on August 4, the National Assembly—as the new body established by the Third Estate called itself—issued decrees that abolished the last remnants of medieval feudalism, including manorial courts, feudal privileges, and church tithes. It also made provisions for a limited monarchy and an elected legislative assembly. The decrees of the National Assembly became part of the Constitution of 1791. It was prefaced by the 1789 Declaration of the Rights of Man and Citizen, which was modeled on the American Declaration of Independence (chapter 23). A Declaration of the Rights of Woman and Citizen, drafted in 1791 by a butcher's daughter Olympe de Gouges, demanded equal rights for women, the sex de Gouges described as "superior in beauty and courage." (Indeed, in October of 1789 six thousand courageous women had marched on Versailles to protest the lack of bread in Paris.) For the first time in history women constituted a collective revolutionary

---

[45]The regiment from the city of Vintimille in Northern Italy.
[46]A salaried man-at-arms. Thirteen years later, in 1792, France established its first national army conscripted from among all classes of men.

force, making demands for equal property rights, government employment for women, and equal educational opportunities—demands guaranteed by the Constitution of 1793 but lost less than two years later by the terms of a new Constitution.

Enlightenment idealism, summed up in Rousseau's slogan "Liberty, Equality, Fraternity" had inspired armed revolt. Nevertheless, from the time of the storming of the Bastille through the rural revolts and mass protests that followed, angry, unreasoning mobs controlled the course of the Revolution. Divisions among the revolutionaries themselves led to a more radical phase of the Revolution, called the Reign of Terror. This phase ensured the failure of the government established in 1793 and sent Louis XVI and his queen to the guillotine. Between 1793 and 1794, over forty thousand people (including Olympe de Gouges) met their death at the guillotine. In 1794, a National Convention devised a system of government run by two legislative chambers and a five-man executive body of directors, one of whom, Napoleon Bonaparte, would turn France into a military dictatorship some five years later. If, indeed, the French Revolution defended the Enlightenment bastions of liberty and equality, its foundations of reason and rationality ultimately crumbled to the forces of extremism and violence. The radicals of this and many other world-historical revolutions to follow rewrote the words of the *philosophes* in blood.

Summary

The Enlightenment faith in the promise of reason, the cornerstone of eighteenth-century optimism, was tempered by an equally enlightened examination of the limits of reason. Among the keenest critics of Enlightenment idealism were Oliver Goldsmith, Jonathan Swift, and Voltaire. These three masters of satire found their Asian counterpart in Li Ju-chen, whose witty prose attacked long-standing Chinese traditions. Voltaire's *Candide* remains the classic statement of comic skepticism in Western literature. Voltaire's contemporary, William Hogarth, brought the bitter invective of the satirist to the visual arts. His engravings exposed the social ills and class discrepancies of British society, even as they mocked universal human pretensions.

Questioning the value of reason for the advancement of the human condition, Jean Jacques Rousseau argued that society itself corrupted the individual. He rejected the artificiality of the wig-and-silk-stocking

culture in which he lived and championed "man in his primitive state." Rousseau's treatises on social history, government, and education explored ways in which individuals might retain their natural goodness and remain free and self-determining. In Germany, the philosopher Immanuel Kant examined the limits of the mind in the process of knowing. He argued that human beings have knowledge of the world through certain innate capabilities of mind. Kant appealed to "good will" as the basis for moral action.

While Enlightenment ideals fueled armed revolt in both America and France, the revolutions themselves blazed with antirational sentiment. In France especially, the men and women who fired the cannons of revolt abandoned reason as inadequate to the task of effecting social and political reform. Operating according to the dictates of their passions and their will, they gave dramatic evidence of the limits of reason to create a heaven on earth. The shift away from reason and the rational was to have major repercussions in the centuries to follow.

GLOSSARY

caricature   exaggeration of peculiarities or defects to produce comic or burlesque effects
idealism   in philosophy, the theory that holds that reality consists of the mind and its ideas

SUGGESTIONS FOR READING

Babbitt, Irving. *Rousseau and Romanticism.* New York: Meridian, 1957.
Bernier, Olivier. *Words of Fire, Deeds of Blood: The Mob, the Monarchy, and the French Revolution.* Boston: Little, Brown, 1989.
Durant, Will and Ariel. *The Age of Voltaire.* Vol. IX of *The Story of Civilization.* New York: Simon and Schuster, 1965.
Gershoy, Leo. *From Despotism to Revolution, 1763–1789.* Westport, Conn.: Greenwood Press, 1983.
Jarrett, Derek. *England in the Age of Hogarth.* London: Hart-Davis MacGibbon, 1974.
Leith, James A. *The Idea of Art as Propaganda in France 1750–1799: A Study in the History of Ideas.* Toronto: University of Toronto Press, 1965.
Lindsay, Jack. *Hogarth: His Art and His World.* New York: Taplinger, 1979.
Richter, Peyton, and Ilona Ricardo. *Voltaire.* Boston: Twayne, 1980.

26

EIGHTEENTH-CENTURY ART, MUSIC, AND SOCIETY

The arts of eighteenth-century Europe responded to the dynamics of class and culture. European aristocrats found pleasure in an elegant and refined style known as the *rococo*. Toward the end of the century, middle-class bonds to Enlightenment idealism and a new appreciation of ancient Greece and Rome ushered in the *neoclassical* style. In music too, the era witnessed notable turns from the ponderous baroque to the more delicate and playful rococo, and then, in the 1780s, to the formal and measured sounds of the *classical* symphony and the string quartet. An increased demand for secular entertainment called forth new genres in instrumental music and a wide range of subject matter in the visual arts. Despite their stylistic diversity, the arts shared a spirit of buoyant optimism and vitality that ensured their endurance beyond the Age of the Enlightenment.

The Rococo Style

The rococo style was born in France among members of the leisured nobility that had outlived Louis XIV. At Versailles and in the elegant urban townhouses (*hôtels*) of Paris, where the wealthy gathered to enjoy the pleasures of dancing, dining, and conversing, the rococo provided an atmosphere of elegant refinement (figure 26.1). The word "rococo" derives from a combination of *rocailles* and *coquilles* (French for "pebbles" and "seashells")—objects that were commonly used to ornament aristocratic gardens and grottoes.

Rococo interiors display the organic vitality of seashells, plants, and flowers. And while rococo artists preserved the ornate and luxuriant features of the baroque style, they favored elements of play and intimacy that were best realized in works of a small scale, such as porcelain figurines, furniture, and paintings suitable for domestic quarters.

The Salon de la Princesse in the Hôtel de Soubise in Paris typifies the rococo style (figure 26.2): its interior is airy and fragile by comparison with a Louis XIV *salon* (figure 23.9). Brilliant white walls accented with pastel tones of rose, pale blue, and lime replace the deep reds and royal blues of the baroque *salon*. The geometric regularity of the baroque interior has given way to an organic network of curves and countercurves, echoed in elegant mirrors and chandeliers. The walls, ornamented with gilded tendrils, cupids, and floral garlands, melt into sensuously painted ceiling vaults crowned with graceful moldings.

Rococo furnishings are generally more delicate than baroque furnishings, and chairs are often fully upholstered—an innovation of the eighteenth century. Bureaus and tables may be fitted with panels of porcelain (figure 26.3)—a Chinese technique that Marie Antoinette, the consort of Louis XVI, introduced at Versailles. Aristocratic women, especially such notable females as Marie Antoinette in France, Catherine in Russia, and Maria Theresa in Austria, helped to shape the rococo style.

FIGURE 26.1　The Grand Ball. © The Bettmann Archive.

FIGURE 26.2　Salon de la Princesse, Hotel de Soubise, Paris, Germain Boffrand, ca. 1740. Oval, 33 ft. × 26 ft. Giraudon/Art Resource, New York.

FIGURE 26.3 *Lady's desk,* Martin Carlin (master 1766–85) ca. 1775. Decorated with Sèvres porcelain plaques; tulipwood, walnut, and hardwood veneered on oak. Height 31 7/8 in., width 25 7/8 in., diameter 16 in. The Metropolitan Museum of Art, New York City, gift of Samuel H. Kress Foundation, 1958 (58.75.49).

Beyond the *salon,* the garden was the favorite setting for the leisured elite. Unlike the geometrically ordered garden parks at Versailles, rococo gardens imitated the calculated naturalism of Chinese gardens (chapter 23). They featured undulating paths that gave false impressions of scale and distance. They also often included artificial lakes, small colonnaded temples, ornamental pagodas, and other architectural "follies." Both outdoors and in, the fascination with Chinese objects, which began as a fashion in Europe around 1720, preserved the cult of *chinoiserie* (chapter 23).

Although the rococo style originated in France, it reached spectacular heights in the courts of secular princes at Wurzburg, Munich, Salzburg, and Vienna. In Austria and in the German states, it became the favorite style for the ornamentation of rural pilgrimage churches. In the Benedictine Church of Ottobeuren

in Bavaria, designed by the German architect Johann Michael Fischer (d. 1766), walls seem to disappear beneath a riot of stucco "frosting" as rich and sumptuous as any wedding cake (figure 26.4). The more restrained elegance of French rococo interiors here gives way to a dazzling array of organic forms that sprout from the moldings and cornices like unruly flora. Shimmering light floods into the white-walled interior through oval windows, and pastel-colored frescoes turn ceilings and walls into heavenly antechambers. Illusionism reigns: wooden columns and stucco cornices are painted to look like marble; angels and cherubs, tendril and leaves, curtains and clouds—all made of wood and stucco that has been painted and gilded—come to life as props in a theater of miracles (figure 26.5). At Ottobeuren, the somber majesty of the Roman baroque church has given way to a bright vision of paradise that is as well a feast for the senses.

Rococo Painting in France

The pursuit of pleasure—a major eighteenth-century theme—dominates the paintings of the four rococo masters: Antoine Watteau (d. 1721), François Boucher (d. 1770), Marie-Louise-Élisabeth Vigée-Lebrun (d. 1842), and Jean-Honoré Fragonard (d. 1806). The Flemish-born Watteau began his career by painting theatrical scenes. In 1717, he submitted to the French Academy the *Departure from the Island of Cythera,* a painting that pays tribute to the fleeting nature of romantic love (figure 26.6). Its subject was the *fête galante* (literally, "elegant entertainment"), a festive diversion featuring fashionably dressed men and women in a parklike setting. Here, on the mythical island of Cythera, birthplace of Venus, a party of richly dressed aristocrats pays homage to the Goddess of Love, whose rose-bedecked shrine appears at the far right. Amidst fluttering cupids, the pilgrims of love linger in groups of twos as they wistfully take leave of their florid hideaway. Watteau repeats the serpentine line formed by the figures in the delicate arabesques of the trees and rolling hills. And he bathes the entire panorama in a misty, golden light. Not since Giorgione and Titian had any painter indulged so deeply in the pleasures of nature or the voluptuous world of the senses.

Watteau's fragile forms and delicate colors, painted with feathery brushstrokes reminiscent of Rubens, capture affections of reverie and nostalgia. His

FIGURE 26.4   Benedictine Abbey, interior, Johan Michael Fischer, Ottobeuren, Bavaria, 1736–66. Vanni/Art Resource, New York.

doll-like men and women provide sharp contrast with Rubens' physically powerful figures (figure 23.17) or, for that matter, with Poussin's idealized heroes (figure 23.14). Watteau's art conveys no noble message; rather, it evokes a mood of melancholy. That mood is superbly realized in the sketches he executed in **pastels**, a chalk medium suited to capturing fleeting effects. In one red and black chalk drawing, Watteau offers an intimate view of a nude female whose casual gesture evokes a sense of languor and dancelike grace (figure 26.7).

If Watteau's world was wistful and poetic, that of his contemporary François Boucher was sensual and indulgent. Boucher, a specialist in designing mythological scenes, became director of the royal Gobelins tapestry factory in 1755. He was first painter to King Louis XV and a good friend of the king's favorite mistress, Madame de Pompadour. In the idyllic *Venus*

FIGURE 26.5   Cherubs, Ottobeuren. Marburg/Art Resource, New York.

FIGURE 26.6 *Departure from the Island of Cythera,* Jan Antoine Watteau, 1917. Oil on canvas, 51 in. × 76 in. Louvre, Paris. Art Resource, New York.

FIGURE 26.7 *Half-Nude Women,* Antoine Watteau, ca. 1720. Red and black chalk on yellow paper, 11 in. × 9 in. Louvre, Cliché des Musée Nationaux, Paris. Photo: © R.M.N.

FIGURE 26.8 *Venus Consoling Love,* François Boucher, 1751. Oil on canvas, 42 1/8 in. × 33 1/8 in. National Gallery of Art, Washington, D.C. Gift of Chester Dale.

Consoling Love, Boucher flattered his patron by portraying her as Goddess of Love (figure 26.8). Surrounded by attentive doves and cupids, the nubile Venus reclines on a bed of sumptuous rose and satin draperies laid amidst a bower of leafy trees and windswept grasses. Boucher delighted in the sensuous contrasts of flesh, fabric, feathers, and flowers. And his girlish women, with their unnaturally tiny feet, rosebud pink nipples, and wistful glances were coy symbols of erotic pleasure.

Boucher also produced designs for eighteenth-century tapestries and porcelains. From the Sèvres porcelain factory, located near Paris and sponsored by Madame de Pompadour, came magnificent porcelains ornamented with gilded wreaths, arabesque cartouches, and playful cupids floating on fleecy clouds

(figure 26.9). Outside of France, in Germany and Austria, porcelain figurines of shepherds and shepherdesses advertised the eighteenth-century enthusiasm for the pastoral life.

Fashion and fashionableness—clear expressions of self-conscious materialism—were major themes of rococo art. Marie-Louise-Élisabeth Vigée-Lebrun (d. 1842), the most famous of a number of eighteenth-century female artists, produced refined portrait paintings for an almost exclusively female clientele. Her glamorous likeness of Marie Antoinette, the consort of Louis XVI, is a tribute to the fashion industry of the time (figure 26.10). Plumed headdresses and low-cut gowns bedecked with lace, ribbons, and tassels turned the aristocratic female into a conspicuous

FIGURE 26.9 Sèvres porcelain potpourri vase. Gondola-shaped body, scrolled handles, 4 lobed cover, height 14 1/8 in., length 14 1/2 in., width. 8 in. This vase, purchased by Mme. Pompadour, is one of the finest products of the Sèvres porcelain factory that she sponsored and patronized. The Metropolitan Museum of Art, New York City, gift of Samuel H. Kress Foundation, 1958 (58.75.88 a,b,c).

FIGURE 26.10 *Marie Antoinette,* **Elizabeth Vigée-Lebrun, 1778. Oil on canvas, 36 3/4 × 29 7/16 in. Versailles Chateau, France. Giraudon/Art Resource, New York.**

ornament: the size of her billowing skirt required that she turn sideways to pass through open doors. In response to the upper-class infatuation with pastoral and idyllic themes, Vigée-Lebrun also painted more modest portraits of women in muslin skirts and straw hats. Unlike Boucher, Vigée-Lebrun did not cast her subjects as goddesses, but she imparted to them a *chic* sweetness and artless simplicity. These talents earned her the equivalent of over $200,000 a year and allowed her an independence uncommon among eighteenth-century women.

Jean-Honoré Fragonard, the last of the great rococo artists, was the undisputed master of translating the art of seduction into paint. In the works he completed shortly before the French Revolution, he captured the pleasures of a waning aristocracy. In

FIGURE 26.11 *The Swing*, Jean-Honoré Fragonard, 1768. Oil on canvas, 32 in. × 35 in. The Wallace Collection, London. Art Resource, New York.

1766, a wealthy aristocrat commissioned Fragonard to paint a scene that showed the patron's mistress seated on a swing being pushed by a friendly old clergyman. *The Swing* depicts a flirtatious encounter that takes place in a garden bower filled with frothy trees, classical statuary, and delicate light. The young woman, dressed in yards of satin and lace, kicks her tiny shoe into the air in the direction of a statue of Cupid, while her lover, hiding in the bushes below, peers delightedly beneath her billowing skirts (figure 26.11). Whether or not the young lady is aware of her lover's presence, her coy gesture and the irreverent behavior of the *ménage à trois* (lover, mistress, and cleric) create a mood of erotic intrigue similar to that found in the comic operas of this period. Fragonard's deft brushstrokes caress the figures and render the surrounding foliage in delicate pastel tones. Although Fragonard immortalized the union of wealth, privilege, and pleasure enjoyed by the upper classes of the eighteenth century, he captured a spirit of sensuous abandon that has easily outlived the particulars of time, place, and social class.

FIGURE 26.12 *The Intoxication of Wine,* Claude Clodion, ca. 1775. Terra-cotta, height, 23 1/4 in. The Metropolitan Museum of Art, New York City, bequest of Benjamin Altman, 1913 (14.40.687).

Rococo Sculpture

Rococo sculpture was small in scale, intimate in mood, and almost entirely lacking in the dramatic urgency and religious fervor of baroque art. Intended for the *boudoir* or the drawing room, rococo sculpture usually depicted elegant dancers, wooing couples, and other lighthearted subjects. The French sculptor Claude Michel, known as Clodion (d. 1814), who worked almost exclusively for private patrons, was among the favorite rococo artists of the late eighteenth century. His *Intoxication of Wine* revived a classical theme—a celebration honoring Dionysus, the Greek god of wine and fertility (figure 26.12). Flushed with wine and revelry, the **satyr** (a part-bestial woodland creature symbolic of Dionysus) embraces a **bacchante,** an attendant of Dionysus. Clodion made the piece in terra-cotta, a clay medium that requires rapid modeling, thus inviting the artist to capture a sense of spontaneity. Rococo painters sought similar effects through the use of loose and rapid brushstrokes and by sketching with pastels (figure 26.6). The expressive impact of *The Intoxication by Wine* belies its tiny size—it is just under two feet high.

Eighteenth-Century French Genre Painting

Many of the *philosophes* found the works of Boucher, Clodion, and other rococo artists trivial and morally degenerate. Diderot, for example, denounced rococo *boudoir* imagery and demanded an art that made "virtue attractive and vice odious." The French artists Jean-Baptiste Greuze (d. 1805) and Jean-Baptiste-Siméon Chardin (d. 1779) heeded the plea for art with a moral purpose. These artists abandoned the indulgent sensuality and frivolity of the rococo; instead they painted realistic scenes of everyday life among the middle and lower classes. In the spirit of eighteenth-century bourgeois novelists (chapter 24), they described human emotions and day-to-day events.

Greuze, Diderot's favorite artist, exalted the simple life and natural virtues of ordinary people. He painted such moralizing subjects as *The Father Reading the Bible to His Children, The Well-Beloved Mother,* and *The Effects of Drunkenness.* In the manner of Hogarth (whose works Greuze admired), he chose themes that sometimes required a series of paintings. Greuze's *Village Betrothal* of 1761 tells the story of an impending matrimony among hardworking, simple-living rustics: the father, who has just given over the dowry to the humble groom, blesses the couple; the mother laments losing a daughter; while the other members of the household, including the hen and chicks (possibly a symbol of the couple's prospective progeny), look on approvingly (figure 26.13). Greuze's painting could easily have been an illustration of a scene from a popular eighteenth-century novel. Greuze shunned the intellectualism of Poussin (figure 23.14), the sensuality of Fragonard (figure 26.11), and the satirical acrimony of Hogarth (figure 25.1). His melodramatic representations appealed to common emotion and sentiment. Understandably, they were among the most popular images of the eighteenth and nineteenth centuries.

The art of Greuze's contemporary Chardin was less steeped in sentimentality. Chardin painted still lifes and scenes showing nurses, governesses, and kitchen maids at work (figure 26.14). Unlike Greuze, who illustrated his moral tales as literally as possible, Chardin avoided both explicit moralizing and anecdotal themes. Yet Chardin's paintings bear a deep concern for commonplace humanity, and they carry an implicit message—that of the ennobling dignity of work and the virtues of domesticity. The forthright qualities of Chardin's subjects are echoed in his style: His figures are simple and monumental, and his compositions reveal an uncanny sense of balance reminiscent of the works of de Hooch and Vermeer.

FIGURE 26.13 *Village Betrothal,* Jean Baptiste Greuze, 1761. Oil on canvas, 46 1/2 in. × 36 in. Louvre, Paris. Alinari/Art Resource, New York.

Each object in the painting seems to assume its proper and predestined place. Executed in mellow, creamy tones, Chardin's paintings evoke a mood of gentility and gravity.

Greuze and Chardin brought painting out of the drawing room and into the kitchen. Their work had enormous popular appeal and was in such demand that their pieces were sold widely in engraved copies. Ironically, while Chardin's subjects were humble and commonplace, his patrons were often bankers, foreign ambassadors, and royalty itself—Louis XV owned at least two of Chardin's paintings.

Eighteenth-Century Neoclassicism

Neoclassicism, the self-conscious revival of Greco-Roman culture, belonged to a tradition that stretched at least from the early Renaissance through the Age of Louis XIV. During the seventeenth century, the European Academies had resurrected this culture by way of Raphael, the High Renaissance standard-bearer of classicism. The neoclassicism of the eighteenth-century, however, differed from earlier revivals in that

FIGURE 26.14 *The Kitchen Maid,* Jean Baptiste Siméon Chardin, 1738. Oil on canvas, 18 1/8 in × 14 3/4 in. National Gallery of Art, Washington, D.C., Samuel H. Kress Collection.

FIGURE 26.15 *View of the Forum*, #15, Giovanni Battista Piranesi, ca. 1748–78. From *Views of Rome*. Etching. The Metropolitan Museum of Art, New York City, Rogers Fund, 1941. (41.7.1 [16]).

for the first time in history, artists and antiquarians made clear distinctions between the artifacts of Greece and those of Rome. The result was a more austere and archaeologically correct neoclassicism than any previous to the eighteenth century.

Rome had been a favorite attraction for well-educated tourists and students of art since Renaissance times. But during the eighteenth century, the old imperial capital received renewed attention. Architects studied the monuments of antiquity (figure 7.11), and artists made topographic sketches, often reproduced in copper engravings that were sold cheaply—in the manner of modern-day postcards. In 1740 the Venetian architect and engineer Giovanni Battista Piranesi (d. 1778) established himself in Rome as a printmaker. Piranesi's engravings of Rome's architectural treasures were widely bought and appreciated (figure 9.8), while his precise studies of Roman ruins exerted considerable influence on French and English architects (figure 26.15). Piranesi's later works—nightmarish visions of dungeons inspired by the Roman sewer system—abandoned all classical canons of objectivity and emotional restraint. Nevertheless, with European artists more eager than ever to rediscover antiquity through the careful study of its remains, the neoclassical revival was under way.

In 1738, two years before Piranesi came to Rome, the king of Naples sponsored the first archeological excavations at Herculaneum, one of the Roman cities in Southern Italy buried under volcanic ash by the eruption of Mount Vesuvius in A.D. 79. These excavations, followed by European archeological expeditions to Greece and Asia Minor in 1750, aroused widespread interest in classical culture and inspired scholars to assemble vast collections of Greek and Roman artifacts (figure 26.16). Shortly after the first English expeditions to Athens, the German scholar Johann Joachim Winckelmann (d. 1768) began to study Greek and Roman antiquities. He published the results in magnificently illustrated and widely circulated texts such as his *History of Ancient Art* (1764).

FIGURE 26.16 *Picture Gallery, (Roma Antica)*, Giovanni Paolo Panini (copy after), Italian (Roman), 1691–1765. Pen and black ink with brush and gray wash and watercolor over graphite on ivory laid paper, 17 1/4 × 27 3/16 in. Emily Crane Chadbourne Collection, 1955.7.45. © 1991 The Art Institute of Chicago. All rights reserved.

Although Winckelmann himself never visited Greece, he was infatuated with Hellenic and Hellenistic sculpture. He argued that artists of his time could become great only by imitating the ancient Greeks, whose best works, he insisted, betrayed "a noble simplicity and a quiet grandeur." Of his favorite ancient statue, the *Apollo Belvedere* (figure 26.19, *left*), Winckelmann proclaimed, "In the presence of this miracle of art, I forget the whole universe and my soul acquires a loftiness appropriate to its dignity." Winckelmann's reverence for antiquity typified the eighteenth-century attitude toward classicism as a vehicle for the elevation of human consciousness. Here, finally, was a style that mirrored the Enlightenment program of reason, clarity, and order, a style that equated Beauty with Goodness, Virtue, and Truth. Winckelmann's publications became an inspiration for artists and aesthetes all over Europe. In England, Sir Joshua Reynolds (d. 1792), the British painter and founder of the British Royal Academy of Art, lectured on the Grand Manner; his *Discourses* were translated into French, German, and Italian. The lofty vision of a style that captured the nobility and dignity of the Greco-Roman past fired the imagination of intellectuals across Western Europe and America.

Neoclassical Architecture

The classical revival of the eighteenth century was unique in its accuracy of detail and its purity of design. Neoclassical architects made careful distinctions between Greek and Roman buildings and between the various Renaissance and post-Renaissance styles modeled upon antiquity. Simple geometric masses—spheres, cubes, and cylinders—became the bases for a new, more abstract classicism. Neoclassical architects rejected the illusionistic theatricality of the baroque style—its broken pediments, cartouches, and ornamental devices—along with the stucco foliage, cherubic angels, and "wedding-cake" fantasies of the rococo. The ideal neoclassical exterior was free of frivolous ornamentation, and its interior consisted of clean and rectilinear wall planes, soberly accented with engaged columns or pilasters, geometric motifs, and shallow niches that housed copies of antique statuary (figures 24.2 and 26.19).

In France, the leading architect of the eighteenth century was Jacques Germain Soufflot (d. 1780). Soufflot's Church of Saint Geneviève (figure 26.17), the patron saint of Paris, follows a strict central plan with four shallow domes covering each of the arms. A massive central dome, supported entirely on pillars, rises

FIGURE 26.17 Church of Saint Geneviève (renamed the Panthéon during the French Revolution), Paris, Jacques Germain Soufflot, 1757–92.

over the crossing (compare Saint Paul's in London, figure 21.1). The facade of Saint Geneviève resembles the portico of the Panthéon in Rome (figure 7.8), while the interior of the church (figure 26.18)—which entombs, among others, Voltaire and Rousseau—recalls the grandeur of Saint Peter's in Rome. As the "Panthéon" illustrates, Soufflot did not slavishly imitate any single classical structure; rather, he selected specific features from a variety of notable sources and combined them with clarity and reserve. In contrast with its baroque and rococo ancestors, the Church of Saint Geneviève was no theater of miracles but rather a rationally ordered, this-worldly shrine.

Some of the purest examples of the classical revival are found in late eighteenth-century English country homes. The interiors of these sprawling symbols of wealth and prestige reflect close attention to archeological drawings of Greek and Roman antiquities. Kedleston Hall in Derbyshire, England, designed by the Scottish architect Robert Adam (d. 1792), reflects a pristine taste for crisp contours and the refined synthesis of Greco-Roman motifs (figure 26.19). In such estates as this, the neoclassical spirit touched everything from sculpture (figure 26.20) and furniture to tea services and tableware. Among the most popular items of the day were the ceramics of the English potter Josiah Wedgewood (d. 1795), which were modeled on Greek and Roman vases and embellished with raised, white surface designs (figure 26.21).

The austerity and dignity of neoclassicism made it the ideal style for public monuments and offices of state. In Paris, Berlin, and Washington D.C., neoclassical architects borrowed Greek and Roman temple designs for public and private buildings, including

FIGURE 26.18   Saint Geneviève (Panthéon) interior, Paris. Photo: A. F. Kersting.

FIGURE 26.19   Marble Hall, Robert Adam, 1763–77. Kedleston Hall, Derbyshire, England. (Note copy of the Apollo Belvedere in niche at left.) Photo: A. F. Kersting.

FIGURE 26.20 *Pauline Borghese as Venus,* Antonio Canova, 1808. Marble, life size. Galleria Borghese, Rome. Alinari/Art Resource, New York.

FIGURE 26.21 Apsley Pellot-Rickman copy of the Portland vase (#7), Josiah Wedgwood and others. Black and white jasper ware, height, 10 in. Museum of Fine Arts, Boston. Gift of Lloyd E. Hawes.

and especially banks, where the modern-day gods of money and materialism took the place of the ancient deities. In some instances, the spirit of revival produced architectural hybrids. In England, for instance, the Scottish architect James Gibbs (d. 1754) designed churches that combined a classical portico with a Gothic spire (figure 26.22). This scheme, which united the baroque love of contrast with the neoclassical rule of symmetry, became extremely popular in America, especially in congregational churches built across New England.

Neoclassicism in America

A tour of the city of Washington in the District of Columbia will convince any student of the impact of neoclassicism on the architecture of the United States. The neoclassical movement in America did not originate, however, in the capital city, whose major buildings date from the nineteenth century, but, rather, among the Founding Fathers. One of the most passionate devotees of Greco-Roman art and life was the Virginia lawyer and statesman Thomas Jefferson (d. 1826), whose Declaration of Independence was discussed in chapter 24. Farmer, linguist, educator, in-

FIGURE 26.22   Saint Martin-in-the-Fields, James Gibbs, London, 1721–26. Photo: A. F. Kersting.

ventor, architect, musician, and politician, the man who served as third president of the United States was an eighteenth-century *uomo universale* (figure 26.23). Jefferson was a student of ancient and Renaissance treatises on architecture and an apostle of neoclassicism. In 1786, he designed the Virginia State Capitol (figure 7.14) modeled on the Maison Carrée (figures 7.13 and 26.31). For his own country estate in Monticello and for the University of Virginia—America's first state university—he drew on the Pantheon of Rome, which he greatly admired. Jefferson reconstructed this ancient temple ·at two-thirds its original size in the Rotunda, which housed the original library of the University of Virginia (figure

26.24). Considerably smaller than Soufflot's "Panthéon," the stripped-down Rotunda is also purer in form. Jefferson's tightly organized and geometrically correct plan for the campus of the University of Virginia reflects the basic sympathy between neoclassical design and the ideals of Enlightenment rationalism. The "academical village," as Jefferson described it, was a community of the free-thinking elite—exclusively white, wealthy, and male—yet, it provided both a physical and a spiritual model for nonsectarian education in the United States.

   The young American nation drew on the heritage of the ancients, and especially the history of the Roman Republic, to symbolize its newly forged commitment to the ideals of liberty and equality. The

FIGURE 26.23 *Thomas Jefferson*, **Jean Antoine Houdon, 1789. Marble, New York Historical Society.**

leaders of the American Revolution regarded themselves as descendants of ancient Roman heroes and some even adopted Latin names, much as the Italian Renaissance humanists had done. On the Great Seal of the United States, as on the earliest American coins and paper currency, the Latin phrase *"E pluribus unum"* ("out of many, one") and the *fasces* (the bundle of rods and an axe that signified Roman authority) identified America as heir to republican Rome (figure 26.25).

Neoclassical Sculpture

Neoclassical sculptors heeded the Enlightenment demand for an art that perpetuated the memory of illustrious men. Jean-Antoine Houdon (d. 1828), the leading portrait sculptor of Europe, immortalized the features of his contemporaries in stone. His portrait busts, which met the popular demand for achieving a familiar likeness, revived the realistic tradition in sculpture that had reached its high watermark among the Romans. Houdon had a special talent for catching characteristic gestures and expressions: Diderot, shown without a wig, surveys his world with inquisitive candor (figure 24.3), while the aging Voltaire addresses us with a grim smile (figure 25.2). While visiting America, Houdon carved portraits of Jefferson (figure 26.23), Franklin, and other "virtuous men" of the republic. His life-size statue of George Washington renders the first president of the United States

FIGURE 26.24 **University of Virginia, rotunda, Thomas Jefferson. Prints Collection, Special Collections Department, University Archives, University of Virginia Library.**

FIGURE 26.25 *Great Seal of the United States.* Courtesy of the Bureau of Printing and Engraving, U.S. Treasury Dept.

as country gentleman and eminent statesman (figure 26.26). Resting his hand on a columnar *fasces,* the poised but slightly potbellied Washington recalls (however faintly) the monumental dignity of the Greek gods (figure 26.19) and the Roman emperors (figure 7.2).

While Houdon invested neoclassicism with a strong taste for realism, most of his contemporaries followed the Hellenic impulse to idealize the human form. Such was the case with the Italian-born sculptor Antonio Canova (d. 1822). Canova's life-size portrait of Napoleon Bonaparte's sister, Pauline Borghese, is a sublime example of neoclassical refinement and restraint (figure 26.20). Canova casts Pauline in the guise of a reclining Venus. Perfectly proportioned and flawless, she shares the cool elegance of classical statuary and Wedgewood reliefs (figure 26.21). In contrast to the vigorously carved surfaces of baroque sculpture (recall, for instance, Bernini's *Ecstasy of St. Teresa,* figure 20.1), Canova's figure is smooth and neutral—even stark. A comparison of Canova's Venus with Clodion's *Intoxication of Wine* (figure 26.12) is also revealing: both depend on classical themes and models, but whereas Clodion's piece is intimate, sensuous, and spontaneous, Canova's seems remote, controlled, and calculated. Its aesthetic distance is intensified by the ghostlike whiteness of the figure and its "blank" eyes—eighteenth-century sculptors seem to have been unaware that classical artists painted parts of their statues to make them look more lifelike.

FIGURE 26.26 *George Washington,* Jean Antoine Houdon. Marble, height, 74 in. State capitol, Richmond, Virginia. Virginia State Library and Archives.

Neoclassical Painting and Politics: The Art of David

During the last decades of the eighteenth century, as the tides of revolution began to engulf the indulgent life-styles of the French aristocracy, the rococo style in painting gave way to a soberminded new approach to picture-making led by the French artist Jacques-Louis David (d. 1825). David's early canvases were executed in the rococo style of his teacher and distant cousin, Boucher. But after winning the coveted Prix de Rome, which sent him to study in the foremost city of antiquity, David found his place among the classicists. In 1782 he completed the painting that would launch him to fame: the *Oath of the Horatii* (figure 26.27). The painting was commissioned by the French king some eight years before the outbreak of the Revolution; ironically, however, it became a symbol of the very spirit that would topple the royal crown.

FIGURE 26.27 *Oath of the Horatii,* Jacques Louis David, 1785. Oil on canvas, 10 ft. 10 in. × 14 ft. The Toledo Museum of Art. Gift of Edward Drummond Libbey.

The *Oath of the Horatii* illustrates a dramatic event recorded by Livy in his *History of Rome.* It depicts the moment when the sons of the noble Horatius Proclus swear to oppose three members of the treacherous Curiatii family in a win-or-die battle that would determine the future of Rome. In France, Livy's story had become especially popular as the subject of a play by the French dramatist Pierre Corneille (d. 1684). David captured the spirit of the story in a single image: the three brothers lift their arms in a dramatic military salute, thus committing themselves to their destiny as the defenders of liberty. Bathed in a golden light, the sculpturesque figures stand along the strict horizontal line of the picture plane. The body of the left-most warrior forms a rigid triangular shape that is subtly repeated throughout the composition—in the arches of the colonnade, for instance, and in the group

of grieving women (one of whom represents the fiancée of a Curiatii). According to the tale, her victorious brother, the sole survivor of the combat, returned home to find her mourning for her dead lover and murdered her in a fit of rage.

The painting was an immediate success. People lined up to see it while it hung in David's studio in Rome, and the city of Paris received it enthusiastically when it arrived there in 1785. The huge canvas (over 10 by 14 feet in size) was a clear denunciation of aristocratic pastimes: It replaced the lace cuffs, silk suits, and powdered wigs of the rococo with the trappings of war. It presented life as serious drama rather than frivolous pleasure. It proclaimed the importance of reason and the intellect over and above feeling and sentiment. And it defended the noble ideals of heroism and self-sacrifice in the interest of one's country. Stylistically too, the painting was revolutionary: David rejected the luxuriant sparkle of rococo art for sober

FIGURE 26.28 *The Death of Socrates,* Jacques Louis David, 1787. Oil on canvas, 77 1/4 in. × 51 in. The Metropolitan Museum of Art, New York City, Catharine Lorillard Wolfe Collection. 1931. (31.45)

simplicity. He replaced the pliant forms, sensuous textures, and pastel tones of rococo art with rectilinear shapes, hard-edged contours, and somber colors—features that recalled the art of Poussin (whom David deeply admired). His technique was austere, precise, and faithful to archeological detail—witness the Roman helmets, sandals, and swords.

Three years after painting the *Oath of the Horatii,* David conceived the smaller but equally popular *Death of Socrates* (figure 26.28). The scene is a fifth-century B.C. Athenian prison. It is the moment before Socrates, the father of Greek philosophy, will drink the fatal hemlock. Surrounding Socrates are his students and friends, posed in various expressions of lament, while the apostle of reason himself—illuminated in the style of Caravaggio—rhetorically lifts his hand to heaven. Clarity and intellectual control dominate the composition: figures and objects are arranged as if plotted on a grid of lines horizontal and vertical to the picture plane. This ideal geometry, a metaphor for the ordering function of reason, complements the grave and noble message of the painting: Reason guides human beings to live and, if need be,

to die for their moral principles. In the *Death of Socrates,* as in the *Oath of the Horatii,* David put neoclassicism at the service of a morality based on Greco-Roman Stoicism, self-sacrifice, and stern patriotism.

Ingres and the Neoclassical Line

David's most talented pupil was the brilliant draftsman Jean-Auguste-Dominique Ingres (d. 1867). Ingres was famous for his polished depictions of classical history and myth and for his accomplished portraits. He worshipped, as he himself admitted, "Raphael, his century, the ancients, and above all the divine Greeks." But Ingres departed from academic dictums in certain matters of style. He abandoned the weighty realism of David and sought a purity of line similar to that found in Greek vase paintings. Drawing, he insisted, is the true basis of art, while color "is no more than a handmaiden." Intrigued by the exoticism of Turkish culture (publicized by Napoleon's campaigns in North Africa), Ingres painted in 1814 his greatest work, *La Grande Odalisque* (figure 26.29).

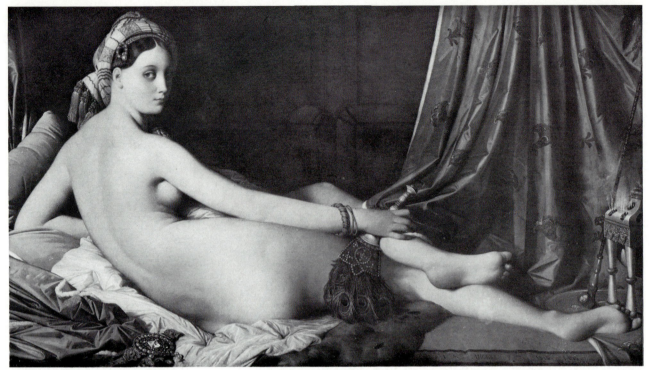

FIGURE 26.29 *Grand Odalisque*, Jean Auguste Dominique Ingres, 1814. Oil on canvas, 35 1/4 in. × 63 3/4 in. Louvre, Paris. Alinari/Art Resource, New York.

The langorous harem slave, a distant kin of Titian's reclining Venus (figure 17.32), is the quintessential image of the seductive female. Ingres rejected neoclassical canons of proportion and elongated the limbs of his nude in ways reminiscent of the Italian mannerists (figure 20.3). The flatness and "incorrect" anatomy of Ingres' *Odalisque* drew strong criticism from his colleagues, who claimed his subject had three too many vertebrae and called his style "primitive" and "Gothic." However, the painting remains one of the most arresting images of womanhood in Western art.

Neoclassicism under Napoleon

While neoclassicism was the "official" style of the French Revolution, it soon became the vehicle of French imperialism. Under the leadership of Napoleon Bonaparte (d. 1821), the imagery of classical Greece and republican Rome was abandoned for the more appropriate imagery of Augustan Rome. Like the Roman emperors, Napoleon used the arts to magnify his greatness. He appointed David to commemorate his military achievements and he commissioned architects to redesign Paris on the order of Rome. Paris became a city of straight, wide avenues and huge, impressive squares. Imaginary axes linked the various monuments raised to honor the emperor, and older buildings were remodeled in the Empire style. Pierre Alexander Vignon (d. 1828) redesigned the Church of Saint Mary Magdalene (called "La Madeleine") as a Roman temple dedicated to the glory of the French army (figure 26.30). Fifty-two Corinthian columns, each sixty-six feet tall, surround the temple, which rises on a twenty-three-foot-high podium like a gigantic version of the Maison Carrée in Nîmes (figure 26.31). Vignon's gloomy interior—a nave crowned with three domes—falls short of reflecting the majesty of the exterior, despite his use of the Corinthian and Ionic orders in the decorative scheme.

Elsewhere, Napoleon's neoclassicism was more precise. The Arc du Carrousel, which stands adjacent to the Louvre, is faithful to its Roman model, the Arch of Constantine in Rome. And the grandest of Paris' triumphal arches, which occupies the crossing of twelve avenues at the end of the famous Avenue des Champs-Elysées (figure 26.32), closely resembles the Arch of Titus in the Roman Forum (figure 7.18). Designed by Jean-François-Thérèse Chalgrin (d. 1811), the 164-foot-high commemorative monument—like the French army to which it was dedicated—was larger than any arch built in ancient times. Napoleon would become one of the nineteenth century's most celebrated romantic heroes (chapter 28), but the monuments he commissioned for Paris were stamped unmistakably with the classical spirit.

FIGURE 26.30 Church of Mary Magdalene ("La Madeleine"), Paris, Pierre Vignon, 1807–1842. Length, 350 ft., width, 147 ft., height of podium, 23 ft. Arch. photo/ S.P.A.D.E.M.

FIGURE 26.31 Maison Carrée, Nîmes, France, 16 B.C. Marburg/Art Resource, New York.

FIGURE 26.32 Arc de Triomphe, Paris, Jean François Thérèse Chalgrin and others, 1806–36. Height 164 ft. J. Feuillie/ © CNMHS/S.P.A.D.E.M., Paris/ARS, New York © 1992.

Eighteenth-Century Music

The eighteenth century was as rich in music as it was in the visual arts. Music filled the courts and concert halls. Religious compositions were still in demand, but church music was overshadowed by the vast amounts of music composed for secular entertainment. Composers sought the patronage of wealthy aristocrats, at whose courts they often served. At the same time, composers wrote music for amateur performance and for the public concert hall. While opera remained the favorite type of vocal music, new forms of instrumental music emerged. Social constraints still determined specific types of music, but inevitably, music began to free itself from religious and ceremonial functions.

During the eighteenth century certain distinctive characteristics of Western music converged. These characteristics included the idea that harmony was proper and essential to music, that a piece of music should be thoughtfully (and individually) composed, and that it should be studiously rehearsed and performed in much the same manner each time it is played. These traits, which stressed control and formality over spontaneity and improvisation, set Western musical culture apart from that of Africa, Asia, and the rest of the world.

Rococo Music

By the middle of the eighteenth century, the rococo (or *galant*) style began to replace the music of Bach and Handel. Rococo composers abandoned the intricate counterpoint and dense textures of the baroque in favor of light and graceful melodies organized into short, distinct phrases. As with rococo art, rococo music was delicate in sound, thin in texture, and natural in feeling. These qualities dominated the works of the French composer François Couperin (d. 1733).

Couperin, a contemporary of Johann Sebastian Bach, wrote in both the baroque and rococo styles, as did many composers of the early eighteenth century. In 1716, Couperin published one of the most important musical treatises of the period, *The Art of Playing the Clavecin,* which offered precise instructions for keyboard fingering and for the execution of musical ornaments known as *agréments.* The rococo preference for intimate forms of expression cast in miniature is reflected in Couperin's suites for harpsichord (in French, *clavicin*).♭ The individual sections of these suites often bear playful titles based on women's names, parlor games, or human attributes, such

as Languor, Coquetry, and Jealousy. Couperin's suites were written for solo instruments or for ensembles and accompanied such dances as the *courante,* the *minuet,* and the *sarabande,* all of which were performed in fashionable eighteenth-century *salons* (figure 26.1). Embroidered with florid *agréments,* Couperin's music shares the lighthearted spirit and fragile elegance of the rococo style in the visual arts.

Classical Music

The word *classical,* when used in reference to music, has two principal meanings. In its broadest sense, it describes that which is of lasting value (see "The Classical Style," chapter 5); hence, "classical" is commonly used to distinguish serious (or "art") music from "popular" (or "folk") music. "Classical" is also employed, however, to describe a specific musical style that emerged in the West between approximately 1760 and 1820—one that, as with Greco-Roman art, featured symmetry, balance, and formal restraint. Unlike neoclassical art and architecture, classical music had little to do with the heritage of Greece and Rome, for European composers had no surviving evidence of Greek and Roman music and therefore, no antique musical models to imitate. Nevertheless, classical music was unique in its clarity of form and purity of design. Classical composers, most of whom came from Germany and Austria, completed the liberation of melody from baroque polyphony, a process clearly anticipated in rococo music. They wrote homophonic compositions that featured easy-to-grasp melodies, which were repeated or developed according to a definitive formal structure.

Although classical composers retained the fast/slow/fast contrasts of baroque instrumental forms, they rid their compositions of many baroque features. They replaced, for instance, the abrupt changes from loud to soft with more gently graduated contrasts. They eliminated the unflagging rhythms and ornate embellishments of baroque polyphony in favor of clear-cut musical phrases. Although counterpoint continued to play an important role in classical music, the intricate webs of counterpoint typical, for instance, of a Bach fugue, gave way to a new harmonic clarity. Classical music reflects an infatuation with formal structure that parallels the neoclassical architect's quest for reasoned clarity, balance, and purity of design.

♭See Music Listening Selections at end of chapter.

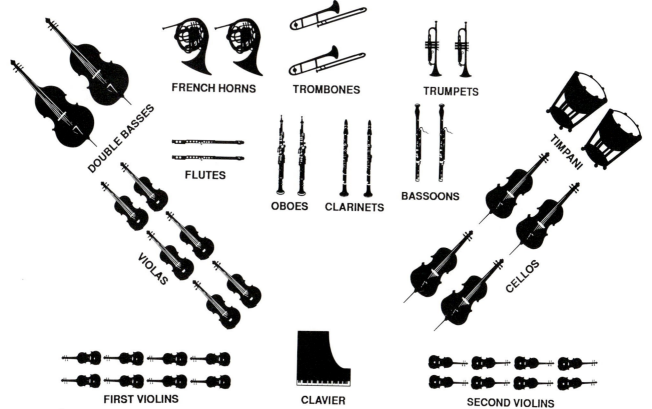

FRENCH HORNS   TROMBONES   TRUMPETS

DOUBLE BASSES

FLUTES

OBOES   CLARINETS   BASSOONS

TIMPANI

VIOLAS

CELLOS

FIRST VIOLINS   CLAVIER   SECOND VIOLINS

FIGURE 26.33   The classical symphony orchestra.

The Birth of the Orchestra

Eighteenth-century instrumental music served as secular entertainment in public theaters and in the *salons* of courtly residences. The most important instrumental grouping to emerge at this time was the orchestra. The Bohemian composer Johann Stamitz (d. 1757), who settled in the south German town of Mannheim in the 1740s, organized what is thought to have been one of the earliest forms of the classical orchestra. It consisted of groups of related instruments, each with its own character or personality. The **strings**, made up of violins, violas, cellos, and bass viols, formed the nucleus of the orchestra, since they were the most melodious and most lyrical of the instrumental families. The **woodwinds**, consisting of flutes, oboes, clarinets, and bassoons, specialized in mellow harmonies. The **brass** section, made up of French horns and trumpets (and, at the end of the century, trombones), added volume and resonant punctuation. And the **percussion** section, comprised of kettledrums, functioned as rhythm markers. Stamitz's orchestra was small by modern-day standards. It included some thirty-five pieces, many of which were

still rudimentary: Brass instruments lacked valves, and the clarinet was not perfected until roughly 1790. The piano, which was invented around 1720, remained until 1775 more closely related to the clavichord than to the modern grand piano. During the last quarter of the century, however, as the piano underwent technical refinement, it came to be the favorite solo instrument.

As musical instruments became more sophisticated, the orchestra, capable of an increasingly expressive and subtle range of sounds, grew in size and popularity. The eighteenth-century orchestra was led by a musician (often the composer) who played part of the composition on the keyboard instrument located at the place now occupied by the conductor's podium (figure 26.33). The string section was seated to the right and left, while the other instruments were spread across the middle distance, in a pattern that has persisted to this day.

To facilitate the conductor's control over the music, the Mannheim orchestra used a **score**, that is, a record of musical notation that indicated every sound to be played by each instrument. Each musical part appeared in groups of five-line staffs that enabled the conductor to "view" the composition as a whole. Separate instrumental parts were written out for each instrument as well. In the eighteenth century, both instrumentation and methods of scoring became standardized. Scores included a time signature, which indicated the number of beats per measure, a key signature, which noted the number of sharps or flats in the specified key, and abbreviations of the Italian words that indicated the dynamics of specific passages: *f* for *forte* ("loud") and *p* for *piano* ("soft"). Interpretive directions, such as *scherzando* ("sprightly") and *affettuoso* ("with feeling"), signified the intentions of the composer as to how a musical passage should be performed. All these notational devices served the principle of formality that governed eighteenth-century music and Western musical composition in general.

Classical Instrumental Compositions

Classical composers wrote music for a variety of instrumental groupings. The most challenging of these was the orchestral form known as the **symphony**. The Italian word *sinfonia* was used during the seventeenth century to describe various kinds of instrumental pieces; but, by the mid-eighteenth century, the word came to mean an independent instrumental composition for full orchestra. In addition to the symphony, three other instrumental genres dominated the classical era: the **string quartet**, a composition for four stringed instruments, usually two violins, a viola, and a cello; the **concerto**, a composition featuring one or more solo instruments and an orchestra; and the **sonata**, a composition for an unaccompanied keyboard instrument or for another instrument with keyboard accompaniment. Although the concerto and the sonata originated earlier (see chapter 22), they now took on a new formality. Indeed, all four instrumental forms—the symphony, the string quartet, the classical concerto, and the classical sonata assumed a singular formal structure: They were divided into three or four sections, or movements, each of which followed a specific tempo, or musical pace. The first movement was played in *allegro* or fast tempo; the second in *andante* or *largo,* that is, moderate or slow tempos; the third movement (usually omitted in concertos) was written in dance tempo (usually in three-quarter time); and fourth was again *allegro.*

Classical composers used a special form for the organization of the first and fourth movements of classical symphonies, string quartets, concertos, and sonatas. This form, known as the **sonata form** (or **sonata allegro form**), calls for the division of the movement into three parts: the exposition, the development, and the recapitulation. In the exposition, the composer "exposes," or introduces, a theme in a certain key, then contrasts it with a second theme. Musical effect is based on the tension and resolution of two opposing key centers. In the development, the composer moves to the contrasting key, expanding and altering the themes stated in the exposition. Finally, in the recapitulation, the themes from the exposition are restated in the original key, adding, perhaps a **coda** ("tail") as a summarizing end piece.

Although classical composers frequently deviated from the sonata form, they used that form to provide the "rules" of musical design—the architectural guidelines, so to speak, for musical composition. Just as neoclassical artists and writers favored clear definitions and an Aristotelian "beginning, middle and end," so classical composers delighted in the threefold balance of the sonata form, the repetition of simple harmonies, and the crisp phrasing of an appealing melody.

The Development of the Classical Style: Haydn

Whether a symphony, string quartet, sonata, or concerto, classical music is usually bright, melodic, and free-flowing. These features characterize the music of the Austrian composer Franz Joseph Haydn (d. 1809). Of peasant birth, Haydn was recruited at the age of eight to sing in the choir of Saint Stephen's Cathedral in Vienna. As a young man, he taught music and struggled to make a living. Finally, in 1761, at the age of twenty-nine, Haydn became musical director to the court of the powerful and wealthy Hungarian nobleman Prince Paul Anton Esterhazy, who was also an accomplished musician. The magnificent Esterhazy country estate (modeled on Versailles) included two theaters—one for opera and one for puppet plays—and two richly appointed concert halls. There, for almost thirty years, Haydn took charge of all aspects of musical entertainment: he composed music, trained choristers, oversaw the repair of instruments, and rehearsed and conducted an orchestra of some twenty-five musicians. At the princely court, Haydn produced music for various instrumental groups. Tailoring his creative talents to suit special occasions and the tastes of his wealthy patron, he wrote operas, oratorios, solo concertos, sonatas, overtures, and liturgical music. But his most original works were those whose forms he himself helped to develop: the classical symphony and the string quartet. The Father of the Symphony, as

Haydn is often called, wrote 104 symphonies and 84 string quartets. The string quartet, a concentrated instrumental form, met the need for elite entertainment in a small room or chamber—hence the term "chamber music." Unfortunately, such works are today often performed in huge music halls, rather than in the intimate surroundings for which they were intended.

After the death of Prince Esterhazy in 1790, Haydn was invited to perform in London, where he composed his last twelve symphonies. In the London symphonies, which Haydn wrote for an orchestra of some sixty players, he explored an expanded harmonic range and a wealth of dramatic effects. For some of the symphonies he used folk melodies as basic themes, inventively repeating key fragments in different parts of the piece. Among the most memorable of the London symphonies is the Symphony No. 94,♪ nicknamed "The Surprise," because Haydn introduced an unexpected *fortissimo* ("very loud") instrumental crash on a weak beat in the second movement of the piece. Tradition has it that the chord was calculated to waken a drowsy audience and entice them to anticipate the next "surprise"—which never does occur. Haydn brought a lifetime of musical experience to his last works. Their witty phrasing and melodic effects made these symphonies enormously popular, so popular, in fact, that eighteenth-century music publishers often sold compositions that they falsely attributed to Haydn. A celebrity in his old age, "Papa Haydn" (as he was affectionately called) was one of the first musicians to attain the status of a culture hero during his own lifetime.

The Genius of Mozart

The foremost musical genius of the eighteenth century—and for some critics, of all time—was Haydn's younger contemporary and colleague, Wolfgang Amadeus Mozart (d. 1791). Mozart brought to music an amazing natural talent. A child prodigy, he wrote his first original composition at the age of six. During his brief (thirty-five-year) life, he produced a total of some 650 works, including forty-one symphonies, sixty sonatas, twenty-three piano concertos, and twenty operas. (These were catalogued and numbered in the late nineteenth century by Ludwig von Köchel, hence the "K." numbers used to identify Mozart compositions.)

Wolfgang, the son of a prominent composer was born in Salzburg, Austria. With his father, he toured Europe, performing hundreds of public and private concerts before he was thirteen (figure 26.34). He

♪See Music Listening Selections at end of chapter.

FIGURE 26.34 *The Mozarts in Concert: Leopold, Wolfgang (age seven), and Nannerl,* Louis Carmontelle, 1764. © The Bettmann Archive.

often performed his own pieces, particularly his piano concertos, which constitute some of the most important contributions of his musical career. Unlike Haydn, Mozart did not invent any new forms. However, he brought to the instrumental genres of his time unparalleled melodic inventiveness. He borrowed melodies from popular dance tunes and transformed them into elegant compositions appropriate for garden parties, weddings, and balls. One such piece is the *Serenade* in G major, K. 525, also known as *Eine kleine Nachtmusik* ("A Little Nightmusic"), a work for a small string orchestra.♪ He incorporated popular melodies into his symphonies as well, three of which (K. 543, K. 550, and K. 551) were written in a six-week period in 1788. These pieces remain among the most eloquent examples of the classical symphonic form.

After leaving Vienna in 1781, Mozart sought appointments in the aristocratic courts of Europe, but he never received adequate patronage and had difficulty supporting himself and his family. When he died in Vienna in 1791, he was buried in a pauper's grave.[1]

[1]For a fascinating interpretation of Mozart's life, see the play *Amadeus* by Peter Shaffer (New York: Harper & Row, 1981) and the Academy Award–winning film version of the play produced in 1984.

CHAPTER 26: EIGHTEENTH-CENTURY ART, MUSIC, AND SOCIETY **161**

During the last six years of his life, Mozart wrote four of his finest operas, receiving commissions for all but the first. These works are among the best loved in the Western operatic repertory: *Le Nozze di Figaro* (*The Marriage of Figaro,* 1786), *Don Giovanni* (1787), *Cosi Fan Tutti* (*Thus Do All Women,* 1790), and *Die Zauberflote* (*The Magic Flute,* 1791).

The Marriage of Figaro is an example of **opera buffa,** a type of comic opera that was popular during the eighteenth century. Mozart transformed the stock characters of the Italian *opera buffa* into psychologically penetrating studies of human nature. At the same time, he leveled a pointed attack on the decadence of the European aristocracy. The central intrigue of *Figaro* features the maid Susanna and her fiancé, the valet Figaro, in a plot to outwit their master Count Almavira, who seeks to seduce Susanna. In an era dominated by aristocratic privilege, and one that still honored the feudal claim to "first night rights" over a female servant, *The Marriage of Figaro* was sharp satire: it championed the wit and ingenuity of lower-class servants over the self-serving arrogance of the nobility. And while such a theme might seem less than controversial today, it stirred heated debate in Mozart's time—Napoleon called the play by Pierre Augustin Beaumarchais (d. 1799), on which the opera was based, "revolution already in action." Certainly Mozart was more interested in music than in political reform—he even agreed to temper Beaumarchais' scolding satire by way of Lorenzo da Ponte's Italian *libretto.* But his scorn for the upper classes—perhaps stemming from his own personal difficulties with aristocratic patrons—is readily apparent in the piece.

Politics aside, the enduring beauty of *The Marriage of Figaro* lies in its lyrical force and its expressive ingenuity. Mozart had a special talent for shaping personalities by way of music. While the characters in the operas of Monteverdi and Lully were allegorical or mythological, Mozart's appeal to us as real human beings. They convey a wide range of human expression, from grief and despair to hope and joy. Mozart's vocal music is never sentimental; it retains the precision and clarity of the classical style and invests it with melodic grace. Only by listening to his music can one appreciate the reason why Haydn called Mozart "the greatest composer known to me either in person or by name."

Summary

Eighteenth-century European art and music reflected the changing character and tastes of its various social classes. The fashionable rococo style reflected the aristocratic affection for ornamental delicacy, intimacy, and playful elegance. The rococo style dominated the *salons* of Paris and the courts and churches of Austria and Germany. In France, the artists Watteau, Boucher, Vigée-Lebrun, Fragonard, and Clodion evoked a world of physical pleasure and sensuous delight.

By mid-century, a reaction against the rococo style occurred among members of a growing middle class, who identified their interests with the rational ideals of the European Enlightenment. Encouraged by the *philosophes'* demand for an art of moral virtue, Greuze and Chardin produced genre paintings that gave dignity to the life and work of ordinary individuals. At the same time, archeological investigations in Greece and Southern Italy encouraged new interest in the classical past. The neoclassical style swept away the rococo in the same way that the French Revolution swept away the Old Regime. David's stirring pictorial recreations of Greek and Roman history invoked a message of self-sacrifice and moral purpose.

The neoclassical style symbolized the Enlightenment ideals of reason and liberty. In America neoclassicism was best expressed in the architectural achievements of Thomas Jefferson. In Europe, neoclassicism influenced all of the arts, from Adam's English country houses and Soufflot's Panthéon to the portraits by Houdon and the ceramics of Wedgewood. During the reign of Napoleon, neoclassicists turned to the arts of imperial Rome to glorify Paris and the emperor himself.

The period between 1760 and approximately 1820 witnessed the birth of the orchestra and the development of the classical forms of Western instrumental music. Classical music was characterized by balance, symmetry and intellectual control—features similar to those admired by neoclassical writers, painters, sculptors, and architects. Composers used the sonata form to govern the composition of the symphony, the string quartet, the sonata, and the concerto. Haydn shaped the character of the classical symphony and the string quartet; Mozart moved easily between rococo and classical styles, investing both with extraordinary melodic grace. In his operas, as well as in his symphonies, Mozart achieved a balance between lyrical invention and technical control that brought the classical style to its peak. In the decades that followed, the polite formalism of the European Enlightenment would yield to the seductive embrace of the Romantic Era.

GLOSSARY

allegro (Italian, "cheerful") a fast tempo in music

andante (Italian, "going," i.e., a normal walking pace) a moderate tempo in music

bacchante a female attendant or devotee of Dionysus

brass a family of wind instruments that usually includes the French horn, the trumpet, the trombone, and the tuba

coda (Italian, "tail") a passage added to the closing section of a movement or musical composition in order to create the sense of a definite ending

concerto see Glossary, chapter 22; the classical concerto, which made use of the sonata form, usually featured one or more solo instruments and orchestra

fete galante (French, "elegant entertainment") a festive diversion enjoyed by aristocrats, a favored subject in rococo art

fortissimo (Italian, "very loud") a directive indicating that the music should be played very loud; its opposite is *pianissimo* ("very soft")

largo (Italian, "broad") a very slow tempo; the slowest of the conventional tempos in music

opera buffa a type of comic opera usually featuring stock characters

pastel a chalk medium used for sketching and drawing; a drawing in that medium

percussion a group of instruments that are sounded by being struck or shaken, used especially for rhythm

satyr a part-bestial woodland creature symbolic of Dionysus

score the musical notation for all of the instruments or voices in a particular composition; a composite from which the whole piece may be conducted or studied

sonata a composition for an unaccompanied keyboard instrument or for another instrument with keyboard accompaniment; see also Glossary, chapter 22

sonata form (or **sonata allegro form**) a structural form commonly used in the late eighteenth century for the first and fourth movements of symphonies and other instrumental compositions

string quartet a composition for four stringed instruments, each of which plays its own part

strings a family of instruments that usually includes the violin, viola, cello, double bass, and viol (which are normally bowed), and the harp, guitar, lute, and zither (which are normally plucked)

symphony an independent instrumental composition for orchestra

woodwinds a family of wind instruments, usually consisting of the flute, oboe, clarinet, and bassoon

SUGGESTIONS FOR READING

Bernier, Olivier. *The Eighteenth-Century Woman.* New York: Doubleday, 1981.

Conisbee, Philip. *Painting in Eighteenth-Century France.* Ithaca, N. Y.: Cornell University Press, 1981.

Harries, Karsten. *The Bavarian Rococo Church: Between Faith and Aestheticism.* New Haven, Conn.: Yale University Press, 1983.

Hawley, Henry. *Neoclassicism: Style and Motif.* New York: Abrams, 1964.

Hildesheimer, Wolfgang. *Mozart.* Translated by Marion Faber. New York: Farrar, Straus, Giroux, 1982.

Honour, Hugh. *Neoclassicism.* New York: Harper, 1979.

Jones, Stephen. *The Eighteenth Century.* Cambridge: Cambridge University Press, 1985.

Kalnein, Wend G., and Michael Levey. *Art and Architecture of the Eighteenth Century in France.* New York: Penguin, 1972.

Levey, Michael. *From Rococo to Revolution: Major Trends in Eighteenth-Century Painting.* New York: Praeger, 1966.

Messing, Scott. *Neoclassicism in Music.* Ann Arbor, Mich.: UMI Research Press, 1988.

Pauly, Reinhard. *Music in the Classic Period.* Englewood Cliffs, N.J.: Prentice-Hall, 1965.

MUSIC LISTENING SELECTIONS

Cassette II Selection 8. Couperin, *Ordre,* No. 22, "Le Crocen-jambe," 1730.

Cassette II Selection 9. Haydn, *Symphony No. 94* in G Major, "Surprise," 2d Movement, Andante, 1791.

Cassette II Selection 10. Mozart, *Serenade No. 3* in G Major, K 525, *"Eine Kleine Nachtmusik,"* 1st Movement, Allegro, 1787.

SELECTED GENERAL BIBLIOGRAPHY

Anderson, Bonnie S., and Judith P. Zinsser. *A History of Their Own: Women in Europe from Prehistory to the Present.* Vol. 2. New York: Harper, 1988.

Artz, F. B. *From the Renaissance to Romanticism: Trends in Style in Art, Literature, and Music, 1300–1830.* Chicago: University of Chicago Press, 1962.

Bridenthal, Renate, and Claudia Koonz, eds. *Becoming Visible: Women in European History.* Boston: Houghton Mifflin, 1977.

Bronowski, Jacob, and Bruce Mazlish. *The Western Intellectual Tradition: From Leonardo to Hegel.* New York: Harper, 1960.

Brown, Calvin S. *Music and Literature: A Comparison of the Arts.* Athens, Ga.: University of Georgia Press, 1948.

Bugner, Ladislas, ed. *The Image of the Black in Western Art.* Vol. 3, *From Sixteenth-Century Europe to Nineteenth-Century America.* Cambridge, Mass.: Harvard University Press, 1986.

Chadwick, Whitney. *Women, Art and Society.* New York: Norton, 1991.

Chang, H. C. *Chinese Literature: Popular Fiction and Drama.* New York: Columbia University Press, 1973.

Clark, Kenneth. *Civilisation: A Personal View.* New York: Harper, 1970.

Clarke, Mary, and Clement Crisp. *The History of Dance.* New York: Crown, 1981.

Copland, Aaron. *What to Listen for in Music.* rev. ed. New York: New American Library, 1957.

Craven, Roy C. *Indian Art.* London: Thames and Hudson, 1976.

Fitzgerald, C. P. *The Horizon History of China.* New York: American Heritage, 1969.

Fleming, William. *Concerts of the Arts: Their Interplay and Modes of Relationship.* Gainesville, Fl.: University of West Florida Press, 1990.

————. *Musical Arts and Styles.* Gainesville, Fl.: University of West Florida Press, 1990.

Harman, Carter. *A Popular History of Music.* rev. ed. New York: Dell, 1973.

Held, Julius S., and Donald Posner. *Seventeenth and Eighteenth-Century Art.* Englewood Cliffs, N.J.: Prentice-Hall, 1972.

Kitson, Michael. *The Age of the Baroque.* New York: McGraw-Hill, 1967.

Kostoff, Spiro. *A History of Architecture: Settings and Rituals.* New York: Oxford University Press, 1985.

Million, Henry A. *Baroque and Rococo Architecture.* New York: Brazillier, 1965.

Nelson, Lynn H., and Patrick Peebles, eds. *Classics of Eastern Thought.* San Diego: Harcourt, 1991.

Orrey, Leslie. *Opera: A Concise History*. London: Thames and Hudson, 1968.

Pevsner, Nikolaus. *An Outline of European Architecture*. 6th ed. Baltimore, Md.: Penguin, 1960.

Raynor, Henry. *A Social History of Music: From the Middle Ages to Beethoven*. New York: Schocken Books, 1972.

Russell, Bertrand. *A History of Western Philosophy*. 2d ed. New York: Simon and Schuster, 1984.

Sadie, Stanley, ed. *The New Grove Dictionary of Music and Musicians*. New York: Macmillan, 1980.

Sorrell, Walter. *The Dance Through the Ages*. New York: Grosset and Dunlap, 1967.

Spence, Jonathan D. *The Search for Modern China*. New York: Norton, 1990.

Sterling, Charles. *Still Life Painting from Antiquity to the Twentieth Century*. 2d rev. ed. New York: Harper, 1981.

Sypher, Wyle. *Rococo to Cubism in Art and Literature*. New York: Random House, 1960.

Tapie, Victor L. *The Age of Grandeur: Baroque Art and Architecture*. Trans. A. Ross Williams. New York: Praeger, 1960.

Weiss, Piero, and Richard Taruskin. *Music in the Western World. A History in Documents*. New York: Schirmer Books, 1984.

Wiener, Philip P., ed. *Dictionary of the History of Ideas*. New York: Scribners, 1973.

Books in Series

Great Ages of Man: A History of the World's Cultures. New York: Time, Inc., 1965–69.

Library of Art Series. New York: Time-Life Books, Inc., 1967.

Time-Frame. 25 vols. (projected). New York: Time-Life Books, 1990–.

CREDITS

Chapter 20

Reading 71 (p. 6): From *The Spiritual Exercises of St. Ignatius,* 1951 Loyola University Press, Chicago.

Reading 72 (p. 7): Source: "St. Teresa's Visions," in *The Complete Works of Saint Teresa of Jesus,* Volume I, translated by E. A. Peers. Copyright © 1957 Sheed and Ward, Ltd., London.

Reading 73 (p. 8): From *The Poems of Richard Crashaw,* edited by L. C. Martin. Copyright © 1957 Oxford University Press, Oxford, England. Reprinted by permission of Oxford University Press.

Chapter 21

Reading 74 (p. 24); **Reading 75** (p. 25); and **Reading 76** (pp. 25–26): Excerpts from *The College Survey of English Literature,* Shorter Edition by Alexander Witherspoon, reprinted by permission of Harcourt Brace Jovanovich, Inc.

Reading 77 (pp. 26–27): Excerpts from PARADISE LOST by John Milton, A Norton Critical Edition, Edited by Scott Elledge, are reprinted with the permission of W. W. Norton & Company, Inc. Copyright © 1975 by W. W. Norton & Company, Inc.

Figure 21.2 (p. 28): From Ronald Gray, *Christopher Wren and St. Paul's Cathedral.* Copyright © 1979 Cambridge University Press, New York. Reprinted by permission.

Figure 21.4 (p. 30): From Richard Phipps and Richard Wink, *Invitation to the Gallery.* Copyright © 1987 Wm. C. Brown Publishers, Dubuque, Iowa. All Rights Reserved. Reprinted by permission.

Chapter 22

Map 22.1 (p. 37): Reproduced from *World Civilizations, Their History and Their Culture,* Fifth Edition, Volume II, by Edward McNall Burns and Philip Lee Ralph. Cartography by Harold K. Faye. By permission of W. W. Norton & Company, Inc. Copyright © 1974, 1969, 1964, 1958, 1955 by W. W. Norton & Company, Inc.

Reading 78 (pp. 38–39): From Sir Francis Bacon, "Novum Organum" in *The Complete Works of Francis Bacon,* translated by James Spedding (London: Longman, 1960). Modernized by the author.

Reading 79 (pp. 39–40): From Sir Francis Bacon, "Of Studies" in *The Works of Francis Bacon,* translated by James Spedding (London: Longman, 1960). Modernized by the author.

Reading 80 (pp. 40–41): Reprinted by permission of Charles Scribner's Sons, an imprint of Macmillan Publishing Company from *Descartes Selections,* edited by Ralph M. Eaton. Copyright 1927 Charles Scribner's Sons; copyright renewed © 1955.

Reading 81 (pp. 42–43): From John Locke, "An Essay Concerning Human Understanding" in *The Philosophic Works of John Locke,* edited by J. A. St. John (London: George Bell & Sons, 1892). Modernized by the author.

Chapter 23

Reading 82 (p. 70): Source: *The Maxims of la Rochefoucauld,* translated by Louis Kronenberger. Copyright © 1959 Random House, Inc., New York.

Reading 83 (pp. 71–80): From Molière, *Le Bourgeois Gentilhomme (The Tradesman Turned Gentleman),* translated by Curtis Hidden Page (New York: G. P. Putnam's Sons, 1908). Modernized by the author.

Chapter 24

Reading 84 (pp. 98–100): Reprinted by permission of Macmillan Publishing Company from Thomas Hobbes, *Leviathan,* edited by Herbert W. Schneider. Copyright © 1985 by Macmillan Publishing Company. Copyright © 1958.

Reading 85 (pp. 100–101): From John Locke, "Two Treatises on Government" in *The Works of John Locke.* (London: Thomas Tegg, 1823.) Modernized by the author.

Reading 87 (p. 102): From Adam Smith, *An Inquiry into the Nature and Causes of the Wealth of Nations.* (London: George Routledge and Sons, Ltd., 1913.)

Reading 86 (pp. 103–4): From *The Declaration of Independence.*

Reading 88 (pp. 106–7): Reprinted by permission of Macmillan Publishing Company from *Diderot: Encyclopedia, Selections,* translated by Nelly S. Hoyt and Thomas Cassirer. Copyright © 1985, 1963 by Macmillan Publishing Company.

Reading 89 (pp. 108–9): From Antoine Nicolas de Condorcet, *Sketch for a Historical Picture of the Progress of the Human Mind,* translated by June Barraclough. Copyright © 1955 George Weidenfeld and Nicholson Ltd., London. Reprinted by permission.

Reading 90 (pp. 110–11): From Alexander Pope, "Essay on Man" in *Poetical Works of Alexander Pope.* (Boston: Little, Brown, 1854.)

Chapter 25

Reading 91 (p. 114): From Oliver Goldsmith, *The Citizen of the World.* (London: Everyman's Library, 1934.)

Reading 92 (pp. 117–26): "Candide" in *The Best Known Works of Voltaire.* New York: Blue Ribbon Books, 1927, with notes by G. K. Fiero. Modernized and edited by G. K. Fiero.

Reading 93 (pp. 128–29): From *A Discourse on Inequality* by Jean-Jacques Rousseau, translated by Maurice Cranston, Translation copyright © 1984 by Maurice Cranston. Used by permission of Viking Penguin, a division of Penguin Books USA Inc. and the Peters, Fraser & Dunlop Group Ltd., London.

Reading 94 (pp. 131–32): From "The Taking of the Bastille: July 14, 1789" by Jacques Godechot, in *The Journee of J. B. Humbert,* translated by Jean Stewart. Copyright © 1965 by Editions Gallimard. Translation Copyright © 1970 by Faber & Faber, Ltd., London.

Chapter 26

Figure 26.33 (p. 159): From *A Popular History of Music* by Carter Harmon. Copyright © 1956 by Carter Harmon. Used by permission of Dell Books, a division of Bantam Doubleday Dell Publishing Group, Inc.

Line Art

Alice Thiede
Map 22.1 (p. 37)
Map 23.1 (p. 56)

WCB Graphics
Figure 26.33 (p. 159)

CREDITS

INDEX

C

Calvinism, 23, 29, 101
Camera obscura, 47, **48**
Candide (Voltaire), 96, 116, **116**, 117–26 (text), 133
Canova, Antonio, 150, 153
Cantata No. 80 (''*Ein Feste Burg*'') (Bach), 33; Music Listening Selection II–4
Caravaggio (Michelangelo Merici), 4, 11–12, 14, 17, 20, 22, 29, 65, 155
Castiglione, Baldassare, 129
Catherine II (queen of Russia), 100, 135
Catholic Reformation, 4, 5–22, 23
Cervantes, Miguel de, 109
Ch'ing dynasty (China), 55, 87–91, 107
Chalgrin, Jean-François-Thérèse, 156
Champs-Elysées, Paris, 156
Chardin, Jean-Baptiste-Siméon, 144–45, 162
Charles I (king of England), 23, 68, 98
Chaucer, Geoffrey, 109
China, 3, 4, 35, 48, 55, 105, 107, 109, 114
 architecture, 87–89
 art, 89–92
 drama, 91–92
 government in, 87–88
 literature, 90–91, 109, 115
Chinoiserie, 90, 137
Christianity. *See also* Catholic Reformation
 and the Bible, 24
 and the Enlightenment, 104–5, 107
Church, Christian. *See also* Catholic Reformation and the Scientific Revolution, 36–37, 53
 in England, 24
Citizen of the World, The (Goldsmith), 114 (text)
Civil War (England). *See* War, English
Clavecin, Art of Playing the (Couperin), 158
Clodion (Claude Michel), 144, 153, 162
Comédie-ballet, 71
Commedia del arte, 71
Condorcet, Antoine Nicolas de, 96, 108–9, 111
Confucius, 114
Constitution (United States of America), 102, 130
Constitution of 1793 (France), 133
Copernicus, Nicolas, 35, 43, 53
Corneille, Pierre, 154

Counter-Reformation. *See* Catholic Reformation
Couperin, François, 52, 158; Music Listening Selection II–8
Crashaw, Richard, 7–8, 21
Critique of Pure Reason (Kant), 130
Cromwell, Oliver, 23
Crucifixion of Saint Peter (Caravaggio), 11, **12**

D

Dance, 69–70, 71, 83
David, Jacques-Louis, 96, 153–56, 162
Death of Socrates (David), 155, **155**
Declaration of Independence (Jefferson), 102 (text), 130, 132, 150
Declaration of the Rights of Man and Citizen, 132
Defoe, Daniel, 109, 126
de Gouges, Olympe, 132, 133
de Heem, Jan Davidsz, 44
de Hooch, Pieter, 45, 54, 144
Deism, 41, 104, 116
Delhi, 84, 86, 92
Departure from the Island of Cythera (Watteau), 137, **139**
Descartes, René, 4, 40–42, 53
Dialogue Concerning the Two Principal Systems of the World (Galileo), 36
Diderot, Denis, 105–6, 114, 126, 127, 144, 152
Diderot (Houdon), **105**
Discourse on the Origin of Inequality Among Men (Rousseau), 128–29 (text)
Donne, John, 4, 24–25, 27, 34
Drama
 Chinese, 91–92
 French, 71–80 (text), 92
Dream of the Red Chamber (Ts'ao Hsüeh-ch'in), 91
Dürer, Albrecht, 47
Dutch Courtyard (de Hooch), 45, **46**

E

Ecstasy of Saint Teresa (Bernini), **8**, **13**, 12–14, 22, 153
Education
 and the Enlightenment, 95, 105–7, 129

and philosophy, 38–43
 and religion, 41–42
 and the Scientific Revolution, 38, 53
''*Eine kleine Nachtmusik*'' (Mozart), 161; Music Listening Selection II–10
El Greco (Dominikos Theotokopoulos), 4, 10–11, 20, 22
Elizabeth I (queen of England), 23
Emile (Rousseau), 129–30
Encyclopédie (Diderot and others), 105, 106–7 (text), 111, 126, 127
Enlightenment, European, 95–133, 135, 147, 152, 162. *See also* Deism; *Philosophes;* Philosophy
 and education, 95, 105–7, 129
 and literature, 109–11, 115–26, 127–30
 and religion, 104–5, 107
 and the Scientific Revolution, 97, 107
Erasmus, Desiderius, **114**
Essay Concerning Human Understanding (Locke), 42–43 (text)
Essay on Man (Pope), 110, 110–11 (text), 113
Estates General (France), 55, 57, 131

F

Feuillet, Raoul Auget, 70
Fielding, Henry, 109
First Treatise on Government (Locke), 100
Fischer, Johann Michael, 137–38
Flaming Heart, The (Crashaw), 7, 8 (text)
Flowers in the Mirror (Li Ju-Chen), 115
Forbidden City (Peking), 87–89, 92
Four Seasons, The (Vivaldi), 53; Music Listening Selection II–5
Fragonard, Jean-Honoré, 96, 137, 142–43, 144, 162
Francis I (king of France), 80
Franklin, Benjamin, 152
Frederick II (king of Prussia), 100
French Revolution. *See* Revolution, French
Fugue. *See* Music, baroque
Fugue, Art of the (Bach), 53; Music Listening Selection II–7